CASS SERIES: STUDIES IN AIR POWER
(Series Editor: Sebastian Cox)

WESTLAND AND THE BRITISH HELICOPTER INDUSTRY, 1945–1960

CASS SERIES: STUDIES IN AIR POWER

(Series Editor: Sebastian Cox)

ISSN 1368-5597

1. *A Forgotten Offensive*
   Royal Air Force Coastal Command's Anti-Shipping Campaign, 1940–1945
   by CHRISTINA J. M. GOULTER

2. *Courage and Air Warfare*
   The Allied Aircrew Experience in the Second World War
   by MARK K. WELLS

3. *Despatch on War Operations*
   by SIR ARTHUR T. 'BOMBER' HARRIS

4. *The Strategic Air War Against Germany, 1939–1945*
   Report of the BRITISH BOMBING SURVEY UNIT

5. *Industry and Air Power*
   The Expansion of British Aircraft Production, 1935–41
   by SEBASTIAN RITCHIE

6. *Air Power at the Battlefront*
   Allied Close Air Support in Europe, 1943–45
   by IAN GOODERSON

7. *Russian Aviation and Air Power in the Twentieth Century*
   edited by ROBIN HIGHAM, JOHN T. GREENWOOD AND VON HARDESTY

8. *Sir Frederick Sykes and the Air Revolution, 1912–1918*
   by ERIC ASH

9. *A Life of Marshal of the RAF Lord Tedder of Glenguin*
   by VINCENT ORANGE

10. *The RAF and Aircraft Design*
    Air Staff Operational Requirements, 1923–1939
    by COLIN SINNOTT

11. *Westland and the British Helicopter Industry, 1945–1960*
    Licensed Production versus Indigenous Innovation
    by MATTHEW R.H. UTTLEY

WESTLAND
AND THE
BRITISH HELICOPTER INDUSTRY
1945–1960

Licensed Production Versus Indigenous Innovation

MATTHEW R.H. UTTLEY

Defence Studies Department, King's College, University of London

FRANK CASS
LONDON • PORTLAND, OR

First published in 2001 in Great Britain by
FRANK CASS PUBLISHERS.
Crown House, 47 Chase Side
London, N14 5BP

and in the United States of America by
FRANK CASS PUBLISHERS
c/o ISBS, 5824 N.E. Hassalo Street
Portland, Oregon, 97213-3644

Website: www.frankcass.com

British Library Cataloguing in Publication Data:

Uttley, Matthew
Westland and the British helicopter industry, 1945–1960:
licensed production versus indigenous innovation. –
(Cass series. Studies in air power; no. 11)
1. Westland Aircraft Limited – History 2. Helicopter industry –
– Great Britain – History 3. Helicopter industry –
Government policy – Great Britain
I.Title
338.4'7629133352

ISBN 0-7146-5194-X (cloth)
ISSN 1368-5597

Library of Congress Cataloging-in-Publication Data:

Uttley, Matthew
Westland and the British helicopter industry, 1945–1960: licensed production versus indigenous innovation/Matthew R.H. Uttley.
p. cm. – (Cass series – Studies in air power, ISSN 1368–5597)
Includes bibliographical references and index.
ISBN 0-7146-5194-X (cloth)
1. Westland Aircraft Limited – History. 2. Helicopters – Research – Great Britain – History. 3. Foreign licensing agreements – History. 4. Helicopter industry – Great Britain – History.
I. Title. II. Series.
TL716.9 .W47 2001
338.7'629133352'0941–dc21

2001028372

Typeset by FiSH Books, London
Printed in Great Britain by MPG Books Ltd, Bodmin, Cornwall

This book is dedicated to the late
Lieutenant Colonel David Limb MBE
of the Parachute Regiment:
a soldier, scholar, gentleman, hero and friend.

Contents

Tables and Figures

TABLES

FIGURES

Series Editor's Preface

In addition to exploring the purely military aspects of air power, it has always been the aim of the Studies in Air Power Series to study its industrial and economic foundations. As air power is wielded in the main by nation-states, and as their aerial strength has depended in part on their ability to build and maintain air forces, the industrial aspects are inextricably linked with the attitudes, policies, and indeed constraints, which operate in government. These involve issues of finance, national pride and security of supply, access to and development of new technology, and, in democracies at least, political factors, both local and national, including the vexed question of employment.

Mathew Uttley's systematic analysis of Westland and the British helicopter industry illustrates the complexity of the relationship between the state – as both the procurer of the final product but also as a major influence on research and development, and indeed industrial structure and policy – and the individual companies. It is an ever-present dilemma for companies in the defence industry that they are ultimately reliant on the state to fill a large part of their order books, which makes them vulnerable to both the fickleness of changes in policy or of governments themselves, and to any inherent flaws or inconsistencies in the policy of the day. Hence, as Uttley so ably demonstrates, the paradox of one arm of government in Britain, the Ministry of Supply, being intent on encouraging a wide range of R&D projects, the cost of which was not insupportable, whilst the ultimate 'customer', the armed services, did not have access to funding on anywhere near the scale to see even a minority of the R&D projects into production. This weakness was one of the primary underlying causes of Westland's success, because the firm was able shrewdly to exploit its position as probably the most successful exponent of licensed production of foreign designs in the UK. That the Westland designs utilised US technology, drawing on the vastly greater R&D resources of the US industry, backed by Federal funds on a grander scale, meant that the firm was able to expose the inherent weaknesses of its competitors' position, where small-scale government R&D funding could only be matched by production funding on a commensurate scale.

Dilemmas over funding of expensive defence technology continue to haunt boardrooms and ministerial offices in the UK and elsewhere in Europe. Europe itself is now a factor in the equation, both in terms of the political passions it arouses and as a possible solution to the funding problem. This was clearly demonstrated at the time of the 1984 political crisis so indelibly associated with Westland's name. The long-term roots of this crisis emerge very clearly from this study.

This book will be of enormous value to today's policy-makers, struggling with problems which would not have been unfamiliar to their predecessors half a century ago, not least because it shows both the potential benefits and the shortcomings of licensed production as a procurement strategy.

SEBASTIAN COX

Acknowledgements

I am grateful for the assistance of staff at the Public Record Office, Kew, and the National Archives, Washington, DC. I am also grateful for the support provided by several people. Thanks are due to Philip Towle who first suggested that UK helicopter R&D and production would make an interesting research subject. Geoffrey Till, Keith Hartley, Ian Bellany, Peter Foot, John Pay, Michael Smith, Richard Coopey, Richard Mills and Bill Park were all generous in their encouragement. Norman Polmar's insights into United States wartime helicopter developments were invaluable. I am particularly indebted to Martin Edmonds and Seb Cox for their guidance and inspiration, and Maria for tolerating my hours at the word-processor. I owe special thanks to Sarah Somers for her comments on the proofs and help with the index. Despite the support of colleagues and friends, any deficiencies remain my responsibility.

Abbreviations

ADRD/H	Ministry of Supply Assistant Director of Research and Development (Helicopters)
AFEE	Airborne Forces Experimental Establishment
AOP	Air Observation Post
ARC	Ministry of Supply Aeronautical Research Council
ASR	Air Staff Requirements or Air Sea Rescue
AST	Air Staff Target
ASW	Anti-Submarine Warfare
AUW/auw	All-Up Weight
BAC	British Air Commission
BEA	British European Airways
BOAC	British Overseas Airways Corporation
BuAer	United States Navy Bureau of Aeronautics
CASEVAC	Casualty Evacuation
CLE	Central Landing Establishment
DCIGS	War Office Deputy Chief of the Imperial General Staff
DDARD	Ministry of Supply Deputy Director of Aircraft Research and Development
DMARD	Ministry of Supply Director(ate) of Military Aircraft Research and Development
DOR	Director of Operational Requirements
DRPC	Defence Research Policy Committee
L/AWC	Land/Air Warfare Committee
MAP	Ministry of Aircraft Production
MCA	Ministry of Civil Aviation
MDAP	Mutual Defence Aid Programme
MoD	Ministry of Defence
MoS	Ministry of Supply
NA	Naval Aircraft Requirement
OR	Operational Requirement
QSEs	Qualified Scientists and Engineers
RAE	Royal Aircraft Establishment
SAR	Search and Rescue
shp	shaft horse power
TARC	Transport Aircraft Requirements Committee
USAAF	United States Army Air Forces
USAF	United States Air Force

USN	United States Navy
VTO	Vertical Take-off
WO	War Office

Introduction

The helicopter is a major aviation technology. Its primary characteristics – the ability for vertical take-off and hovering – have facilitated important evolutions in battlefield and naval operations, making it a key element in modern warfare. As Allen observes, 'only one major innovation after 1945 brought with it a whole new form of military mobility: the helicopter'.[1] Helicopters are now firmly established in a range of specialist civilian roles and they comprise some 40 per cent (by number) of the aircraft inventory of the armed services.[2] Moreover, in industrial terms, the current turnover of Britain's helicopter industry is £447m and approximately 9,000 workers are directly employed in research and development (R&D) and manufacture.[3]

At one level, this book is a history of British helicopter procurement between 1945 and 1960. Unlike fixed-wing aviation, early post-war British helicopter industrial policy has largely been neglected by air historians. Though accounts already cover development chronologies of individual helicopter projects, the memoirs of key design personnel, the activities of firms and the operational deployment of helicopters by the British armed services, none addresses systematically the industrial and procurement dimensions.[4] The book, therefore, fills a gap in the historical record of what has become a key branch of post-war aviation.

At another level, this book seeks to understand not just the nature of Britain's helicopter procurement experience *per se*, but also the relevance of this experience for the historiography of early post-war British aircraft industrial policy as a whole and wider government procurement choices. The salient features of this experience are reflected in trends during the period and the issues they generate.

TRENDS IN BRITISH HELICOPTER DEVELOPMENT, 1945–60

After 1945, the objective of the Ministry of Supply (MoS) – the agency responsible for implementing post-war British aircraft industrial policy[5] – was explicitly

> to establish and foster a strong [indigenous] helicopter industry with the design and production capacity to cater for all home markets and bid for... export markets.[6]

Reflecting overall British aircraft procurement policy in microcosm, the rationale was that a self-sufficient helicopter industry founded on domestic R&D and manufacture would generate economic, strategic and political benefits. Implementation involved the MoS in placing R&D contracts with indigenous firms on the explicit assumption that public funding and 'buy-national' procurement policies would generate 'all-British' helicopter technology to meet domestic and export requirements.

Given these policy imperatives, British helicopter R&D and production between 1945 and 1960 reveals a seemingly paradoxical set of statistics. On the production side (Table 1), British firms manufactured a series of commercially successful[7] helicopters. Cumulative output accounted for some 1022 helicopters, of which 79 per cent (809 units) were for home markets and 21 per cent for export.

Table 1: UK Helicopter Production, 1945–60

Firm/Helicopter	*First Service*	*Role*	*Total Military*	*Total Civil*	*Total Export*
Westland Dragonfly[a]	April 1950	Rescue	88	8	41
Bristol Sycamore	Feb. 1953	Rescue	109	2	66
Westland Whirlwind[b]	June 1954	Rescue/ASW	308	20	90
Saunders-Roe Skeeter	Jan. 1957	Army Light	66	2	10
Westland Widgeon	Sept. 1957	Civil	–	6	6
Westland Wessex[c]	April 1960	ASW/Assault	c200		
Total					1022
Total Westland					767

Notes: [a] Westland licensed variant of the Sikorsky S-51 helicopter.
[b] Westland licensed variant of the Sikorsky S-55 helicopter.
[c] Westland licensed variant of the Sikorsky S-58 helicopter. The 1960 figures for the Wessex are approximate, based on 1960 production estimates.

Source: Figures from Report of the Committee of Inquiry into the Aircraft Industry, 1964–65, *Cmnd 2853* (London: HMSO, 1965), pp. 121–2; and R. Hafner, 'British Rotorcraft', *Journal of the Royal Aeronautical Society*, Vol. 70, Part 1, January 1966, p. 241.

The paradox arises when the industry's impressive manufacturing output is contrasted with MoS-sponsored R&D over the same period. Helicopter R&D is characterised by a catalogue of cancelled and unfinished projects (Table 2). Although a large number of helicopter R&D projects were initiated, the majority failed to convert into production orders. Taken together, the record indicates *prima facie* that, by 1960, Britain had demonstrated a helicopter production capability but also a questionable legacy of abandoned development projects.

Table 2: MoS-Sponsored Helicopter R&D Projects, 1945–60

Project/Model	*Company*	*Project Initiation*	*Date of Cancellation*
Sycamore (Type 171)	Bristol	1946	N/A (Entered service in February 1953)
W.9	Cierva	1944	1946
Air Horse	Cierva	1946	1951
Type 173	Bristol	1946	N/A[a]
Gyrodyne	Fairey	1946	1949
Rotodyne	Fairey	1947	1962
Ultra-Light	Fairey	1954	1956
Small Ramjet	Bevan	1948	1953
Gas Turbine	Percival	1952	1956
Crop Sprayer	Cierva	1948	1952
Skeeter	Saunders-Roe	1948	N/A (Entered service in January 1957)

Note: [a]The tandem rotor Type 173 was the precursor to the Bristol B191, B192 and Belvedere helicopters. The last entered service with the Royal Air Force in July 1960.

Source: PRO AVIA 65/6, Statement of Expenditure on Rotary-Wing Aircraft, 10 May 1954.

The paradox is explained when the figures are segregated on a firm/product basis. As Table 1 shows, approximately 75 per cent of British helicopter unit production was attributable to Westland Aircraft Limited. Unlike its UK competitors Westland concentrated on licensed production of helicopter technology developed in the US by Sikorsky, but received negligible British government R&D funding. Westland came to dominate the UK helicopter market, while Fairey, Cierva, Bristol and other companies bound by UK MoS helicopter policy largely failed to enter commercial production. Consequently, the figures indicate a failure of UK government industrial policy to achieve its stated objectives and a serious inability in Britain to develop commercially viable indigenous helicopter technology, leading to a reliance on overseas (American) design.

Westland's manufacturing pre-eminence was the result of two distinct factors. First, by relying on US Sikorsky design expertise, Westland was able to compete for production orders against MoS-sponsored 'all-British' alternatives. Westland's total output was based principally on UK service contracts: in market share terms, the British armed services were the primary customer, purchasing approximately 75 per cent of manufacture (Table 1). After obtaining a licensed manufacturing agreement on 10 January 1947 for the Sikorsky S-51, Westland received Admiralty and Air Ministry orders in 1948.[8] Renamed the Dragonfly, 137 were sold.[9] In 1950, a second license was agreed for the larger S-55, which Westland called the Whirlwind. Again, large-scale UK service orders followed (308).[10] The third licensed agreement signed with Sikorsky in 1955 allowed the company to produce the S-58, which Westland designated the Wessex. Production of these three machines provided the basis of Westland's production success. It also represented approximately three-quarters of UK helicopter manufacturing output.

At each stage when Westland received a British service or civil production contract, a roughly comparable helicopter in terms of size, all-up-weight (AUW) and projected operational role was under development elsewhere in the UK. In 1947, for example, the Bristol Aeroplane Company was developing the Type 171 Sycamore under a MoS Experimental Contract, a helicopter similar in principle to the Sikorsky S-51.[11] In 1955, Bristol again had MoS backing for its B191, a project that shared broadly similar performance characteristics with the S-58. Consequently, while producing US designs under license, Westland was able to compete against 'all-British' customer-specific R&D projects.

Westland's order book was only one element of a more complex picture. The second key factor was the commercial failure of a series of R&D projects, which did not progress beyond the prototype stage (see Table 2) that had been initiated or funded by British governments to meet specific requirements against which Westland did not compete.[12] Importantly, the cancellation of programmes conducted by Cierva, Fairey, Bristol and others, all marked the commercial failure of projects that were protected from direct Westland competition.

To complete the picture, the period was significant for two further reasons. Between 1945 and 1960, the British helicopter industry included four major firms[13] in addition to Westland (Table 3). By 1960, as a result of its cumulative orders, Westland had absorbed these companies through acquisition and merger and had emerged as Britain's sole helicopter manufacturer. Consequently, despite earlier government policy to fund and support 'all-British' helicopter R&D, Britain had by 1960 become dependent on a monopoly domestic supplier which had specialised in manufacturing technology of US design origin. Finally, though Britain did import some civil and military fixed-wing aircraft from the US during this period as stopgap measures, the helicopter sector was unique in being systematically dominated by indigenous manufacture of licensed American technology.

THE ISSUES

These trends raise important questions on two levels. At one level lie the factors that dictated patterns of British helicopter R&D and production between 1945 and 1960. The questions here are essentially of two types. On the one hand, there are the reasons why Westland was able to win substantial service and civil production contracts in the face of British government-financed competition. Questions here include: Why did Westland elect to circumvent government industrial policy and acquire licences from Sikorsky? What was it about licensed production that provided Westland with a competitive edge? To what extent did Westland's commercial success undermine the market potential and innovation rates on MoS-sponsored 'all-British' alternatives? Why, given overtly protectionist MoS industrial policies, was Westland awarded significant domestic civil and military helicopter contracts? And why, given its post-1945 industrial policy objectives, did the British government allow Westland to emerge as the sole national helicopter supplier in 1960?

Table 3: Main UK Helicopter Manufacturing Companies, 1945–60

Firm	Years														1960
	1945 45	1946	1947	1948	1949	1950 50	1951	1952	1953	1954	1955 55	1956	1957	1958	1959	60 onwards
Westland Aircraft																
Cierva Autogiro Co.							Helicopter interests merged as Saunders-Roe Helicopter Division in 1950									
Saunders-Roe																
Bristol Aeroplane Co.								Bristol Aircraft								
Fairey Aviation																

On the other hand, there is the key issue of the technical and commercial failure of MoS-sponsored 'all-British' helicopter alternatives at Fairey, Cierva, Bristol and the other companies. Why were British government industrial policies unable to generate successful indigenous competition against Westland-licensed production? What factors led to the questionable commercial performance of 'all-British' helicopter programmes in sectors of the market immune from direct Westland competition? And why did procurement officials get away with a deluded assessment of indigenous helicopter technology, and a programme of 'all-British' development so unrelated to the needs of service and civil operators?

At another level, the helicopter case is relevant to the broader historiography of early post-war British aircraft procurement and more general discussions about defence industrial policy. The orthodox interpretation is that Britain failed to translate 'promising' civil and military aircraft R&D into large-scale production between 1945 and 1960. This assumption is based on the relatively small proportion of aviation projects initiated, almost exclusively funded by the government, that finally entered scale manufacture. Industry undertook 165 manned aircraft programmes that were 'overtly intended for production, and sale to the widest market attainable'[14] of which just ten were eventually produced in quantities of 500 or more. On these input/output – number of projects initiated/number entering production – statistics, the dominant interpretation is 'one of disappointments: it was a story of grandiose projects gone wrong'.[15] On this basis, aircraft procurement has been held up as a classic example of the 'British disease', or the inability of UK manufacturers to exploit their technological innovations.

Because government contracting was the primary determinant of the size, structure and activities of the aircraft industry,[16] the orthodoxy is that the project cancellations reflected deficiencies in government procurement policies. Studies that underpin this view are diverse in both scope and level of analysis, ranging across individual aircraft programmes, entire branches of aeronautical engineering, aircraft development *in toto*, government procurement policies and processes, as well as 'policy prescriptive' texts advocating organisational and administrative reform.[17] What emerges are two competing explanations that purport to account for Britain's legacy of project cancellations.

The first explanation is essentially that British industry developed good aircraft that were wrongly cancelled by government. The primary exposition of this thesis is Wood's *Project Cancelled*, which claims that,

> since the Second World War Britain has become notorious as the nation which spends time and money embarking on advanced aviation projects and then destroys them by withdrawing support at the eleventh hour.[18]

The main tenets of this thesis are that a combination of inter-service rivalry, the dispersal of development funding, the 'gradual starvation' by government of a potentially profitable industry and political mismanagement meant that the British aircraft industry achieved only a 'dismal fraction of what might have been'. Moreover, aircraft programmes that would have assured Britain's lead, including the Miles M.52 and the TSR-2, 'were never given a chance or were cancelled at the last moment'. In essence, therefore, the 'Project Cancelled' view assumes that British technical excellence and world-beating designs were undermined by the failure of government industrial and procurement policies.

Against this, a second influential thesis argues that the fundamental cause of aircraft programme cancellations lay in the government supporting 'too many' projects and firms. Between 1945 and 1960, government funding sustained 22 major aircraft-design groups with associated manufacturing facilities and nine major aero-engine development teams.[19] This industrial structure was underpinned by a procurement philosophy that assumed benefits from parallel development and technical competition between firms across the spectrum of aircraft types.[20] The 'too many' firms/projects thesis adopts three premises to argue that this procurement philosophy led to the legacy of project cancellations.

The first premise is that increases in the cost and complexity of aircraft during the period meant that Britain could not hope to place in production even a fraction of the R&D projects under government sponsorship with available financial resources. Government industrial policy was deficient, therefore, in that it delayed an inevitable amalgamation of aircraft firms.[21] Correspondingly, had government induced mergers immediately after the Second World War, there would have been two beneficial effects: the 'need to subsidise smaller inefficient firms would have been greatly reduced';[22] while, through concentrating 'design teams and production facilities as well as focusing available resources on fewer development projects, more contracts might have been completed'.[23]

The second premise is that failure to rationalise the aircraft industry militated against economies of scale in production.[24] Throughout the post-war period

> ...governments encouraged the maintenance of a variety of aircraft manufacturers, in order, so it was argued, to preserve security of supply and competition between suppliers. At any rate, ...one outcome was the failure to build firms of sizes comparable to those of the USA.[25]

Consequently, procurement policies were 'detrimental...in spreading the country's industrial and design effort too thinly and in making production expensive because of the small numbers ordered'.[26] Broadly speaking, there are two views that flow from this: on the one hand, scarce resources were misallocated over 'too many' projects;[27] on the other, parallel development was a sound philosophy for reducing development risk, but successive governments failed to recognise the need for an inevitable rationalisation of the aircraft industry.[28]

The third premise of the 'too many' firms/projects thesis is that procurement policies failed to provide adequate innovation incentives in industry. Between 1945 and 1960, an important objective of British aircraft supply ministries was the maintenance of key production and design facilities for a future large-scale war economy.[29] On this basis, the policy was to preserve the existing aircraft-industrial structure for future expansion by spreading research contracts among firms. As a consequence of preserving this capacity, the idea of fostering genuine competition between individual aircraft firms 'played only a minor role in the [government's] deliberations'.[30] According to the 'too many' firms/projects critique, procurement policy created an overriding incentive among aircraft firms to *maximise the number* of government R&D contracts they received, rather than *force the pace* of individual programme innovation. Devons, for example, argues that each firm's response was 'to take on a wide range of [R&D] projects in order to safeguard their own future, especially if they [were] uncertain about the production demand'.[31] Moreover, according to Devons, procurement policy was self-defeating because the resulting dispersion of effort made it almost certain that no project was successful.[32] A key document underpinning this view was the 1956 House of Commons Select Committee on Estimates 'The Supply of Military Aircraft' report. This found, *inter alia*, that procurement officials 'had not been sufficiently selective in their allocation of contracts for military aircraft',[33] 'did not appear to deny' that comparatively inefficient firms were sometimes employed on government contracts, had 'a tendency to carry on too far projects essentially similar',[34] and provided firms with R&D contracts at virtually no risk.[35] By implication, the Select Committee's view was that these deficiencies had adverse implications for innovation on individual projects because scarce resources were often misdirected on obsolete development lines.

These two interpretations that dominate the historiography generate a further set of questions. Was it the case, as the 'Project Cancelled' thesis implies, that British industry developed good helicopters that were wrongly cancelled by government? Conversely, did successive British governments sustain 'too many' 'all-British' helicopter firms and projects, and an inadequate incentive structure for innovation in industry? At issue here are the extent to which the historiography is applicable in the helicopter case, and indirectly, whether deficiencies in procurement policies provided the opportunity for Westland's success via the licensed-production broute.

Finally, Westland's performance raises more general questions about the scope and limitations of licensed production as a procurement strategy for national governments. In the extensive literature on defence technology transfer, licensed production is presented as a discrete national procurement approach.[36] At one extreme, a state may pursue policies of 'national self-sufficiency' – or domestic R&D and production – in a particular area of defence technology. At the other, it may decide to circumvent indigenous R&D and manufacture altogether by importing technology 'off-the-shelf' from a non-national supplier. Within this schema, licensed production is that strategy whereby a firm or government attempts 'to bypass the R&D phase of weapons development completely by entering the [manufacturing] process after R&D has been completed'.[37]

In theory, licensed production offers several potential advantages over policies of domestic R&D and production. By circumventing in-house R&D a licensed producer can avoid the cost and lead-time penalties associated with development, and focus instead on the manufacture of a proven technology. Licensed production also provides the opportunity for a firm to increase its industrial capability through what is essentially a technology-transfer process. Indeed, some national governments have adopted overt policies to establish indigenous self-sufficient industries through a step-by-step strategy in which technology transfer through licensed production forms a 'building block': licences are obtained for domestic assembly of a foreign system which provides the know-how for domestic manufacture of components, which, in turn, generates the ability to produce indigenously designed systems.[38]

Empirical research, however, reveals mixed results. On the one hand, in some states where licensed production has been adopted it has failed to provide the cost savings, lead-time reductions and technological assimilation that recipient firms and governments have envisaged.[39] Conversely, other studies have shown that licensed producers have succeeded in achieving economic gains and industrial benefits in the form of self-sufficiency and technology assimilation through the licensing process.[40]

In the context of these broader debates about the costs and benefits of licensed production, the case of the early post-war UK helicopter industry raises three further questions. MoS helicopter-industrial policies which imagined a self-sufficient helicopter industry could be equated with domestic R&D and manufacture patently failed. Consequently, did the combination of Westland's market dominance via licensed production and the relative failure of 'all-British' projects mark the fundamental loss of an indigenous British technological capability? Moreover, to what extent did Westland's strategy provide a competitive edge in equipment cost and lead-time terms? Finally, what lessons does the UK helicopter case provide about the opportunities that licensed production can provide as a government-mandated procurement strategy?

STRUCTURE AND SOURCE

These questions shape the format, scope and analysis of this book. The first two chapters address the primary industrial, technological and policy antecedents of post-war British helicopter R&D and production before 1940 (Chapter 1) and between 1940 and 1945 (Chapter 2). The subsequent chapters focus on developments over discrete time periods: 1945–47 (Chapter 3), 1947–50 (Chapter 4), 1950–55 (Chapter 5) and 1955–60 (Chapter 6). In part, these chronological subdivisions are designed to simplify presentation, but more importantly, the study reveals that each period formed a distinct phase in the processes dictating overall patterns of UK helicopter R&D and production. Each chapter is structured to address two central issues: first, the factors that accounted for Westland's ability to win helicopter production orders; and, second, the factors behind the relative failure of government-sponsored 'all-British' projects to compete against Westland-licensed variants, but also specific civil and military helicopter requirements for which Westland did not compete. The conclusion summarises the main findings of the case study and relates them to the major questions posed at the outset.

The analysis draws primarily on documents contained in the Public Record Office, Kew, and the United States National Archives in Washington, DC. Research conducted at the Public Record Office was centred on relevant files for the major British ministries with a role in post-war helicopter industrial policy: the Ministry of Supply (MoS), the Ministry of Defence (MoD), the Admiralty, the War Office, the Air Ministry, the Ministry of Civil Aviation (MCA) and HM Treasury. Data collection at the United States National Archives was concentrated on United States Air Corps and Army Air Forces, Joint Chiefs of Staff, State Department and United States War Production Board records. One data constraint lay in access to company records for post-war UK helicopter firms, primarily because 'the take-over by Westland of various other British helicopter companies occurred so long ago' that remaining documents other than 'purely formal documents such as share transfers' were not retained by the Westland Group.[41] Moreover, Companies House retains only fragmentary information. Despite these limitations, however, considerable data on the decisions and activities of individual firms were obtained via documents and correspondence in the Ministry of Supply's industrial files.

NOTES

1. M. Allen, *Military Helicopter Doctrines of the Major Powers, 1945–1992* (London: Greenwood Press, 1993), p. xix.
2. Figures calculated from *The Military Balance 1998–1999* (London: Brassey's, 1998).
3. Figures for 1994 calculated from the European Commission, *The European Aerospace Industry: Trading Position and Figures 1994* (Brussels: European Commission, 1994).
4. This literature is relevant to this study and warrants a brief survey. Important development accounts are contained in R.A.C. Brie (ed.), *A History of British Rotorcraft, 1866-1965* (Yeovil: Westland Helicopters, 1968), which includes the memoirs of key design personnel. Articles published in the *Journal of the Royal Aeronautical Society* between 1945 and 1960 outline day-to-day development and technical aspects of individual projects. The most comprehensive accounts of helicopter firms are P. London, *Saunders and Saro Aircraft since 1917* (London: Putnam, 1988); C.H. Barnes, *Bristol Aircraft since 1910* (London: Putnam, 1988); H.A. Taylor, *Fairey Aircraft since 1915* (London: Putnam, 1974); W.J. Reader, The *Weir Group: A Centenary History* (London: Weidenfeld & Nicolson, 1971); J.W.R. Taylor and M.F. Allward, *Westland 50* (London: Ian Allen, 1965); and, E. Mensforth, *Family Engineers* (London: Ward Lock, 1981). Numerous technical accounts of individual projects have been published, the most comprehensive of which include E.J. Everett-Heath, *British Military Helicopters*

(London: Arms & Armour Press, 1986); C. Gablehouse, *Helicopters and Autogiros* (Philadelphia, PA: J.B. Lippincroft Co., 1967); C.H. Gibbs-Smith, *The Aeroplane: An Historical Survey of its Origins and Development* (London: HMSO, 1960); P. Beaver, *Modern Military Helicopters* (Wellingborough: Patrick Stephens, 1987); and, K. Munson, *Helicopters and Other Rotorcraft since 1907* (London: Blandford Press, 1973). Between 1945 and 1960, the British Armed Services were the primary customer of the helicopter industry. However, commentary has focused almost exclusively on operations rather than procurement issues. Notable texts that do develop some of the procurement themes are J. Dowling, *RAF Helicopters: The First Twenty Years* (London: HMSO, 1992); P.A. Towle, *Pilots and Rebels: The Use of Aircraft in Unconventional Warfare, 1918–1988* (London: Brassey's, 1989); and, A. Farrar-Hockley, *The Army in the Air: The History of the Army Air Corps* (London: Alan Sutton, 1994).

5. Between 1945 and 1959, the Ministry of Supply acted as the procurement agency for military and civil aircraft. Its roles included: drawing up specifications and negotiating contracts for production aircraft, responsibility for the Government's R&D programme on military and civil aircraft, and the running of the Government's research establishments.
6. See, for example, PRO AVIA 65/6, Note on the MoS Helicopter R&D Programme with Special Emphasis on the Civil Transport Role, MoS Air 2(a), 17 October 1953.
7. The term 'commercially successful' describes unit manufacturing output. Unit production of 100 aircraft or more is assumed as a measure of project commercial success.
8. Taylor and Allward, *Westland 50*, p. 109.
9. Report of the Committee of Inquiry into the Aircraft Industry, *Cmnd. 2853* (London: HMSO, 1965), p. 121.
10. Ibid.
11. A. McClements, 'A Review of British Rotorcraft Activities, 1943–46', in R.A.C. Brie (ed.), *A History of British Rotorcraft, 1866–1965*, p. 106.
12. See M.R.H. Uttley, 'British Helicopter Developments 1945–60: Government Technology Policy in a Changing Defence Environment', in R. Coopey, M.R.H. Uttley and G. Spinardi (eds), *Defence Science and Technology: Adjusting to Change* (Reading: Harwood, 1993), pp. 125-41.
13. Table 2 includes projects conducted by Percival Aircraft and Bevan. Percival's involvement was limited to basic design and development. Bevan's activities were restricted to power-plant development.
14. R. Worcester, *Roots of British Air Policy* (London: Hodder & Stoughton, 1966), p. 9.
15. D. Edgerton, *England and the Aeroplane: An Essay on a Militant and Technological Nation* (London: Macmillan, 1991), p. xiv.
16. Evidence cited here is the scale of government expenditure during the period. Between 1950 and 1962, government payments accounted for 70 per cent of the aircraft industry's total output. Likewise, by the mid-1950s, government R&D expenditure in the aircraft industry was only marginally less than what Britain's private and nationalised industries spent on their own R&D. See Edgerton, *England and the Aeroplane*, p. 91; and, K. Hartley, 'The Mergers of the UK Aircraft Industry, 1957–60', *Journal of the Royal Aeronautical Society*, December 1965, p. 847.
17. Texts in these categories are numerous, notable examples of which include: G. Williams, F. Gregory and J. Simpson, *Crisis in Procurement: A Case Study of the*

TSR-2 (London: RUSI, 1969); A. Reed, *Britain's Aircraft Industry: What Went Right? What Went Wrong?* (London: J.M. Dent & Sons, 1973); K. Hayward, *Government and British Civil Aerospace: A Case Study in Post-War Technology Policy* (Manchester: Manchester University Press, 1983) and *The British Aircraft Industry* (Manchester: Manchester University Press, 1989); and, K. Hartley, *A Market for Aircraft: A Critique and Proposal for Radical Reconstruction of British Government Procurement Policy*, Hobart Paper 57 (London: Institute for Economic Affairs, 1974).

18. D. Wood, *Project Cancelled: The Disaster of Britain's Abandoned Aircraft Projects* (London: Tri-Service Press, 1990), p. 5.
19. E. Devons, 'The Aircraft Industry', in D. Burns (ed.), *The Structure of British Industry II* (Cambridge: Cambridge University Press, 1964), pp. 45–92.
20. Between 1945 and 1960, the procurement style was 'parallel development', whereby two or three designs of aircraft were developed in each class at competing firms. The major justification for this approach was the assumption that the investment of small sums of money on parallel projects would produce significant reductions in uncertainty (where uncertainty is measured as the potential for programme failure), because it would provide a hedge against unforeseen technical difficulties on an individual programme. For a discussion, see C.J. Hitch and R.N. McKean, *The Economics of Defense in the Nuclear Age* (Cambridge, MA: Harvard University Press, 1960), pp. 249–50.
21. Devons, *Aircraft Industry*, pp. 45–92.
22. T. Geiger, '"The Next War is Bound to Come": Defence Production Policy, Supply Departments and Defence Contractors in Britain, 1945–57', in H. Mercer, N. Rollings and J.D. Tomlinson (eds), *The Labour Governments and Private Industry: The Experience of 1945 to 1951* (Edinburgh: Edinburgh University Press, 1992), p. 112.
23. Ibid.
24. For a discussion about the significance of scale economies in aircraft production see, for example, G.C. Allen, *British Industries and their Organisation* (London: Longman, 1970), p. 186.
25. P. Gummett, 'Civil and Military Aircraft in the UK', in J. Krige (ed.), *Choosing Big Technologies* (Reading: Harwood, 1993), p. 206.
26. Second Report with Evidence Taken before the Sub-Committee E of the Select Committee on Estimates of Session 1956–57, The Supply of Military Aircraft, *HCP 34* (London: HMSO, 1956), p. xvi.
27. See, for example, Wood, *Project Cancelled.*
28. Indicative of this perspective is F. Gregory and J. Simpson, 'The Acquisition of Military Aircraft in Great Britain and West Germany', in F.B. Horton, A.C. Rogerson and E.L. Warner, *Comparative Defense Policy* (London: Johns Hopkins University Press, 1974), pp. 453–64.
29. Geiger, *The Next War*, p. 99.
30. Ibid.
31. Devons, *Aircraft Industry*, p. 65.
32. Ibid., p. 59.
33. Second Report from the Select Committee on Estimates, *HCP 34*, p. 113.
34. Ibid., p. vii.
35. Ibid., p.14.
36. For a summary, see C. Catrina, *Arms Transfers and Dependence* (London: Taylor & Francis, 1988).
37. R. Head, 'The Weapons Acquisition Process: Alternative National Strategies', in Horton, Rogerson and Warner, *Comparative Defense Policy*, p. 420.

38. See, for example, M. Moodie, 'Defense Industries in the Third World: Problems and Promises', in S.G. Neuman and R.E. Harkavy (eds), *Arms Transfers in the Modern World* (New York: Praeger, 1979), p. 299.
39. See, for example, I. Bellany and J. Richardson, 'Australian Defence Procurement', in H.G. Gelber (ed.), *Problems of Australian Defence* (Melbourne: Oxford University Press, 1970), pp. 255–6; C. Groth, 'The Economics of Weapons Coproduction', in M. Edmonds (ed.), *International Arms Procurement: New Directions* (Oxford: Pergamon Press, 1981), p. 71; W. Struys, 'Offsets and Weapons Procurement: The Belgium Experience', in S. Martin (ed.), *The Economics of Offsets: Defence Procurement and Countertrade* (Reading: Harwood, 1996), pp. 75–105; D. Deng and M.W. Chinworth, 'The Teeth of the Little Tigers: Offsets, Defense Production and Economic Development in South Korea and Taiwan', in Martin, *The Economics of Offsets*, pp. 245–298; S. Markowski and P. Hall, 'The Defence Offsets Policy in Australia', in *The Economics of Offsets*, pp. 49–74; and, B. Udis, 'US–Swiss F-5 Transaction and the Evolution of Swiss Offsets Policy', in *The Economics of Offsets*, pp. 321–36.
40. G.R. Hall and R.E. Johnson, 'Aircraft Co-Production and Procurement Strategy', *RAND Report R-450-PR*, May 1967; M.W. Chinworth and R. Matthews, 'Defense Industrialisation Through Offsets: The Case of Japan', in *The Economics of Offsets*, p. 206; Moodie, 'Defense Industries in the Third World', p. 17; and, A. Redlich and M. Miscavage, 'The Business of Offsets: A Practitioner's Perspective Case Study: Israel', in *The Economics of Offsets*, pp. 381–406.
41. Letter to the author from J.R. Bayley, Westland Group Plc, Yeovil, England, 12 February 1990.

1

Pre-1940 Helicopter Developments

Compared with fixed-wing aviation, the helicopter was a marginal technology at the outbreak of the Second World War. Fixed-wing aircraft were in large-scale manufacture with clearly defined military and civil roles. During 1939, for example, the major industrial powers[1] constructed 41,893 military aeroplanes, and British fixed-wing output in 1939 alone was 7,940 units.[2] By contrast, despite some research effort in Europe and North America, no helicopter design had progressed to production.[3]

However, the period to 1940 provided three important preconditions for patterns of UK helicopter R&D and production after 1945. The first was that experimentation before 1940 revealed inherent technical constraints to helicopter development which had retarded its progress in comparison with fixed-wing types; these constraints remained to be resolved in the post-war period. The second was that, despite the experimental status of helicopter technology in 1940, British technical capabilities were – with government support – state of the art when compared with the most advanced projects under development in the US and continental Europe. Britain arguably entered the Second World War at the forefront of helicopter design and development. The third and most significant occurred in July 1940. Perceptions of the higher priority of other aviation projects and pressures on resources led the British government to suspend all indigenous helicopter work indefinitely, and adopt the policy of relying instead on helicopter technology under development within US industry.

TECHNICAL CONSTRAINTS AND PRE-1939 HELICOPTER DEVELOPMENT

In December 1903, the Wright brothers demonstrated controlled and sustained flight with a fixed-wing aircraft. Some four years later the first manned rotorcraft – the Breguet-Richet Gyroplane No.1 – flew in France on 19 September 1907.[4] Despite the similar stages of initial flight, the pre-1939 period witnessed a considerable divergence between innovation rates in the fixed and rotary-wing sectors. Rapid fixed-wing development after

1903 was a consequence of inherent aerodynamic simplicity: once the feasibility of manned-flight had been established, major advances required incremental technical refinement but no fundamental evolution in principle of flight or aircraft configuration. The rapid evolution of fixed-wing aircraft performance to 1939 has been demonstrated by trends in the key performance indicators of speed, range and endurance, payload, stability and control, reliability and maintainability, and especially with regard to powerplant.[5] Other commentators have measured allied technical advances, including improvements in aircraft construction materials and advances in the precision of aircraft engineering technologies.[6] Irrespective of which indicator is applied, the primary result of the inherent technical simplicity of fixed-wing aircraft was the emergence of classes of aircraft in large-scale manufacture catering for both civil and military markets by 1939.[7]

By contrast, the primary factor accounting for the relatively slow development of the helicopter was its inherent technical complexity. Early manned rotorcraft experiments revealed fundamental engineering problems, the solution to which was essential before the helicopter could be translated into an operational technology. The technical constraints confronting helicopter designers were two-fold. First, unlike fixed-wing aircraft, engineering problems arising from 'torque' meant that the most fundamental issue of the 'optimum' helicopter configuration was far from apparent. Second, experimentation revealed that helicopters required a powerplant of much greater output than fixed-wing aeroplanes of comparable weight, and limitations in contemporary aero-engine technology generated further barriers to development. The result of these 'many interrelated mechanical problems'[8] was to retard helicopter development rates relative to fixed-wing innovation before 1939 and to generate technical debates that remained to be resolved in the post-war period.

Torque, 'Optimum' Helicopter Configuration, and Powerplant Constraints

As early as 1880, experiments with models had identified the adverse effects of 'torque' for helicopter stability. The primary observation was that driving a main rotor by an engine through a rotor shaft created a tendency for the fuselage to move in the opposite direction in accordance with Newton's Third Law, namely, that to every action there is an equal and opposite reaction. For helicopter development, the fundamental issue of how most effectively to neutralise torque effects was the primary technical question. The various theoretical 'solutions' to the torque problem that emerged, however, led to the fragmentation of pre-war rotorcraft designers into a series of contending 'schools of thought', each attempting to identify the 'optimum' anti-torque mechanism. The extent of fragmentation is illustrated by the diverse configurations investigated by European and American designers prior to 1939.

One concept was the 'tail-rotor' configuration, premised on the assumption that by incorporating a tail-rotor of smaller dimensions than the horizontal main rotor, but revolving in a vertical plane, the torque could be neutralised. The technical rationale was that the tail rotor, if provided with sufficient thrust, could compensate for any tendency for the helicopter's fuselage to swing round against the rotation of the main rotor. During the 1930s, proponents of this configuration throughout Europe and North America initiated a series of 'tail-rotor' projects. In the US Baumhauer, for example, produced plans for an experimental programme and conducted theoretical research.[9] Baumhauer's approach was later refined in America by Igor Sikorsky. By 1939, the Sikorsky VS-300 represented the most advanced tail-rotor helicopter under development.[10]

A second approach was the 'coaxial' configuration. This was premised on the assumption that the turning of one half of the rotor system in one direction, and the other half in the other direction on the same axis of rotation, would neutralise torque by balancing the opposite rotor forces.[11] The approach attracted interest because designers recognised that its theoretical benefit over the tail-rotor configuration was that the coaxial rotors dispensed with the need for a tail-rotor which in turn consumed engine power. On this assumption, the Spaniard Pescara built a coaxial rotor helicopter powered by a 180 hp Hispano-Suiza engine during 1923, which was capable of making flights of 10 minutes' duration.[12] Subsequently, during the early 1930s the French Breguet-Dorand Gyroplane Laboratoire applied the coaxial configuration when constructing a helicopter prototype that established a series of endurance records in 1936.[13] Other notable coaxial designs developed during the pre-war period were *inter alia*, by Berliner (USA), Sergievsky (Russia) and Flettner (Germany).[14]

A third configuration was the 'twin-rotor'. Similar in principle to coaxial designs, the twin rotor configuration incorporated two equally sized tandem or side-by-side rotors, each operating in opposite directions on the same axis of rotation. Here, it was assumed that the contra-rotating rotors would generate equal and opposite forces, thereby cancelling the torque reaction. In aerodynamic terms, the attraction of the twin rotor design was that it would not incur the power loss associated with a tail-rotor. The origin of the configuration arose from experimental work by Dieuaide during 1877;[15] before the Second World War, a range of 'twin rotor' prototypes were constructed, of which the most advanced projects were the German Focke-Achgelis Fw-61[16] and the British Weir W.6.[17]

A logical extension of the twin-rotor approach was the 'multi-rotor' configuration. Illustrative was the helicopter project commenced in the US by De Bothezat during the early 1920s with financial support from the US Army Air Service, which incorporated multiple rotors to neutralise torque.[18] Though demonstrating some hovering ability, the project was cancelled in

1923 when the prototype failed to reach its target flight ceiling of 300 feet.[19] Other multi-rotor projects also emerged during the 1920s, the most notable of which was a prototype developed by Oemichen in France which flew during April 1924.[20]

In 1842, Phillips observed that if a helicopter's rotor driving force was applied to the rotor blades themselves rather than the rotor shaft, no torque reaction was experienced.[21] In theory, therefore, providing motive power to the tips of the rotors could neutralise torque and also dispense with the need for a heavy and complex transmission system. These assumptions underpinned the 'tip-jet', or 'pressure jet', configuration. Early designs incorporated motor-driven propellers mounted on the rotor blades, of which the 1932 German Flettner design was illustrative.[22] Though the theoretical benefits of the configuration were not undermined, the Flettner project was unsuccessful because the rugged environment surrounding the mechanical rotors caused the engine to disintegrate.[23] To counteract this problem, the Austrian, Doblhoff, began investigating the viability of blade tip-jets, whereby air was ducted to the tip of hollow rotor blades from a compressor mounted on the fuselage. Though development had not been perfected by 1939, further refinement culminated in the limited production of the Doblhoff WNF-342 during the latter stages of the Second World War.[24]

Throughout the pre-war period, one or another of the five basic configurations achieved short-term design dominance. This is illustrated by the endurance, range and speed records established during the period. During 1924, for example, Oemichen's multi-rotor design established a temporary flight distance record of 360 metres.[25] Throughout the late 1930s, the twin-rotor Focke-Achgelis Fw-61 held helicopter altitude, endurance and distance records.[26] Finally, by 1941 the tail-rotor Sikorsky VS-300 had established a helicopter endurance record of 1 hour 32 minutes.[27] However, the lack of consensus between advocates of the different configurations served to fragment and dissipate experimentation resources and also to retard innovation rates. Moreover, the unattractive performance of pre-1939 helicopters held back commercial support and left potential customers uninterested.

Before 1939, the problem for designers in identifying the 'optimum' helicopter configuration was compounded by practical constraints concerning available engine technology. As Munson points out:

> ... undoubtedly the biggest barrier to the helicopter's progress [has] been that, pound for pound of payload, the helicopter requires a powerplant of much greater output than a conventional [fixed-wing] aeroplane.[28]

A consequence of the very success of fixed-wing aircraft development before 1939 was that aero-engine designers and manufacturers had focused on developing powerplants for 'conventional' aircraft. The problem this created for pre-war helicopter design teams was that they were forced to rely on aero-engines intended primarily for fixed-wing aircraft, rather than designed to meet the more exacting power requirements of helicopters.[29] The outcome was that all pre-war prototypes were installed with under-powered engines that precluded the development of helicopters with adequate range and speed for manufacture and operational use.

Before 1939, these inherent technical complexities meant that the helicopter remained an experimental technology. In short:

> At the beginning of the helicopter era, no one configuration was dominant. Assorted designers weighed differently the advantages and disadvantages of the various arrangements of rotors and types of power plant and as a result produced a wide variety of vertical-flight machines.[30]

UK HELICOPTER TECHNOLOGY AND THE ROLE OF PUBLIC POLICY IN 1939

Despite the experimental status of the helicopter in 1939, two key factors were important as far as British development capabilities were concerned. The first was that UK helicopter teams entered the Second World War at the contemporary state of the art in terms of designs and practical achievements. The second was that shortly before the outbreak of hostilities, the British government assumed responsibility for helicopter development by providing military specifications and financial support for projects in industry.

British Designs and the State of the Art

Table 4 shows performance characteristics for the most advanced helicopter prototypes under development worldwide in 1939. The absence of design dominance is apparent: the US Sikorsky VS-300 was a tail-rotor type, whereas the French Breguet project incorporated coaxial rotors; by contrast, the German Focke-Achgelis and the British Weir W.6 designs were configured with twin-rotors. More important, when measured against the performance indicators of top speed and maximum flight altitude, the British Weir W.6 was the most advanced prototype under construction. At the outbreak of the Second World War, it could reasonably be claimed that the British team 'were on the verge of leading the world in helicopter development',[31] and on the brink of placing the W.6 into scale production.

A further indicator of the leading status of British designers concerned their advanced role in developing and manufacturing non-helicopter forms of rotorcraft. After 1925, the Cierva Autogiro Company in the UK had concentrated on 'autogiro' design and construction, or rotorcraft:

Table 4: Indicators of the Comparative State of the Art in Helicopter Technology, 1939–40

Country	*Model/ Company*	*Year*	*Top Speed* (km/h)	*Range* (km)	*Maximum Altitude* (m)	*Take Off Weight* (lb)	*Config-uration*
France	Breguet-Dorand Gyroplane	1936	100	44	158	4,475	Coaxial
Germany	Focke-Achgelis Fw-61	1939	100	230	3,427	2,100	twin-rotor
USA	Vought-Sikorsky 300	1940	80	121	–	1,150	tail-rotor
UK	Weir W.6	1940	125	–	3,810	2,360	twin-rotor

Source: Figures compiled from K. Munson, *Helicopters and Other Rotorcraft since 1907* (London: Blandford, 1968).

> ...pulled through the air by a propeller like a conventional fixed-wing aircraft, but it was sustained by a rotor, from the actions of air flowing through it (auto-rotation, windmilling). As distinct from the helicopter rotor the autogiro rotor was not power driven. This enabled the autogiro to perform over a much wider range of speeds than the fixed-wing aircraft but it could not truly hover like the helicopter.[32]

Between 1925 and 1939, the significance of the autogiro was that it remained the only operational rotary-wing aircraft in existence, and the pre-eminent role of UK designers was evident in a series of refinements to its configuration. Cierva's early autogiros employed conventional fixed-wing aircraft controls, of which the most advanced model of the series was the 1932 C.19 Mk. IV.[33] The next important British development was the introduction of 'direct control', whereby all fixed-wing controls were discarded and replaced with direct controls to tilt the rotor hub and provide rotor thrust. The first successful direct control autogiro manufactured in quantity was the Cierva C.30, of which 100 were built after 1934.[34] The final technical refinement was 'direct take-off',[35] which provided the basis for the Cierva C.40 autogiro design that entered production in 1938. A measure of the capability of the C.40 was that it could operate into and out of a 'tennis-court-sized area', and cruise at over 120 knots (222km/h).[36]

The importance of Cierva's technical achievements was that they provided a clear UK lead in practical rotorcraft development and manufacture. Throughout the 1930s, Cierva's innovations, coupled with Air Ministry[37] and Admiralty[38] procurement orders, led a number of UK firms to obtain licenses for Cierva designs. What emerged was a cluster of firms and design teams that formed the basis of the embryonic British helicopter industry. These included G. & J. Weir (W.1, W.2, W.3, W.4, W.5 and W.6 designs), de Havilland (C.24 design), Comper (C.25 design), Westland (CL.20 and C.29 designs) and the AR III Construction (Hafner Gyroplane) Company (ARIII design).[39]

An equally significant measure of the UK technological lead was the fact that Cierva licences were taken out by the Autogiro Company of America, which catered for US Army battlefield observation and liaison autogiro requirements.[40] Consequently, on the basis of their achievements in helicopter and autogiro development and construction, British helicopter firms entered the Second World War not only at the technical state of the art, but also as an industry that had penetrated overseas helicopter markets through the export of rotorcraft and licensed production agreements.

Role of UK Public Policy

Before 1938, the British Air Ministry's policy approach had been to take a 'technical interest'[41] in the development of rotary-wing aircraft. This 'interest' took two forms. The first was limited financial support for proposals by individual designers before 1925. During 1915, for example, Brennan at the Royal Aircraft Establishment (RAE) had requested funding for a multi-rotor helicopter design, which the Air Ministry provided after 1919. Despite some progress, Brennan's prototype crashed on 2 October 1925 and Air Ministry support was withdrawn. The crash was important because it:

> ...caused the Air Ministry to call for advice on helicopters in general and Brennan's in particular from the Aeronautical Research Committee. This committee reported that there was no point in proceeding with helicopters of the Brennan type, that is with driven rotors.[42]

The second form of 'technical interest' was small-scale Air Ministry financing for and procurement of British-built autogiros after 1925. In October 1925, the Air Ministry agreed to sponsor tests of the Cierva C.6A.[43] Subsequently, during November 1925, the Secretary of State for Air announced that he had decided to have several types of autogiro built in the UK for further trials and evaluation by the RAF. A series of Air Ministry autogiro specifications[44] followed, and cumulative orders for 75 military production aircraft were issued by 1939.[45]

During 1938, however, the Air Ministry adopted a more systematic approach towards helicopter industrial policy when:

> ...it became clear that, like every other important project in aviation, it [helicopter development] could not be run as a commercial undertaking and that Air Ministry control was essential if this country were to retain its position in relation to other countries.[46]

The primary stimulus was Air Ministry concern that the emerging German helicopter industry and developments by the Focke-Achgelis firm, in particular, were threatening to establish a technological lead.[47] By late 1938, the result was Air Ministry helicopter specifications and funding for three British helicopter projects. The first contract, to meet the Fleet Air Arm's requirements for 'Night Shadowing' duty, was placed with the AR III Construction (Hafner Gyroplane) Company for the firm's 'Gyroplane' AR.5 proposals to fulfil Specification No. 22/38.[48] The second contract, again to meet Specification No. 22/38, was given to G & J Weir for the development of the company's W.7 design. Finally, during December 1938, the Air Ministry placed contracts with the Hafner company for the design and construction of a single-seater, single-rotor experimental helicopter to Specification No. S.10/39.[49] After late 1938, these contracts meant that the projects were formally incorporated into the government's aircraft industrial policy and were in receipt of official development support.

HELICOPTER POLICY AFTER 1940: ABANDONING A CAPABILITY

In September 1939, the deployment of British troops to France brought renewed Air Ministry interest in the operational utility of rotorcraft. To optimise the use of available assets in support of the war effort, two Cierva C.40 autogiros were despatched to France with the British Expeditionary Force to support Army observation work. Early in 1940, RAF and requisitioned civilian-owned C.30 and C.40 autogiros were assembled at RAF Duxford as No. 1448 Rota Calibration Flight for radar calibration duties.[50] This unit, later to become No. 529 Autogiro Squadron, was moved to Henley-on-Thames where it remained until 1945.[51]

Throughout 1939, with the immediate imperative of mobilising existing aircraft stocks, longer-term issues over the future of indigenous helicopter development were initially ignored. Instead, official attention focused on rationalising aircraft production and the creation of a new organisation – the Ministry of Aircraft Production (MAP) – to relieve the Air Ministry of certain procurement functions. The establishment of the MAP on 17 May 1940 resulted in part from the necessity to relieve the Secretary of State for Air from the responsibility of organising the aircraft industry, and leave the Air Staff free to concentrate on air operations, training and the day-to-day conduct of the air war.[52] The Ministry was also created to rationalise and regulate the supply of aircraft *matériel* as between the RAF and the Royal Navy, and to rationalise experimental research and development work between the two services. In terms of former Air Ministry duties, whereas the Air Ministry retained the role of formulating operational requirements for the RAF and the Army, the MAP acquired formal responsibility for the supply (including research and development), inspection and repair of aircraft, aircraft armaments, and aircraft storage pending issue to operational squadrons.

After the clarification of bureaucratic roles in early 1940,[53] agreement was reached between the MAP and the Admiralty on aircraft supply questions by mid-1940. The major roles allocated between the MAP and the Admiralty relating to aircraft development can be summarised as follows:

(i) The Ministry of Aircraft Production will be responsible for meeting Admiralty requirements as regards research, experiment, development and supply of airframes, engines, spares, equipment and armaments...
(ii) The Admiralty will have absolute right to determine the types of aircraft, engines and equipment to be produced for the Fleet Air Arm.
(iii) The Ministry of Aircraft Production will allocate, for the purposes of meeting Admiralty requirements, such a proportion of the available resources as decided from time to time by the policy of HM Government.[54]

The major organisational implication was that responsibility for aircraft R&D, of which helicopter activities were a part, had been centred in the new Ministry. In terms of indigenous helicopter activities, therefore, the MAP was now to be the primary focus of decision-making for the duration of the war.

The MAP evaluated the scope and requirements for a domestic helicopter programme during July 1940. Rather than continuing to support industrial R&D, the MAP's revised position was summarised by the Deputy Director of Scientific Research:

> [the Ministry]... is not able at present to declare for a policy of helicopter development irrespective of definite war application and irrespective of parallel development in America...[55]

Despite Air Ministry recognition in 1938 that government funding was essential for embryonic British manufacturers, by the end of July 1940 all helicopter development had been suspended indefinitely.

The primary impetus to abandon helicopter work arose from Air Ministry and MAP perceptions of the higher priority of other aviation projects given the pressure on resources after Dunkirk.[56] To maximise operational capability, the MAP policy was to halt all contracts not directly linked to fixed-wing aircraft production.[57] As a 'developmental' technology, helicopter contracts were given the lowest possible priority in the competition for scarce funds. The low-priority status was compounded by Air Ministry scepticism about the helicopter *per se*. The RAF had been experiencing technical problems with autogiro operations in France. As MAP documents indicate, 'poor performance of existing (autogiro) types' and 'maintenance difficulties' contributed to an 'unwillingness to divert production manpower engaged in making "normal" RAF types of aircraft'.[58] More significant was the more general view in the RAF that there was no demonstrable specific need for aircraft of the helicopter type.[59] Implicit here was the assumption that, in its primary transport role in support of the Army, fixed-wing aircraft would be adequate for foreseeable requirements.

On the industrial side and independent of overt MAP policy, work on the Air Ministry contracts at Weir and Hafner had effectively ceased by late June 1940. Throughout 1940, the Weir W.6 had undergone flight trials, but in July the company's Board had concluded '...they could not continue under the pressure of other work more immediately productive from the war point of view'.[60] Part of the problem for Weir was that significantly increased project funding was required if the W.6 was to meet Specification S.22/38 for the three-seat shipborne observation aircraft.[61] Though the MAP Director of Scientific Research later claimed that Weir stopped work 'against our [the Ministry's] better judgement',[62] the low priority already assigned to helicopter work meant that no direct incentives could be provided by the Ministry to preserve the company's design capacity by, for example, diverting non-helicopter commitments elsewhere. The Weir design team was disbanded and the experimental machine and equipment were stored in a hangar at Thornliebank, Glasgow.[63]

In the case of the Hafner contract (in conjunction with Shorts/Pobjoy), work ceased on the Ministry-sponsored AR.5 Rotaplane in May 1940.[64] As an Austrian national, Hafner had been interned by the authorities on nationality grounds.[65] Without his expertise, the work on the experimental rotorcraft for Specification S.22/38 (FAA Night Shadowing Duties) was wound up, despite existing contracts for the production of two prototypes.[66] With the exit of both Weir and Hafner from the field, the two industrial centres of UK pre-war helicopter activity had been dismantled.

As British development effectively ceased, helicopter designers, engineers and administrative personnel making up the pre-war industry were re-employed elsewhere. Table 5 shows the pre-1940 activities and subsequent deployment of key individuals in the Cierva/Weir and Hafner organisations. As the information indicates, an immediate implication of the decision to halt rotorcraft development was the fragmentation and redirection of expertise to non-helicopter-related functions. For example, C.G. Pullin, the Weir pre-war Chief Designer, was redeployed for research into fighting vehicles. Likewise, K. Watson – a Cierva/Weir designer of considerable experience – was also subsequently redeployed, in his case on fixed-wing activities at Power Jets (Research & Development) Ltd.

Clearly, the strains on financial and manpower resources within these firms, and the relatively low official priority given to helicopters in the face of more pressing military requirements, led to the demise of British projects and the fragmentation of the emerging British helicopter industry. Under these constraints, a new MAP approach emerged which had the objective of optimising British access to helicopter technology under development within US industry.[67]

Table 5: Post-1940 Wartime Activities of Key UK Helicopter Development Personnel

Name	*Role in 1940*	*Post-1940 Employer*	*Post-1940 Employment*
J.A.J. Bennett	Chief Designer, Cierva	Chief Technical Officer, CLE/AFEE (1940); US helicopter liaison (1940–44)	Rotachute work; US helicopter liaison
O.L.L. Fitzwilliams	Designer on the W.6 at Weir	Not known (1940–42); CLE/AFEE (1942–45)	Rotachute work with Hafner
R.Hafner	Chief Designer, ARIII Construction	CLE/AFEE (1940–44); Bristol Aeroplane Co. Ltd. (1944–45)	Rotachute work (1940–44); helicopter design (1940–45)
A. Marsh (1940–45)	Chief Test Pilot, Cierva		Royal Air Force
T. Nesbit	Designer, Weir/Cierva	CLE/AFEE (1940–44); Bristol Aircraft Company Ltd. (1944–45)	Rotachute work (1940–44); helicopter design (1944–45)
C.G. Pullin	Chief Designer, Weir	Fighting Vehicles Research Centre; Power Jets; Cierva (1944–45)	Non-helicopter work
J.S. Shapiro	Chief Technical Officer, Cierva	Not known (1940–43); Weir (1943–45)	Helicopter experimental work after 1943
G.E. Walker	Designer, Cierva/Weir	CLE/AFEE (1940–44); Bristol Aeroplane Company Ltd. (1944–45)	Rotachute work (1940–44); helicopter design (1944–45)
K. Watson	Designer, Cierva/Weir	Power Jets (1940–45)	Fixed-wing design
S.B. Weller	Designer, Cierva/Weir	CLE/AFEE (1940–44); Bristol Aeroplane Company Ltd. (1944–45)	Rotachute work (1940–44); helicopter design (1944–45)

Source: Information compiled from R.A.C. Brie, 'The Cierva Autogiro Company, 1930–40'; K. Watson, 'Activities of Weir, Cierva and Saunders-Roe 1933–1962'; and G.E. Walker, 'Activities of Weir, Hafner and Bristol, 1933–1960', all in R.A.C. Brie (ed.), *A History of British Rotorcraft 1866–1965* (Yeovil: Westland Helicopters, 1968).

The Ministry's revised strategy had four elements. First, signals were dispatched to the US authorities expressing British interest in purchasing any 'promising' types that might subsequently be developed by American firms.[68] To this end, the MAP made enquiries to the US authorities about the mechanisms by which any future British requirements could be met by allocations from American production.[69] Second, recognising that any technical advances made by American firms were '... the only way in which ... [the UK] shall get helicopters for war use',[70] the decision was made to place British design and development knowledge at the disposal of the US authorities. An early example of this technology transfer was the dispatch of all drawings for the rotor and transmission systems of the Weir W.6 to the US during late 1940.[71] Third, because the MAP's assumption was that 'if a [British Service helicopter] requirement should arise it will have to be met by allocations from American production',[72] it became a policy tenet that,

> if... machines from the US are satisfactory and have definite operational value, an attempt will be made to interest one of the American firms in our needs so that it may carry out our rotaplane development.[73]

The MAP's thinking was that because it was assisting US efforts through technology transfer, then leverage could be applied to the US authorities to provide production types for the UK in the form of a *quid pro quo*. In this regard, the Ministry's perception was of the potential for an Anglo-US relationship of collaboration in the helicopter field, rather than British reliance on the production priorities of US forces. The final element of policy was a series of initiatives to monitor helicopter developments in US industry and analyse their operational potential for British forces. Despite Air Ministry ambivalence about helicopter technology, the Admiralty was becoming interested in the possibility of using helicopters in the vital area of convoy protection. Under the instruction of the Director of Naval Development and Production, Wing Commander R.A.C. Brie (formerly Cierva's Chief Test Pilot and on secondment from the RAF) was posted to the British Air Commission in Washington to liaise with US services and encourage American interest in the use of rotorcraft in the anti-submarine role.[74]

In 1940 the MAP did make a minor concession in its blanket policy on indigenous helicopter R&D activity. Released from internment in September, Hafner was posted to the Central Landing Establishment (CLE) with a small group of designers and technicians (see Table 5) to work on a small rotary wing glider.[75] Designated the 'Rotachute', the primary objective of the project was the development of a one-man rotary-wing parachute for use by airborne forces in conjunction with troop-carrying aircraft.[76] The requirement and justification for development of a rotary parachute had arisen because of the Army's view that, with the increasing need for parachutes, subsequent shortages of silk might arise.[77] By the latter part of 1940, despite small-scale rotary work at the CLE,

Britain had abandoned indigenous helicopter development and now relied on US industry to meet foreseeable Allied requirements.

SUMMARY

Up to 1940 the helicopter remained an experimental technology and crucial design issues relating to 'optimum' configuration and powerplant remained largely unresolved. Despite limited practical achievements, however, the capabilities of British design teams were at the state of the art in terms of their success with both helicopter prototypes and autogiro manufacture. Moreover, Air Ministry perceptions of the operational potential of the helicopter during 1938 had resulted in an industrial policy that provided both operational requirement specifications and government R&D funding. The consequence was that UK helicopter designers entered the Second World War with a technological edge, government financial backing and prototypes that were on the verge of entering scale production.

By July 1940, pressures on technical resources and RAF perceptions that the helicopter was likely to be of limited wartime utility led the British government to abandon indigenous development and to rely instead on potential helicopter innovations in US industry. Measured by short-term operational considerations, British defence planners were to be proved correct: helicopters were to have only a marginal impact on Allied wartime operations. However, the 1940 decision to halt helicopter work was to have profound longer-term implications for Britain: it was to enable US firms using UK technological advances and knowledge to gain a significant lead in helicopter design, development and manufacturing capacity.

NOTES

1. Defined as Great Britain, France, Germany, Italy, the USSR, the USA and Japan.
2. Figures obtained from R. Overy, *The Road to War* (London: Macmillan, 1989), p. 319.
3. Figures include prototypes. Compiled from E.J. Everett-Heath, *British Military Helicopters* (London: Arms & Armour Press, 1986), pp. 214–15.
4. For a detailed analysis of the Breguet-Richet Gyroplane, see, for example, K. Munson, *Helicopters and Other Rotorcraft since 1907* (London: Blandford, 1968), p. 107.
5. For a detailed analysis, see, for example, R. Miller and D. Sawers, *The Technical Development of Modern Aviation* (London: Routledge & Kegan Paul, 1968). Miller and Sawers chart innovation against these performance indicators and the factors accounting for the development of cost-effective aircraft for civil and military roles.
6. See, for example, D. Edgerton, *England and the Aeroplane: An Essay on a Militant and Technological Nation* (London: Macmillan, 1991), pp. 33–5.

7. Miller and Sawers, *Technical Development*.
8. PRO AVIA 15/954, Rotary Wing Aircraft Development, Report by J.A.J. Bennett, 23 December 1940.
9. USNA, War Production Board Collection, The Helicopter and its Future by Grover Loening, Chairman of the Helicopter Committee of the National Advisory Committee for Aeronautics, 3 December 1943, File No. 314.248.
10. For more detail, see W.R. Young, *The Helicopter* (Alexandra, VA: Time-Life, 1982), pp. 79–82.
11. For a more detailed discussion, see R.W. Prouty, *Military Helicopter Design Technology* (London: Jane's, 1989), p. 35.
12. C.H. Gibbs-Smith, *Aviation: An Historical Survey from its Origins to the End of World War II* (London: HMSO, 1985), p. 190.
13. Munson, *Helicopters and Other Rotorcraft*, p. 109.
14. USNA, War Production Board Collection, The Helicopter and its Future by Grover Loening, Chairman of the Helicopter Committee of the National Advisory Committee for Aeronautics, 3 December 1943, File No. 314.248.
15. For a more detailed discussion, see Gibbs-Smith, *Aviation*, p. 50.
16. See R.A.C. Brie and C.F. Caunter, 'References to Rotary Wing Aircraft in the Annual Reports and Journals of the Royal Aeronautical Society, 1866-1965', in R.A.C. Brie (ed.), *A History of British Rotorcraft, 1866–1965* (Yeovil: Westland Helicopters, 1968), p. 8; and PRO AVIA 15/954, Rotary Wing Aircraft Development, Report by J.A.J. Bennett, 23 December 1940.
17. See Everett-Heath, *British Military Helicopters*, pp. 26–7.
18. For a detailed account of the project, see Prouty, *Military Helicopter Design*, pp. 1–2.
19. Ibid.
20. Munson, *Helicopters and Other Rotorcraft*, p. 106.
21. Gibbs-Smith, *Aviation*, p. 28.
22. For more details, see PRO AVIA 15/954, Rotary Wing Aircraft Development, Report by J.A.J. Bennett, 23 December 1940.
23. See N. Polmar and F.D. Kennedy, *Military Helicopters of the World: Military Rotary-Wing Aircraft since 1917* (London: Arms & Armour Press, 1981), pp. 46–53.
24. Ibid., p. 44.
25. Munson, *Helicopters and Other Rotorcraft*, p. 106.
26. For more details, see: PRO AVIA 15/954, Rotary Wing Aircraft Development, Report by J.A.J. Bennett, 23 December 1940.
27. Munson, *Helicopters and Other Rotorcraft*, p. 116.
28. Ibid., p. 10.
29. For a discussion, see I. Cheeseman, M. Edmonds and J. Simpson, 'The Procurement of Military Combat Aircraft, 1945–1970', in F. Gregory, M. Imber and J. Simpson (eds), *Perspectives Upon British Defence Policy, 1945–1970* (Southampton: Southampton University Press, 1978), p. 194.
30. Prouty, *Military Helicopter Design*, p. 35.
31. Everett-Heath, *British Military Helicopters*, p. 27.
32. R. Hafner, 'British Rotorcraft', *Journal of the Royal Aeronautical Society*, Volume 70, January 1966, p. 235.
33. Ibid.
34. Everett-Heath, *British Military Helicopters*, p. 16.
35. For a technical description, see Hafner, 'British Rotorcraft', p. 236.
36. Prouty, *Military Helicopter Design*, p. 3.
37. For a more detailed account of Air Ministry autogiro procurement and policy,

see E.J. Everett-Heath, G.M. Moss, A.W. Mowat and K.E. Reid, *Military Helicopters* (London: Brassey's, 1990), p. 5; and J. Dowling, *RAF Helicopters: The First Twenty Years* (London: HMSO, 1992), p. 19.
38. See R.A.C. Brie, 'The Cierva Autogiro Company 1930–1940', in R.A.C. Brie (ed.) *A History of British Rotorcraft 1866–1965* (Yeovil: Westland Helicopters, 1968), pp. 41–4.
39. Details compiled from Hafner, 'British Rotorcraft', pp. 235–7. For a more detailed description of firms and projects, see R.N. Liptrot, 'Rotary Wing Survey 1842–1954', in R.A.C. Brie (ed.), *A History of British Rotorcraft 1866–1965* (Yeovil: Westland Helicopters, 1968), pp. 23–34.
40. Prouty, *Military Helicopter Design*, pp. 3–4.
41. PRO AVIA 15/954, Rotary Wing Aircraft Development, Report by J.A.J. Bennett, 23 December 1940.
42. Everett-Heath, *British Military Helicopters*, p. 13.
43. Ibid.
44. For a detailed account, see R. Sturtivant, *British Research and Development Aircraft: Seventy Years at the Leading Edge* (Yeovil: Haynes, 1990), pp. 29–42. Official documentation relating to autogiro specifications is contained in PRO AIR 20/690, Development of the Autogiro and Helicopter for Operational Purposes (1933–1936).
45. Figures calculated from Everett-Heath, *British Military Helicopters*, p. 214. For a detailed description, see O. Thetford, *Aircraft of the Royal Air Force since 1918* (London: Putnam), 1962, p. 559; and, Royal Air Force, 'Rotary Wings in the RAF', *The Aeroplane and Astronautics*, 18 March 1960, pp. 336–9.
46. PRO AVIA 15/954, Rotary Wing Aircraft Development, Report by J.A.J. Bennett, 23 December 1940.
47. Ibid.
48. Ibid.
49. PRO AVIA 15/954, Letter from the Air Ministry to ARIII Construction (Hafner Giroplane), 29 December 1938.
50. Royal Air Force, 'Rotary Wings', p. 336.
51. Hafner, 'British Rotorcraft', p. 236.
52. Naval Staff History of the Second World War, *The Development of British Naval Aviation, 1919–1945*, Vol. 1 (London: Historical Section, Admiralty, 1954), p. 206.
53. Ibid.
54. Ibid. Air Branch Acquaint of 11 September 1940, pp. 206–7.
55. PRO AVIA 15/954, Minute from the Deputy Director of Scientific Research, 12 January 1943.
56. PRO AVIA 15/954, Minute from Director of Scientific Research, 2 February 1943. For a more general discussion of this point, see Cheeseman *et al.*, *The Procurement of Military Combat Aircraft*, p. 192.
57. PRO AVIA 15/954, Minute from Deputy Director of Research, Development and Technology, 14 January 1943.
58. PRO AVIA 15/954, Minute from MO9, 9 December 1940.
59. Dowling, *RAF Helicopters*, p. 5.
60. PRO AVIA 15/954, Minute from the Director of General Research and Development, 6 February 1941.
61. Everett-Heath, *British Military Helicopters*, p. 27.
62. PRO AVIA 15/954, Minute from the Director of Scientific Research, 2 February 1943.
63. PRO AVIA 15/954, Rotary Wing Aircraft Development, Report by J.A.J. Bennett, 23 December 1940.

64. PRO AVIA 15/954, Minute from the Director of General Research and Development, 6 February 1941.
65. PRO AVIA 15/954, Rotary Wing Aircraft Development, Report by J.A.J. Bennett, 23 December 1940.
66. Ibid.
67. PRO AVIA 15/954, Minute from the Director General of Research and Development, 6 February 1941.
68. Ibid.
69. PRO AVIA 15/954, Minute from the Chief Executive, 4 February 1943.
70. PRO AVIA 15/954, Minute from the Director of Scientific Research, 2 February 1943.
71. L.B. Bryson, F.E. Heenan and C.A, Johnson, 'Helicopters in the Royal Navy', *Aeronautical Journal*, Vol. 76 (August 1972), p. 471.
72. PRO AVIA 15/954, Minute from the Chief Executive, 4 February 1943.
73. PRO AVIA 15/954, Rotary Wing Aircraft Development, Report by J.A.J. Bennett, 23 December 1940.
74. Bryson *et al.*, 'Helicopters in the Royal Navy', p. 471.
75. PRO AVIA 15/954, Minute from the Deputy Director of Scientific Research, 12 January 1943.
76. For a detailed discussion of the Rotachute project, see Hafner, 'British Rotorcraft', p. 236; and R. Hafner, 'Four Decades of Rotating Wing Activity, 1928–1965', in R.A.C. Brie (ed.), *A History of British Rotorcraft 1866–1964* (Yeovil: Westland, 1968), pp. 37–41.
77. G.E. Walker, 'Activities of Weir, Hafner and Bristol 1933–1960', in R.A.C. Brie (ed.), *A History of British Rotorcraft*, p. 70. The MAP file covering developments on the project is PRO AVIA 44/536, Work of the AFEE, 1940–45.

2

The Wartime Legacy, 1940–45

Wartime events after July 1940 were central determinants of the subsequent post-war success of Westland's licensed production and the comparative failure of indigenous British helicopter R&D. In 1940, constraints and short-term expediency led the British government to abandon a concerted programme of indigenous helicopter R&D. By 1945, a considerable divergence between US and British helicopter development and production capabilities had emerged. On the one hand, US firms had completed large-scale production of helicopter types. This had two implications. First, it provided the basis for US firms to enter post-war helicopter manufacture with a clear technological lead over British firms. And second this lead, later transferred to Westland as a licensed producer, created key conditions for Westland's subsequent domination of post-war British helicopter production. On the other hand, British government policy measures throughout the war had had opposite implications: to create conditions that were to retard indigenous British helicopter research and development throughout the 1940s and 1950s.

US HELICOPTER DEVELOPMENTS, 1940–43: THE ACQUISITION OF A TECHNOLOGICAL LEAD

Until 1940, the relative status of British and US helicopter designs were comparable. In Britain, flight performance with Weir W.6 prototypes indicated scope for future production.[1] Across the Atlantic, Sikorsky had flown the VS-300 in September 1939 – a prototype demonstrating both controllability and production potential.[2] The exit of Weir and Hafner from the helicopter field, however, was followed by an immediate divergence between British and US helicopter design and production capabilities. By 1943, Sikorsky had made dramatic technical advances and anticipated large-scale production orders for a range of helicopter types.

Between 1940 and 1943 Sikorsky had developed three helicopter types, each of which was derived from, and an improvement upon, the original VS-300. By mid-1943, these types had received large-scale production contracts from the US Army Air Force (USAAF) (67 units) and the British Government (267 units), and a small-scale contract from the US Navy (4 units).[3]

Igor Sikorsky achieved a series of technical breakthroughs. By September 1939 he had flown the VS-300 helicopter and demonstrated its controllability, after which the design team continued development work and finally accomplished 'a reasonable degree of stability'.[4] In view of the success with the VS-300 project, Sikorsky commenced development of three derivative models.[5] The first, the XR-4, a larger variant of the VS-300, was initiated during 1940 and a prototype was successfully flown during January 1941. The XR-4 type was designed around a 165 horsepower engine with a unit weight of 1,500 lb and an all-up-weight of 2,050 lb.[6] By March 1943, provisional orders for 29 XR-4s had been placed.[7] The second model, designated the XR-6, had a larger 225 hp Lycoming engine. This had a gross weight of 2,355 pounds, of which 600 lb was to be useful load. Initial XR-6 testflights took place during October 1943.[8] Provisional orders by March 1943 totalled five units, of which two were to be for the USAAF and three for the US Navy.[9] The third type was the much larger XR-5 powered by a 450 hp engine and with a gross weight of 5,300 lb. It was first flight-tested in August 1943,[10] and the anticipated order was for 304 units, of which 52 were to be for the USAAF and 252 for the UK Armed Services.[11] In each case, Sikorsky had improved upon the basic configuration established in the VS-300. The major technical innovation incorporated in the post-1940 models was a more powerful powerplant with commensurate increases in payload, and improvements in design and reliability to the extent that large-scale manufacture could be undertaken.

In contrast to British MAP priorities in 1940, three factors were responsible for Sikorsky's transformation of the helicopter from an experimental to a production technology with its ability to win significant production contracts. First, *responsibility* for wartime rotorcraft development lay with the USAAF,[12] an organisation that was to provide urgent operational requirements and incentives for rapid helicopter production. Secondly, and somewhat paradoxically, it was the British Admiralty that provided further requirements and incentives for helicopter production. And, thirdly, perception within the USAAF and the British Admiralty that the helicopter would prove to be an important operational technology served to channel significant US government financial support.

USAAF Helicopter Requirements and Sikorsky Innovation

The cessation of UK helicopter development work after 1940 had been attributable in part to RAF concerns about the operational utility and reliability of rotary-wing aircraft. The overriding priority of the RAF's strategic bombing mission was premised on high-speed, fixed-wing aircraft in fighter and bomber roles – priorities against which rotorcraft as 'transport types' were perceived to be of marginal utility. Crucial for the subsequent debate over helicopter development in the UK, RAF priorities emphasised the strategic rather than the tactical use of air power, for which fixed-wing aircraft were judged by the Air Staff to be most appropriate. In contrast, shortly before the outbreak of the Second World War, the Norris-Dorsey Bill had placed responsibility in the US for the development of rotary-wing aircraft with the USAAF.[13] Like the RAF, the USAAF was oriented almost completely towards strategic heavy bombers in 1940. However, unlike the RAF, the USAAF was part of the US army. After the outbreak of war in Europe, the emerging USAAF view reflected ground forces' beliefs that the helicopter offered a range of tactical opportunities for land-based forces. Unlike the Air Ministry ambivalence in Britain, the US Army policy assessment was one of 'keen interest in the Helicopter . . . and most branches desire[d] to test its characteristics'.[14] Because the army wanted to acquire ground-cooperation rotary-wing aircraft, the USAAF had no choice but to support this approach.

After flight testing of the Sikorsky VS-300 in 1939, USAAF attention focused on the battlefield potential of helicopters and operational requirements were beginning to be defined. On the basis of early VS-300 performance trials, the USAAF communicated to the War Production Board the roles for which it considered helicopters offered potential superior to that of fixed-wing aircraft. These included air-ambulance duties, rescue of personnel and critical materials from inaccessible locations, liaison and general cooperation with ground forces, specialised radio missions for the signals corps and the adjustment of artillery fire.[15] An indication of USAAF enthusiasm at the highest levels is the endorsement from Brigadier General Chidlaw, the USAAF Assistant Chief of Staff, that:

> The above gives only a partial list of possible military missions now foreseen, however, it is believed with service experience many new missions will be discovered.[16]

Emerging USAAF operational interest provided important incentives for intensive development at Sikorsky. Recognising the potential for large-scale USAAF orders, Sikorsky abandoned all fixed-wing aircraft work in 1940 and concentrated on improving the basic design configuration of the VS-300.[17] The USAAF enthusiasm after the tests on the VS-300 led to the provision of development funds of $265,000 for the Sikorsky XR-4.[18] This larger single-seater had been initiated by the company on a private venture basis in 1940.[19] By January 1941, after a period of extensive development, Sikorsky successfully demonstrated the XR-4 to the USAAF.[20] Following further prototype demonstrations,[21] USAAF contracts were placed in January 1941 and flight tests of the XR-4 began at the Vought-Sikorsky plant in March 1942. After 17 hours of flying, the machine was delivered to the USAAF for acceptance tests at Wright Field, Dayton, Ohio.[22] It was accepted on 30 May 1942.

The subsequent rate of technical progress on the XR-4 during 1942 was enhanced by USAAF procurement strategy. With the impetus of developing helicopters for urgent war use, the USAAF ordered a service test quantity of 13 XR-4As, a further one for the US Navy and 15 for British forces. In addition to forcing the pace of the programme by allowing simultaneous development and production in industry, the machines were used for the instruction of USAAF personnel and limited tactical training to provide service experience of helicopter operation.[23] By the end of 1942, the aircraft had flown a further 143 hours during which time seven pilots were instructed to the solo stage.

In parallel, after the XR-4 was successfully flown in January 1941, the USAAF formulated a development programme that provided yet further incentives at Sikorsky. First, procurement contracts were let for an experimental helicopter, the XR-6, of the same size as the XR-4 but of refined design, with increased power and performance, to serve as a prototype of a second production helicopter.[24] Second, as a result of testing on the XR-4, contracts were also placed for the construction of an even larger type, the Sikorsky XR-5, for operational deployment.

By April 1943, Vought-Sikorsky's longer-term production plans had been consolidated for foreseeable wartime requirements. During February 1943 the US Joint Aircraft Committee had approved production of the XR-5, redesignated the R-5.[25] By March, cumulative orders had been placed with the firm for some 338 helicopters to include production models of the R-4, R-5 and a refined version of the XR-6, designated R-6. Whilst the firm were obtaining these specific contracts, the Joint Aircraft Committee were approving in principle potential orders for a total of 900 Sikorsky helicopters, primarily for the USAAF.[26] In the event, by June 1945 actual production deliveries from Vought-Sikorsky for the range of helicopters on order was to total some 400 units for the USAAF, the US Navy and Coast Guard, and the Royal Navy.[27]

British Admiralty Helicopter Requirements and Incentives for Sikorsky Innovation

A further factor leading to a concerted programme of helicopter development by Sikorsky was the British Admiralty's requirements for helicopters. By late 1940, the Admiralty was becoming increasingly concerned with the loss of merchant shipping to German submarines and recognised the potential of ship-borne rotary-wing aircraft. An illustration of initial concern was a request by the British Purchasing Commission on behalf of the Admiralty to the US Government for seven Pitcairn PA-39 autogiros on 13 December 1940 at a cost of $130,000.[28]

During early 1941, Wing Commander R.A.C. Brie, the former commander of No. 1448 Flight, was released to the Admiralty, which had become interested in the possibility of employing autogiros for anti-submarine convoy protection. At this stage it was considered that autogiros operating from merchant ships could potentially locate submarines and provide prior warning of enemy activity. Given that all indigenous British helicopter R&D had been abandoned, Captain Caspar John (later Admiral of the Fleet Sir Caspar), Director of Naval Development and Production, posted Brie to the British Air Commission (BAC) in Washington to interest American forces in the use of autogiros in the anti-submarine role.[29]

Whereas Brie's initial remit was to investigate autogiro developments, he was invited to see tests of the Sikorsky VS-300 during early 1942. Afterward:

> Brie went straight to the head of the British Air Commission in Washington, Air Marshal Sir Roderic Hill, and explained that a helicopter had at last appeared which effectively eliminated the only serious disability of the autogiro – the inability to hover ... An order for YR-4s was placed on behalf of the Admiralty and this marked the beginning of the Naval involvement in helicopters for anti-submarine and, later, SAR [Search and Rescue] duties.[30]

The successful trials of the Sikorsky prototype, coupled with Brie's technical evaluation, clearly generated immediate interest at the BAC and at the Admiralty. By this stage, the USAAF had already placed contracts for 50 Sikorsky helicopters and the BAC then began the process of arranging procurement of Sikorsky types for RN use. By 15 December 1942, under the terms of Anglo-American agreements affecting the allocation of US-produced or financed aircraft, British access to US production had been clarified.[31] During December the BAC placed preliminary orders for 25 Sikorsky R-4s for future joint RN/RAF use[32] with an anticipated delivery date of late 1943.[33] Against the ever-growing priority of securing convoy protection and on the basis of Sikorsky plans to develop the larger R-5, the British order was subsequently extended to include 250 R-5s[34] for the RN 'to certain minimum Admiralty requirements'.[35]

Throughout early 1943, the existence of British helicopter orders increased the American resources assigned to Sikorsky development and production. The primary factor here was the pressure for rapid delivery and early in-service date generated by Brie and the BAC. The impact of Brie's communications to the US War Production Board during March 1943 is illustrated by internal correspondence at the Board. After receiving correspondence from Brie, the Board noted that the RN

> ... is now very interested in helicopters, and ... the Bureau of Aeronautics has been instructed by Admiral King [US Navy] to get [the RN] helicopters as soon as possible.[36]

More significant impetus was provided shortly after at a meeting of Admiral Davidson (RN), Sir Richard Fairey of the BAC and officials from the US War Production Board on 23 March 1943. During the meeting:

> All of these concurred in the immediate necessity of getting some production with a minimum of delay. Sir Richard advised that he had received instructions from the Prime Minister to place particular emphasis on the larger size, type R-5 . . . Considerable discussion was also given to plant location, manpower situation and the quantities to be produced.[37]

The specific interest of Prime Minister Churchill in the progress of the Sikorsky helicopter developments was to create added incentives at the War Production Board for the rapid developments of Sikorsky types *per se* and the R-5 in particular. Tests at sea were planned[38] and modifications of Sikorsky designs to meet Admiralty requirements, including provision for mounting a British single-lug bomb, were put in train.[39] The size of the anticipated RN order, totalling 250 R-5s alone, coupled with American commitments under wartime aircraft production agreements, were therefore instrumental in the priority that the US War Production Board and the USAAF assigned to helicopter development.

Resources for Sikorsky Development and Technical Innovation

USAAF and British Admiralty production demand increased the priority of Sikorsky projects. This priority translated into US Government funding for development and production, industrial infrastructure to enable rapid testing, refinement and large-scale manufacture, and provision of qualified technical personnel.

In the USA, as in Britain, government funding had been released for helicopter development before the outbreak of war in Europe. Under the Public Act No. 787 of 30 June 1938, the US Congress had appropriated $2,000,000 'to remain available for the research, development, procurement, experimentation, and operation for service testing of rotary-wing aircraft'.[40] In accordance with the Act, Government agencies had been invited to submit plans to the Secretary of War for funding allocations.[41] During 1939, the sum of $299,459 was assigned directly to the USAAF to support its helicopter interests.[42] Provisions from these Congressional resources initially enhanced Sikorsky development of the VS-300. After recommendations by the USAAF on 17 December 1940, some $60,000 was allocated to Sikorsky for rotary wing development.[43] At this stage, 'the manufacturer was willing to absorb a large proportion of the development costs'; subsequently, Sikorsky 'submitted figures showing that the development of this aircraft totalled $265,000',[44] – the balance being later reimbursed by the USAAF. Importantly, after funding the VS-300 and with growing USAAF interest in operational aspects of helicopter development, all subsequent Sikorsky helicopter programme 'expenses, procurement costs, engineering... and flight testing [were] charged to Air Corps funds'.[45] The willingness for the USAAF to absorb this expenditure resulted from

> ... a very definite interest by the Army Air Forces in the helicopter and belief in its practicable and potential uses... evidenced by the procurement programme that has been initiated and which is expected to increase as actual service proves theory.[46]

Aggregated data on USAAF funding for Sikorsky helicopter developments are not available.[47] However, an indication of its magnitude for the R-5 helicopter development alone is provided by Air Forces Materiel Center documents.[48] At a meeting held on 23 February 1943, Sikorsky representatives submitted their plans for organisation and sub-contracting on the R-5. Sikorsky officials requested $3,000,000, approximately $2,000,000 of which was concerned with the procurement and rehabilitation of buildings for manufacture, and $1,000,000 for the costs of special factory machinery and equipment.[49] Whilst the subsequent allocation of these funds by the USAAF is not documented, the Sikorsky bid is indicative of the scale of expenditure during 1943 alone. By comparison, infrastructure costs on the R-5 in 1943 exceeded total US Government rotorcraft development funding at the outbreak of hostilities in 1939. Consequently, unlike the pre-war environment affecting rotorcraft development in Europe and the USA, the mobilisation of financial resources in support of wartime American and British operational needs was a primary variable accounting for Sikorsky's success.

An important factor impeding pre-war helicopter development in the USA and elsewhere had been the fragmentation of development between small groups of competing designers and the limited interest shown by large fixed-wing aircraft manufacturers. Rivalry between teams and the lack of access to testing and development facilities that a fixed-wing manufacturer could provide had retarded innovation. Urgent operational requirements after 1939, however, were to lead to a consolidation of Sikorsky helicopter activities within a large fixed-wing concern, which in turn hastened the pace of development on Sikorsky helicopter types.

Before March 1939, the primary activity of Igor Sikorsky had been the design of passenger flying boats under the Sikorsky Division of the United Aircraft Corporation.[50] At this stage, helicopter development constituted a small and unofficial sideline to the Division's main activities. As part of United Aircraft's rationalisation plans in response to the outbreak of hostilities in Europe, it was decided to optimise fixed-wing capabilities and amalgamate the Sikorsky Division with the Chance Vought plant of United Aircraft at Stratford, Connecticut.[51] At this stage, Chance Vought had been primarily concerned with propeller manufacture. Shortly after the consolidation, Igor

Sikorsky asked permission to undertake helicopter development on the VS-300 project. The Board of United Aircraft took the view that:

> Mr. Sikorsky and the small group of Russian *émigrés* surrounding him had shown unusual original and creative skills [in helicopter design]. The Corporation therefore agreed to support the development.[52]

An implication of the merger process was that it provided the Sikorsky helicopter team with access to the development facilities at Stratford, and the assets of United Aircraft more generally. Equally important, initial development work on the VS-300 was supported financially by the parent firm. Subsequently, when the Materiel Division of the USAAF took an active interest in development, United Aircraft were prepared to undertake and support work on the XR-4 and subsequent variants.

Early co-location with Chance Vought had been a source of synergism. By early 1943, United Aircraft made a further decision that was to have implications for technical progress on Sikorsky designs. On 1 January 1943, the Sikorsky Division, having proven its development competence, was reconstituted as a separate entity from Chance Vought 'in order that each might operate to greater advantage in its own field'.[53] A primary reason was further to optimise Sikorsky's access to specialist expertise within the United Aircraft Corporation, given the urgency of USAAF and British production requirements. The rationale and implications of this decision were summarised by E.E. Wilson, President of United Aircraft, in correspondence with the USAAF:

> The new Sikorsky Division was set up by action of the Board of Directors as of January 1 1943 and shortly after Mr J. Reed Miller was made its General Manager. Mr. Miller is one of our most experienced executives... In order to bring competent manufacturing experience into this Division we have transferred Mr. John L. Brown... to the new Division. Mr. Brown is one of the outstanding manufacturing executives of the Corporation. On the production engineering side we have obtained from Nash-Kelvinator the services of Mr Meade Moore... Mr Moore is well trained in the field of quantity production.[54]

In addition, and under the growing pressure to fulfil helicopter orders, the Sikorsky Division was relocated to the Hartford area of Connecticut where the bulk of United Aircraft's aviation activities were based. This provided Sikorsky with access to a further range of technical facilities and experience. As the President of United Aircraft observed in March 1943:

> The desirability of this is apparent. The vast amount of engineering and development work essential to the prompt and effective solution of the difficult fundamental rotor problems required the assistance of experienced personnel in the other United Divisions. For instance, the

> Hamilton Standard Propeller engineering department has already set up a small group to do the fundamental research and the subsequent design work on the rotor and rotor drives. In addition, the whole problem is under study by the Research Division of the Corporation located in Hartford under the direction of Mr. Frank Caldwell, one of the outstanding propeller authorities in the world... It was clear that the development could be expedited under the close supervision of United management.[55]

Wartime requirements, coupled with Sikorsky's relationship with the United Aircraft Corporation, were key factors behind the rapid development of the Sikorsky helicopter types that took place between 1940 and 1943. Further links between Sikorsky and other firms in the US aircraft industry also enhanced the helicopter production process. By May 1943, in order to meet exacting production schedules of 50 helicopters per month, the Sikorsky Division elected to engage in extensive subcontracting under 'Engineering Assistance Agreements', notably with Hamilton Standard and Nash-Kelvinator.[56] It was the pressures imposed for rapid manufacture that enabled Sikorsky to gain access to these other production facilities, which, in turn, enhanced the rate of output and further refined the production engineering process.

In addition to funding and technical facilities, Sikorsky developments were enhanced by its accumulation of qualified scientists and engineers (QSEs) on a previously unprecedented scale in helicopter terms. Whereas pre-war helicopter teams had contained fewer than ten QSEs, the urgency of wartime production requirements after 1940 meant that by May 1943 the Sikorsky Division was employing some 550 personnel.[57] As production orders for fifty R-5s per month were consolidated throughout the year, provision was made for Sikorsky manpower to peak in mid-1944. Manpower estimates for May 1943 were that some 1,368 employees were to be assigned to Sikorsky development, of which 435 were QSEs specialising in experimental, development and production technologies.[58] A further 875 individuals were experienced technicians in final assembly and inspection.[59]

The urgency and scale of US and British helicopter requirements, therefore, provided the impetus for rapid Sikorsky helicopter development. These requirements facilitated industrial reorganisation, access to specialist plant and facilities, and the provision of large-scale development expertise at Sikorsky. Collectively, this forced the pace of innovation by the firm and its translation of the helicopter from an experimental programme to a production contract between 1940 and 1943.

Other US Developments – Technology on a Broad Front

Though the USAAF recognised that Vought-Sikorsky was the most likely source of helicopters for war use,[60] Army-sponsored R&D was undertaken in other organisations. Whereas the activities of Sikorsky are of primary concern in the context of the post-war UK helicopter industry, analysis of US wartime activities *in toto* indicates the scale of American efforts. During December 1943, the overall situation was summed up by the Chairman of the Helicopter Committee on the National Advisory Committee for Aeronautics as follows:

> The [US] government, through the War Production Board, is granting materials to and designating laboratories for several pioneering young engineers who have good new ideas in this [the helicopter] field. The Army, Navy and Coast Guard are now placing strictly military orders and developing strictly military uses for the helicopter . . . The National Advisory Committee for Aeronautics is proceeding now with an ambitious program of research to make sure that no stone is left unturned in exploring the fundamentals of this problem in the interests of safety for the helicopter pilot and success for the technical development of this field in America.[61]

As well as early USAAF contracts for the Sikorsky XR-4, the other major locus of government-funded activity was Platt LePage Aircraft. After the issue of tender documents in 1939, the company received two USAAF contracts for experimental helicopters designated XR-1 and XR-1A during early 1940. Both types were flown in May 1941 and, despite technical problems with the control system, deliveries to the USAAF were originally expected in the spring of 1943.[62] Of a similar weight and class to what was to become the Sikorsky XR-5, the USAAF view in late 1943 was that the Platt LePage machines would 'prove to be of definite tactical utility . . . [when] . . . the control trouble is satisfactorily cured'.[63]

As a longer-term option, USAAF funding was also provided to the Kellet Autogiro Company for the highly experimental XR-8 helicopter. Employing two rotors in tandem – in contemporary terms a radical departure from the conventional single-rotor configuration – which was designed to eliminate power-loss in the tail-rotor, flight tests were scheduled for the autumn of 1943.[64]

While USAAF requirements and funding were forcing the pace of development at companies in receipt of R&D and production contracts, clear military interest also encouraged private venture initiatives in both pre-war autogiro manufacturers and larger fixed-wing firms. As Table 6 illustrates, 19 firms were involved in helicopter developments of one form or another, four of which had considerable technical experience in the autogiro field and ten in conventional aircraft design and manufacture.

By 1942, American policy-makers had also considered an issue largely ignored in Britain until the mid-1950s: the relative merits of amalgamating helicopter design expertise as opposed to separate and competitive enterprises. At the War Production Board, for example, concern had been voiced about the fact that '. . . there is a great deal of work going on [in the US] on helicopters . . . [From] the war standpoint it is somewhat scattered and disconnected'.[65] The Board noted that strong arguments existed for the merger of Kellett, Platt LePage and PV Engineering with Vought-Sikorsky, and deploying designers Arthur Young (Bell) and Bossi (Higgins Industries) with the Sikorsky team. In the event, however, after a technical assessment of progress at Sikorsky, the policy was adopted of encouraging competition between design teams as a mechanism for stimulating longer-term technical innovation.[66]

Table 6: US Helicopter Activities, 1939–43

Company	*Project(s)*	*Comments*
Autogiro Company of America	Studies for a single-rotor helicopter with 450 hp engine	
G. & A. Aviation	Two-seater autogiro	USAAF-funded contract
Kellett Autogiro Company	Two-seater autogiro; XR-8 helicopter	In receipt of USAAF helicopter, autogiro and rotor research contracts
Platt LePage Aircraft	XR-1 and XR-1A helicopters	In receipt of USAAF contracts
Bell Aircraft	Single-seat helicopter	Initial flight tests during 1943
Consolidated Aircraft	Small single-rotor helicopter	Advanced stage of construction in early 1943
Curtiss Wright	Rotor blade research	
Vought-Sikorsky	XR-4, XR-5 and XR-6 helicopters	In receipt of USAAF contracts
Fleetwing Incorporated	H-10 helicopter	Hovering tests in early 1943
P-V Engineering Forum	PV2 Piasecki helicopter	First flight in 1942
Fred Landraf	Twin-rotor helicopter	In development during 1943
R.T. Machine Shop	Tandem-rotor helicopter	In development during 1943
Hillier Industries, Inc.	Coaxial helicopter	In development during 1943
Aeronautical Products Company	Helicopter	Flight tests during 1943
Dow Chemical Company	Jet-propelled helicopter	Design stage during 1943
Nash-Kelvinator Company	R-6 rotor testing	
Higgins Industries, Inc.	EB-1 helicopter	Flight testing during March 1943
McDonnell Aircraft Corporation	Twin-rotor helicopter	Design stage at March 1943
General Electric Company	Jet-propelled helicopter	Design stage at March 1943

Source: Table constructed from information contained in USNA, War Production Board Collection, Inspection of Helicopter Projects in the United States, March 1943, 314.242; and, PRO AVIA 15/954, Report on Rotating Wing Aircraft Activities in the United States, 22 January 1943.

US Protectionism in the Helicopter Field

After 1940, MAP officials assumed the Anglo-US arrangement for helicopter procurement was one of collaboration. Indeed, an element of MAP strategy had been explicitly to assist US technical developments through the transfer of British designs to the US government on the expectation of operational helicopters in return. In direct contrast to British officials' perceptions of a cooperative relationship, by June 1943 the US administration had become preoccupied with consolidating its industry's hold on helicopter technology obtained from the UK and protecting the longer-term and post-war commercial interests of American firms.

After US entry into the war, the Truman Committee was established by the Senate under Harry S. Truman of Missouri not only to scrutinise domestic war plants for fraud and waste, but also to consider the longer-term, post-war commercial opportunities offered by wartime technical advances and innovations.[67] In early June 1943, the Truman Committee conducted a scrutiny of helicopter activities within US firms that were in receipt of military contracts. At a meeting with the USAAF Materiel Department on 2 June 1943, the issue of patents affecting US helicopter projects in train was raised.[68] The Committee found during the hearing that patents applying to all US helicopter programmes, including those of Sikorsky, stemmed 'from the Cierva Autogiro Company Ltd., of London, which company owns the basic rotary wing patents'.[69] Moreover, it transpired that the sole licensee of Cierva in the US was the Autogiro Company of America, from whom the Sikorsky Division had taken a license.[70]

On receipt of this information Senator Brewster, a Truman Committee member,

> ...stressed the importance of protecting American interests on any patent developments that might grow out of American initiatives, and he stated that it would be the purpose of the Truman Committee to see that none of the benefits from such developments would accrue to outside interests except on an equitable basis.[71]

In response, measures were adopted to protect US helicopter programmes from the potential implications of existing patent arrangements. After the meeting with the Truman Committee, USAAF investigations were conducted into the patent details as they related to Cierva and its US licensee. By 24 June 1943, Brigadier General B.W. Chidlaw was informed of the situation:

> Any improvements or developments by a licensee of the American Co. (such as Sikorsky's) becomes the property of the British Co. [Cierva] as far as foreign rights are concerned... In as much as the foreign rights to any development 'flow back' to the British Co., it would mean if Sikorsky were to manufacture and sell in England in post war years, they would have to pay the English Co. for the privilege to use their own developments and improvements.[72]

Moreover, he was made aware of a further 'tying-in' clause whereby all rotor-blade developments in the US would automatically flow back to the Cierva Autogiro Company.[73]

Given Truman Committee and USAAF concern to protect longer-term US commercial interests, measures were adopted to challenge and, if necessary, circumvent the legal provisions of patent agreements with the British firm. By 25 June 1943, pressure had been brought to bear on the Autogiro Company of America. At a meeting between USAAF, United Aircraft and Autogiro Company of America officials, the last was informed that:

> ...strenuous objections...had been raised by the Truman Committee, Senator Brewster in particular, at their last hearing. Also the army was prepared to go through with production arrangements with United [Sikorsky Division] regardless of the patent situation and if necessary, the Government would let any license agreement go by default, in which case the licenser would have to go to court to collect any royalties or fees that might be due him...[Moreover] ...in fact the British rights [Cierva's] might be considered as suspended for the duration due to the fact that the British Government itself was buying helicopters in this country on Lend Lease funds.[74]

Under this high-level political scrutiny, the American Autogiro Company Chairman responded on 26 June that it was possible to waive the 'flow back' arrangement to Cierva on any developments or improvements by Sikorsky and that the royalty terms of Sikorsky's licences from American Autogiro could be renegotiated.[75]

By mid-August, the patent situation had been clarified and US post-war commercial interests protected. After a further meeting of relevant officials on 11 August 1943, United Aircraft renegotiated its licence with the Autogiro Company of America to the extent that royalty fees on Sikorsky types were reduced to '85 hundredths of 1 per cent for War Department contracts for the duration', and that '"flow-back" of patents [to Cierva were] eliminated'.[76] With regard to the US helicopter programme as a whole, the Department of Justice had also initiated court action to dissolve all helicopter licences previously agreed with the Autogiro Corporation on what the Department claimed to be restrictive practices under the Anti-Trust Act.[77]

By August 1943, therefore, US government officials had introduced measures to protect the impressive advances made by Sikorsky and other US firms. In direct contrast to British MAP perceptions of Anglo-American cooperation and technology exchange in the helicopter field, the Truman Committee had stemmed any legal claim that British firms might have to American wartime developments and protected the post-war commercial interests of the emerging US helicopter industry.

RESUMING BRITISH HELICOPTER R&D IN 1942: THE DEBATE

Throughout this period of considerable development within US industry, British rotorcraft activities were by contrast confined to two areas. First, while Sikorsky was accumulating design and production staff and expertise, Hafner and his small design team were continuing work on Rotachute prototypes for use with airborne forces. Work had been transferred to the Airborne Forces Experimental Establishment (AFEE) in 1942 and had reached the prototype-testing phase by June of the same year. Earlier model testing had been completed in October 1940, enabling full-scale versions to be towed behind a car in February 1942. On 17 June 1942, the first flight test was conducted and the results transferred to the MAP, confirming that the system would be ready for service release by late 1943. Secondly, in the US, Wing Commander Brie, under the aegis of the BAC, was monitoring American innovations and assessing their potential for British wartime requirements. Sikorsky's development of the R-4 and R-5 helicopters, the careful monitoring by British officials and the subsequent allocation of American types, all appeared to vindicate the MAP's post-1940 strategy of reliance on US industry for production helicopters. However, the apparent success of Sikorsky brought a central question to the fore in 1942: how, when and in what form should indigenous British helicopter research and development be resumed?

The 'Weir/Sikorsky Controversy'

Between 1940 and 1942, the MAP and the organisations comprising the pre-war industry largely ignored the issue of resuming indigenous helicopter R&D.[78] On the industrial side, helicopter designers and technicians were either deployed in support of the war effort or seconded directly to military scientific establishments. In the MAP, the major preoccupation was fixed-wing aircraft production and the 1940 policy on indigenous helicopter R&D remained extant. The Admiralty orders for 250 Sikorsky R-5s, however, reopened the debate. On hearing of the R-5 procurement decision, Mr J. Weir, pre-war Chairman of G. & J. Weir Ltd., put forward proposals to the MAP advocating support for concerted British helicopter R&D work and the reversal of its 1940 policy directive.

Weir raised three arguments in correspondence to the MAP during early 1942. First, he protested against Admiralty procurement of the Sikorsky R-5 helicopters on safety grounds: '...an element of danger in the Sikorsky type which may arise from the vigorous use of controls during high-speed flight in gusty weather'.[79] As evidence, Weir cited three instances of blade failure during pre-war trials of the W.5 and W.6 Weir helicopters, although he considered the danger was avoidable by not operating the machine at maximum efficiency.[80] Under these circumstances, Weir advocated that the order with Sikorsky should be cancelled and urgent work should commence on his own alternative design – the W.9.[81] To implement the W.9 programme, Weir suggested that two men 'skilled in the detailed design of helicopters' be released from service duties to start preliminary investigation.[82] Second, later supported in correspondence to the Ministry from Hafner's previous employers, AR III Construction,[83] Weir launched a broader attack on MAP rotorcraft policy. Pointing out that rapid US innovation had been directly facilitated by MAP policy and Admiralty orders, Weir argued that similar encouragement should have been provided to British firms. Finally, Weir pointed to longer-term dangers in MAP policy: that the UK was being 'left behind' by the American industry with the likelihood of a 'post-war situation that would find the UK entirely dependent on the Americans, with no organised body in this country engaged in helicopter work'.[84]

Despite the case put forward by Weir, his proposals and arguments were rejected by the MAP. Though MAP officials recognised that reliance on the US for production helicopters could 'contribute to place [Britain] in an inferior position to the Americans commercially if and when we restart helicopter construction',[85] bureaucratic procrastination and what was to be a dubious assessment of the relative importance of Hafner's work on the Rotachute were to delay the resumption of concerted British efforts until 1945.

The MAP rejection of Weir's thesis was governed by a number of considerations. On the technical question of the safety of the R-5 machine, Weir's claims were discounted. After analysis of available technical and trials data on the Sikorsky machine by the Aeronautical Research Committee in November 1942,[86] 'expert opinion' was

> ... unanimous in saying that although instability is present [in the R-5], it can be overcome by pilot control. Further a simple modification to the design of the XR-5 can be made which will eliminate the instability.[87]

With no technical case against the American machine, the MAP decided that procurement should proceed with the Sikorsky R-5 to fulfil 'pressing Admiralty requirements'. Furthermore, the results of the inquiry also undermined Weir's own proposals: the perception in the MAP was that Weir's attempts to discredit the R-5 were merely a mechanism to reinforce the case for his alternative W.9. The Ministry's decision was that 'Weir's proposals [were] not worth development, either now or in the future ... '.[88]

On the more substantive issue of the resumption of British helicopter R&D *per se*, disagreement emerged within sections of the Ministry which delayed a decisive decision. On the one hand, it was universally accepted that wartime reliance on US firms could impair the competitive position of British firms in any emerging post-war commercial market.[89] On the other hand, opinion differed on the practical issues of how, when and in what form to proceed with indigenous R&D. Clearly, as the MAP's Controller of Research and Development pointed out, resources were available immediately for a 'modest' programme of research and experimentation by Weir.[90] Instead, however, the policy position that was to emerge was based on the Deputy Director of Scientific Research's insistence that:

> ...Hafner has a better appreciation of the problems involved [in helicopter development] than anyone else in this country and the inauguration of any work here should include Hafner as Technical Controller of design.91

Given this insistence on Hafner's involvement in future Ministry-sponsored activity, the policy decision was made that:

> ...commercial interests, headed by Weir..., should be told that they must combine, give the whole technical responsibility to Hafner, and that experimental work only would be authorised.[92]

Since the inclusion of Hafner was central to any MAP-sanctioned helicopter R&D initiative, the central determinant affecting the resumption of British government-sponsored development was Hafner's release from the Rotachute project at the AFEE. However, other considerations led to the decision that Rotachute work had to take precedence over any programme of helicopter work. First, the view at the MAP appears to have been that Rotachute work had priority over helicopter development because the former would have a wartime operational role whereas 'the war would be over before Britain could build a satisfactory production helicopter'.[93] Consequently, the helicopter policy remained that for 'any war use [the UK] shall have to depend on the USA'.[94] Rotachute work was to continue and the question of

> ...an outside organisation...deferred until the war need for further rotaplane development and helicopter development is ascertained by experience with the [American] projects now in hand.[95]

Second, any US threat to post-war British commercial helicopter activities was viewed as marginal, and did not require an immediate programme of development. Though Brie had informed the Ministry of the 'active and intelligent interest' of American firms in post-war markets,[96] his assertions were not acted upon because of MAP perceptions of Hafner's ability as a rotorcraft designer.[97] Expert opinion in the Ministry was that the question of sanctioning British R&D

> ...must be strongly influenced by the fact that we have in Hafner a first class designer whose ideas in many ways are in advance of those of the designers in the USA. He could, after his present work on rotorplane gliders is finished, start the design of a helicopter which would have every

> chance of being as good as or better than anything being produced in the USA.[98]

This approach was reinforced by the MAP Chief Executive's view that '...we [Britain] should be able to take up the threads again without difficulty and doubtless we should learn a lot from the practical difficulties encountered by Sikorsky'.[99]

Finally, concern emerged that resuming R&D could potentially damage the cooperative arrangements reached with the US Government. News of Weir's activities had reached the USAAF. As a result, the USAAF were unwilling to provide technical data to the British authorities that could be used to criticise the Sikorsky design.[100] Rather than supporting Weir's position, the MAP's response was one of damage limitation: to assist Sikorsky further by sending Dr J.A.J. Bennett, the former Chief Designer at Cierva, to assist US developments and maintain good relations.[101]

By late February 1943, the MAP Chief Executive had taken the decision that '...it would be unjustifiable to pursue...development independently of the Americans'.[102] In the absence of a pressing military need for a production helicopter of British origin, the longer-term issue of formulating post-war civil requirements was passed to the Transport Aircraft Committee under the chairmanship of Lord Brabazon.[103] In effect, the question of British helicopter development was to be shelved until the termination of hostilities.

Between February and July of 1943, the MAP attitude towards indigenous helicopter activities was summed up in a Minute by Sir Henry Tizard:

> ...[to] go on with [helicopter] research and development in a small hole and corner [would] result in very little progress and will not prevent us from lagging behind the USA work...The only thing which might cause [the Ministry] to change [its] opinion would be the agreement of one of our main aeronautical firms to take up research and development. A big firm might push it along.104

On the question of Hafner, despite requests from AR III for his release,[105] the Ministry's position remained that Rotachute work was essential in support of the war effort.

By July of 1943, however, some twelve months after Weir's initial communication with the MAP, the Ministry's antagonism towards Weir's proposals was finally reversed.[106] Ministry orders for two experimental W.9 prototypes were placed, and the two technicians requested by Weir were made available.[107] Though MAP records make no direct reference to why the change in policy occurred, indications are that two factors were responsible. First, after the initial rejection of Weir's W.9 proposals during the controversy over the Sikorsky R-5, a second report from the Aeronautical Research Committee dated 3 July 1943 advocated that the W.9 was worthy of basic research. In the report, the Committee concluded that

> ...the Weir type of helicopter which embodies novel mechanical features in the main rotor should be made the subject of further experimental investigation leading ultimately, if found satisfactory, to experiments in flight.[108]

Second, attempts by MAP officials to limit the scope of Weir's project and the allocation of personnel can be interpreted as a bureaucratic compromise. Given that procurement was going ahead from Sikorsky, the W.9 may have provided the Ministry with a convenient mechanism for avoiding continued and vocal criticism from Weir. To support this assertion, clear indications were given to Weir that MAP support would only be provided for basic experimental work[109] under Ministry of Aircraft Production Specification E.16/43. Equally, Ministry officials may have supported limited work as a mechanism to establish at least some indigenous helicopter capability, or to help the MAP become 'intelligent purchasers' of US machines. In any event, the *de facto* implication was that the MAP had compromised and adopted the 'small hole and corner' approach.

The Aeronautical Research Committee's findings that advocated work on the W.9, however, were to have a more significant implication: to prompt renewed attention at the MAP over priorities for longer-term helicopter development. Until July 1943, the major constraint affecting a serious programme of helicopter development was the MAP's position with respect to Hafner. After July, a more positive strategy had emerged as to how, when 'conditions permitted', development involving Hafner should proceed. Echoing earlier discussion, it was decided that to maximise Hafner's design expertise it was essential that he join 'some established engineering company able to undertake constructional work'.[110] There was thus no question of MAP support or funding for the AR III company in its pre-war form. Hafner, with or without former AR III personnel, was to be strongly encouraged to join a large fixed-wing aircraft concern. In addition, decisions were emerging about technical priorities. Unlike Weir's experimental work, the Ministry envisaged Hafner working on a helicopter of the cyclic pitch type of which the Sikorsky R-5 was representative.[111] Though Hafner was to remain at the AFEE in the interim, arrangements were made for his involvement in experimental tests of Sikorsky designs[112] in addition to rotary-wing glider work. A further indication of the growing interest in the future of UK helicopter activity at the MAP was the consideration given to recalling Bennett from the US to assist Hafner in his investigations.[113]

Despite evidence of practical achievements in the US and agreement in principle that Hafner should be released for a programme of helicopter development, MAP stipulations about Hafner's future employment details after July 1943 were again to delay the resumption of indigenous UK helicopter developments involving the individual that the MAP considered to be Britain's leading rotorcraft designer.

Bristol Aeroplane Company and Weir's Developments, 1944–45

As late as August 1944, 'it was becoming apparent [at the MAP] that the war would not last long and the rota-plane would not be ready in time to take any significant part'.[114] However, the MAP decided that the prototype under development should be tested and on 11 September 1944 towing trials were conducted from a Whitley bomber.[115] As a consequence of the official decision that development of the rotor-plane should proceed after it had been accepted that he should restart substantive helicopter design work, Hafner had been based at the AFEE for some 13 months. Whilst Hafner was also investigating Sikorsky designs during this period, no practical achievements had been made in terms of the resumption of indigenous helicopter development.

After a period of absence of some four years, Hafner recommenced helicopter development in earnest during October 1944. At this stage, as Walker points out, interest in future helicopter development was increasing throughout the aircraft industry, primarily because of the success achieved by Sikorsky in the US.[116] Among these firms were Short Brothers, Handley Page, Percival Aircraft, Morris Motors Ltd. and the Bristol Aeroplane Co. Ltd. By October 1944, with rotary-wing glider work finally ceased, Hafner had visited each of these companies and eventually decided to join the Bristol Aeroplane Company.[117] Shortly after, the firm invited 'several' wartime personnel from the AFEE to help to form a rotary wing department in the company.[118]

With this small design team in place, Hafner continued during early 1945 with the design of a four-seater helicopter (later designated the Type 171) on which he had started preliminary conceptual work at the AFEE.[119] In technical terms, Hafner's approach involved no 'departure from the Sikorsky types'[120] already in manufacture in the US in that it was premised on the basic configuration established with the VS-300. Given the official policy adopted by the MAP after 1940, the project was initiated and funded by Bristol on a private venture basis, and it did not receive an MAP specification on which future production plans could be based. Design work continued on the Type 171 on this basis until the end of hostilities in May 1945.

By late 1944 when Bristol was commencing basic helicopter design work, promising developments had taken place at Weir on the W.9. While limited MAP documentation has emerged, key aspects of the project at this stage have been provided by designers and engineers who were directly involved. During early 1944 a small staff had been recruited to the programme. Mr G.A. Pullin, the pre-war Chief Designer at Weir, was actively involved in experimentation and further personnel had been obtained from the Power Jets firm, including the designer J. Shapiro.[121] In addition, Sir Frank Whittle of Power Jets had loaned Mr. K. Watson, formerly a Weir designer during 1940, to the project for a period of six months.[122] Basic experimentation and development to the criteria contained in MAP Specification E.16/43 continued until the prototype was finally prepared for hover testing during November 1945.[123]

THE WARTIME LEGACY

This analysis has focused on factors surrounding the very different wartime helicopter policies adopted in the USA and the UK, and the developments within each approach. On the one hand, the USAAF priority to acquire helicopters for war use had led to the production of Sikorsky helicopters in the USA by 1945. On the other, constrained by different operational priorities and limited resources, British policy had been to rely on helicopters from America and to suspend the issue of longer-term indigenous helicopter development until the cessation of hostilities. The issue that emerges is the legacy of these policies in 1945 for subsequent post-war UK helicopter R&D and production.

During 1943, the Truman Commission was eager to protect US wartime helicopter advances and the longer-term post-war commercial interests of American firms. Conversely, as we have seen, in 1943 MAP officials were more complacent about the ability of UK firms to compete in post-war markets. At this stage, MAP perceptions were that Hafner's ideas were in advance of those of designers in the USA and that by learning from the practical difficulties encountered by Sikorsky, British designers would be able to 'take up the threads again without difficulty'. Evidence of this complacency was the MAP's approach towards the timing and priority of Hafner's resumption of helicopter work, and transfer of the whole question of possible post-war civil requirements to the Brabazon Committee. In sum, the MAP view by 1945 was that US firms had acquired no significant lead over UK capabilities, and that British designers would have little difficulty in 'catching-up' and entering post-war markets.

Relative UK and US helicopter development capabilities

In contrast to the MAP assessment, this analysis suggests that a legacy of wartime developments had been to facilitate a comprehensive technological lead in US helicopter firms over their British counterparts. The extent of this lead in 1945 is evident against a number of indicators. The first relates to the relative size of the respective industrial capabilities. In the USA, the consequence of USAAF and British Admiralty orders was to create an industry comprising 21 firms actively designing helicopters of various sizes and configurations. Of the larger companies, Sikorsky commanded a design and manufacturing staff of over 1,000 in 1945 and Nash-Kelvinator had 700 employees trained in final assembly of helicopters.[124] Between 1939 and 1945, approximately 80 different helicopter programmes had been initiated by US firms,[125] of which 16 types had undergone flight testing, and for two projects – the Sikorsky R-4 and R-5 – tooling and manufacturing lines had been established for large-scale production. The policy of reliance on US-sourced helicopters rendered indigenous UK infrastructure and achievements marginal by comparison. In 1945, two design teams collectively containing fewer than ten designers represented the extent of the UK helicopter industry.

Moreover, for the majority of the war, the core of Britain's pre-war expertise had been fragmented and dissipated in non-helicopter areas. In contrast to the state of the art in the USA, where scale production had been initiated, the two projects at the Bristol and Weir firms were very much at the basic experimental stage. Consequently, in contrast to MAP perceptions, the scale and scope of US and UK activities by 1945 indicated a clear American technological lead in the helicopter field.

The second indicator of the US lead in 1945 was the relative status of British and American helicopter technology. Manifestly, in terms of their stage of technical development, the status of the two British projects reflected the effects of Britain's exit from R&D in 1940 and the subsequent innovations made by US firms. In 1945, while Sikorsky was producing R-4 and R-5 helicopters in quantity, Weir's technical challenge to Sikorsky's approach on the W.9 project had made only limited experimental progress. Tethered ground tests revealed fundamental limitations in the W.9 design[126] to the extent that the prototype had disintegrated during testing. Control problems were also encountered on the W.9 from the lack of cyclic pitch controls of the type perfected by Sikorsky during the war,[127] controls that Weir had rejected on technical grounds in approaches to the MAP during 1942. More fundamentally, W.9 testing had also revealed that 'torque reaction by a tail jet controlled at source from the centre of the helicopter is too sluggish as a means of directional control as compared with the tail-rotor [adopted by Sikorsky]'.[128] Weir's technical critique of the Sikorsky configuration in 1942, which had led the MAP to sanction basic experimental work on the W.9, had proved to be incorrect. Hafner's design approach at Bristol and the development status of the Type 171 were also indicative of Sikorsky's lead. With the Type 171, Bristol was proceeding with a design 'similar in principle'[129] to the Sikorsky R-4 and R-5 types. Whereas the Sikorsky models were entering scale production in 1945, only preliminary work had been completed on the Type 171 to the extent that a 50ft rotor tower had been constructed for preliminary blade testing.[130]

In addition to the outward manifestations of the comparative US lead, the factors explaining the divergence with UK capabilities were also an important legacy. The first relates to 'design dominance'.[131] As Chapter 1 revealed, a primary characteristic of pre-1939 technical debates over optimising helicopter design had centred on competing configurations of rotor and anti-torque mechanisms. Within the array of US wartime projects, various configurations had been investigated (see Table 6) but the particular success of the Sikorsky approach – mechanically driven single rotor and lateral mechanically-driven anti-torque rotor – had profound implications. The relative success of Sikorsky's wartime innovation, reflected in the entry into production of the R-4 and R-5, created an acceptance by US technologists and policy-makers that the Sikorsky approach was the 'conventional' helicopter configuration; in effect, the configuration had established 'design dominance'. Sikorsky design dominance had wider implications. During 1943, for example, a major criterion in MAP technical evaluations of the Weir W.9 was its potential in comparison to the 'conventional' Sikorsky design. Hafner's technical approach at Bristol after 1944 was an explicit attempt to 'catch-up' with Sikorsky innovations on the 'conventional' configuration.

The second cluster of factors underpinning the situation in 1945 were the facilitators of the comparative US and UK divergence in technological capability. As Rawlins and Sambito point out, 'without military procurement of helicopters, prompted by World War II, it is doubtful that the [US] industry would have blossomed so rapidly'.[132] After 1939, as we have seen, the policy imperative of helicopters for wartime operations augmented by British Admiralty requirements were important catalysts for the rate of US innovation. The combination of specific military requirements, operational urgency, and provision of large-scale government financial and technical resources were central in the US transformation of the helicopter from an experimental to a production technology with an extensive design, engineering and industrial infrastructure. Britain's re-entry into the field in the latter stages of the war through limited MAP funding for two small design teams was thus an attempt to 'catch up' with a US capability that had undergone a fundamental shift after the UK's exit in 1940, a capability that had been the recipient of major innovation incentives and that had been transformed from small and fragmented design efforts into an industry.

Relative US and UK perceptions of helicopter technology

Despite the sanguine view of MAP officials, that US firms in general, and Sikorsky in particular, had established a technological lead over British capabilities in 1945 has become apparent. However, another legacy of the war was the markedly different US and UK governmental and bureaucratic perceptions about the significance of the helicopter as a technology. On the one hand, the USAAF had been quick to recognise the operational potential of the helicopter, had initiated developments in US industry, and had initiated programmes of pilot training and supporting operational infrastructures. Ongoing participation and involvement in industrial developments at the highest levels of the USAAF had served to generate substantial acceptance and support for the helicopter from a major element of the US military establishment. Moreover, the rate of US innovation, coupled with the provision of extensive public funds, had focused policy attention through the Truman Committee on mechanisms to protect US post-war commercial interests in the helicopter field. In addition, throughout the war, the US War Production Board officials had been active and influential in directing, planning and assisting the emerging helicopter industry. The result in 1945 was not only sizeable government, bureaucratic and military acceptance of the potential for the helicopter in civil and military roles but also recognition in industry of these positive official perceptions about post-war markets.

On the other hand, official perceptions in the UK were quite different. The Royal Navy, the only branch of the UK armed services with wartime helicopter interests, had no direct interest in indigenous British helicopter development. Moreover, as a recipient of US helicopter equipment, the Admiralty's exposure to American industrial developments had been restricted to the small body of personnel liaising with the USAAF in Washington. By 1945 therefore, the helicopter *per se*, and British wartime developments in particular, had no extensive or established service support. Consequently, official perceptions about the utility and importance of helicopter technology differed considerably in the UK and the US in 1945. As subsequent chapters demonstrate, this factor, coupled with the US technological lead, was to have decisive and fundamental implications for British post-war developments.

SUMMARY

In 1940, Britain had an indigenous helicopter design capability comparable to teams in the USA. By 1945, the situation had altered radically: despite British complacency about being able to catch up, this analysis suggests that a range of US firms, and Sikorsky in particular, had established a comprehensive design, development and production lead over UK firms and projects. This technological lead was to become a central determinant of longer-term trends in post-war UK helicopter R&D and production. In the meantime, as the next chapter demonstrates, factors that were to affect UK helicopter activities between 1945 and 1947 generated the second determinant.

NOTES

1. E.J. Everett-Heath, *British Military Helicopters* (London: Arms & Armour Press, 1986), p. 27.
2. USNA, Air Corps and Army Air Forces Library Collection, Report from the Truman Committee, 2 June 1943, File No. 452·1.
3. Ibid., Letter from General Chidlaw to the War Production Board, 19 March 1943.
4. Ibid., Letter from the President of the United Aircraft Corporation to the USAAF, 19 March 1943.
5. Ibid.
6. Ibid.
7. Ibid., Letter from General Chidlaw to the War Production Board, 19 March 1943. The breakdown of orders was 13 units for the USAAF, 1 unit for the US Navy and 15 units for UK Services.
8. Ibid., Memorandum for the Assistant Secretary for War from General B.W. Chidlaw, 17 September 1943.
9. Ibid., Letter from General Chidlaw to the War Production Board, 19 March 1943.
10. Ibid., Memorandum for the Assistant Secretary for War from General B.W. Chidlaw, 17 September 1943.
11. Ibid., Letter from General Chidlaw to the War Production Board, 19 March 1943.
12. The USAAF was established on 20 June 1941. From 2 July 1926 until then it was the

US Army Air Corps. For the reader's convenience, the abbreviation USAAF is used throughout for the period after 1940.

13. USNA, Air Corps and Army Air Forces Library Collection, Memorandum for the Assistant Secretary for War from General B.W. Chidlaw, 17 September 1943, File 452.1.
14. Ibid., Letter from Brigadier General B.W. Chidlaw to the War Production Board, 19 March 1943.
15. Ibid.
16. Ibid.
17. Ibid.
18. Ibid., Memorandum on Helicopter Production, War Production Board, 19 March 1943.
19. PRO AVIA 15/954, Report on Rotating Wing Activity in the United States, 23 January 1943.
20. USNA, Air Corps and Army Air Forces Library Collection, War Department Air Corps Materiel Division, Engineering Division Memorandum Report on Helicopter Development, 15 February 1943, File No. 452.1.
21. Ibid., Memorandum from the Engineering Division of the Air Corps Materiel Division: Helicopter Development, 15 February 1943, File 452·1.
22. Ibid.
23. Ibid.
24. Ibid., War Department Air Corps Materiel Division, Engineering Division Memorandum Report on Helicopters for Production, 13 February 1943.
25. Ibid.
26. Ibid., Letter from Col. J.W. Sessums to the president, United Aircraft Corporation, 23 April 1943.
27. R.W. Prouty, *Military Helicopter Design Technology* (London: Jane's, 1989), p. 5.
28. USNA, War Production Board Collection, Memorandum from the Working Subcommittee on Delivery Schedules to the Recorder, Army-Navy British Joint Committee, 13 December 1940, File No. 314.228.
29. L.B. Bryson, F.E. Heenan and C.A. Johnson, 'Helicopters in the Royal Navy', *Royal Aeronautical Society Journal*, Vol. 76, August 1972, p. 471.
30. J. Dowling, *RAF Helicopters: The First Twenty Years* (London: HMSO, 1992), p. 5.
31. PRO AIR 45/21, Review of the Arnold/Evill Agreement, 13 May 1943.
32. Bryson *et al.*, 'Helicopters in the Royal Navy', p. 471.
33. PRO AVIA 15/954, Report on Rotating Wing Aircraft Activities in the United States, 23 February 1943.
34. USNA, Air Corps and Army Air Forces Library Collection, Memorandum from the Air Corps Material Division, 13 February 1943, 452.1.
35. PRO AVIA 15/954, Minutes of Meeting on Helicopter Staff Requirements held by DAWT, 22 February 1943. The Admiralty requirements had been formulated on 22 February 1943. While accepting that British forces would have to accept helicopters that were 'laid out to cover American requirements', the meeting agreed on several requirements that should be forwarded to the USA and incorporated in production helicopters for British use. The recommendations made included *inter alia* that the helicopter should be capable of striking and therefore armament load should be given a high priority; a crew of two as normal should be facilitated; an operational endurance of three hours was desirable; a radio was essential; provision must be made for carrying the 35lb Shaped Charge Bomb; and that the prime requirement was that a ship 'should be capable of launching or landing her Helicopter without having to alter course (and thus quit her station in the convoy) to do so'. Summarizing these requirements in order of priority the Memorandum placed them as follows:
    a) Two in crew.
    b) Radio.

c) Endurance of not less than three-and-a-half hours at economical speed.
d) Offensive load, including provision for carrying flares, equivalent to not less than two Mark XI depth charges (551 lb).
e) ASV.

36. USNA, Air Corps and Army Air Forces Library Collection, Letter from Major Bradbury to Colonel Sessums, 18 March 1943, File No. 452.1.
37. Ibid., Discussion: Helicopters, by the Air Corps Assistant Chief of Staff, 31 March 1943.
38. USNA, War Production Board Collection, Report from Grover Loening, Consultant on Aircraft, War Production Board, 19 May 1943, File No. 314.2.
39. USNA, Air Corps and Army Air Forces Library Collection, Letter from Colonel R.C. Wilson, Chief of Development and Engineering to the Commanding General, Materiel Command, 24 December 1943, File No. 452.1.
40. Ibid., Letter from the War Production Board to Colonel Gregory, I-C, Rotary Wing Section, 24 February 1943.
41. Ibid.
42. Ibid.
43. Ibid., Letter from Brigadier General B.W. Chidlaw to the War Production Board, 19 March 1943, File No. 452.1.
44. Ibid.
45. Ibid.
46. Ibid.
47. This assertion is based on extensive investigation of US public records of the period at the National Archives. Moreover, no information is contained in published commentary.
48. USNA, Air Corps and Army Air Forces Library Collection, Inter-Office Memorandum by Brigadier General Wolfe (Chief of Production Division) to Commanding General, Materiel Command, 24 February 1943, File No. 452.1.
49. Ibid.
50. Ibid., Letter from E.E. Wilson, President of the United Aircraft Corporation to the Chief of the Army Air Corps, 19 March 1943.
51. Ibid.
52. Ibid.
53. Ibid.
54. Ibid.
55. Ibid.
56. Ibid., Memorandum for General Chidlaw by Major A.P. Tappan, 27 May 1943.
57. Ibid., Memorandum from Major Tappan to General Chidlaw: Meeting, Wright Field, Wednesday, 26 May 1943, Production Helicopters, 27 May 1943.
58. The precise personnel breakdown of QSEs was 150 scientists for 'Experimental' work, 181 technologists for 'Development Engineering' and 104 technologists for 'Production Engineering'. *Source:* USNA, Air Corps and Army Air Forces Library Collection, Memorandum from Major Tappan to General Chidlaw: Meeting, Wright Field, Wednesday, 26 May 1943, Production Helicopters, 27 May 1943, File No. 452.1.
59. The precise non-QSE manpower breakdown was: 'Factory' – 825 personnel; 'Inspection' – 50 personnel; 'Accounting' – 48 personnel; and, 'General Administration' – 10 personnel. *Source:* USNA, Air Corps and Army Air Forces Library Collection, Memorandum from Major Tappan to General Chidlaw: Meeting, Wright Field, Wednesday, 26 May 1943, Production Helicopters, 27 May 1943, File No. 452.1.
60. Ibid.
61. USNA, War Production Board Collection, The Helicopter's Limited Future, by Grover Leoning, Chairman, Helicopter Committee, National Advisory Committee

for Aeronautics, 3 December 1943, File No. 314.248.
62. USNA, Air Corps and Army Air Forces Library Collection, Memorandum from Major Tappan to General Chidlaw: Meeting, Wright Field, Wednesday, 26 May 1943, Production Helicopters, 27 May 1943, File No. 452.1.
63. Ibid.
64. Ibid.
65. USNA, War Production Board Collection, Inspection of Helicopter Projects in the United States, March 1943, File No. 314.242.
66. Ibid.
67. See, for example, G.L. Weinberg, *A World at Arms: A Global History of World War II* (Cambridge: Cambridge University Press, 1994), p. 829.
68. USNA, Air Corps and Army Air Forces Library Collection, Summary by Major A.P. Tappan of Truman Committee Hearings held on 2 June 1943, 2 June 1943, File No. 452.1.
69. Ibid.
70. Ibid.
71. Ibid.
72. Ibid., Memorandum to General B.W. Chidlaw by Colonel J.W. Sessum, 24 June 1943.
73. Ibid., Memorandum for General Chidlaw by Major A.P. Tappan, 27 May 1943.
74. Ibid., Memorandum from Major Tappan to General Chidlaw: Helicopter Patent Situation, 26 June 1943.
75. Ibid.
76. Ibid., Memorandum from Major Tappan to General Chidlaw: Helicopter Patents, 12 August 1943.
77. Ibid.
78. This assertion is based on detailed scrutiny of the UK Public Records for this period. MAP files contain no reference to development other than the activities of Hafner.
79. PRO AVIA 15/954, Minute from the Director of Scientific Research, 2 February 1943.
80. Ibid.
81. Ibid., Aeronautical Research Committee: Report of the Helicopter Panel, 3 July 1943.
82. Ibid.
83. See, for example, PRO AVIA 15/954, Letter from ARIII Construction (Hafner Gyroplane) to the Secretary of the Ministry of Aircraft Production, 17 January 1944.
84. Ibid., Minute from the Chief of Research and Development, 4 February 1943.
85. Ibid., Minute from the Director of Scientific Research, 2 February 1943.
86. Ibid., Aeronautical Research Committee: Report of the Helicopter Panel, 3 July 1943.
87. Ibid., Minute from the Director of Scientific Research, 2 February 1943.
88. Ibid.
89. Ibid., Minute from the Controller of Research and Development, 8 March 1943.
90. Ibid., Minute from the Controller of Research and Development, 4 February 1943.
91. Ibid., Minute from the Deputy Director of Scientific Research, 12 January 1943.
92. Ibid.
93. Everett-Heath, *British Military Helicopters*, p. 27.
94. PRO AVIA 15/954, Minute from the Controller of Research and Development, 4 February, 1943.
95. Ibid., Minute from the Deputy Director of Research, Development and Technology, 14 January 1943.
96. Ibid., Letter from the British Air Commission: Rotating Wing Aircraft, 23 January 1943.
97. Ibid., Minute from the Controller of Research and Development, 8 March 1943.
98. Ibid., Minute from the Deputy Director of Scientific Research, 12 January 1943.
99. Ibid., Minute from the Controller of Research and Development, 4 February 1943.

100. Ibid., Minute from the Deputy Director of Scientific Research, 17 June 1943.
101. USNA, Air Corps and Army Air Forces Library Collection, Letter from Colonel H.F. Gregory to General B.W. Chidlaw, 10 December 1942, 452.1.
102. PRO 15/954, Minute from the Chief Executive, 14 February 1943.
103. Ibid., Minute from the Chief of Research and Development, 4 February 1944.
104. Ibid., Minute from Sir Henry Tizard, 9 February 1943.
105. Ibid., Letter from AR III Construction to the Ministry of Aircraft Production, 17 January 1944.
106. Ibid., Minute from the Controller of Research and Development, 15 July 1943.
107. Ibid., Minute from the Controller of Research and Development, 16 July 1943.
108. Ibid., Aeronautical Research Committee: Report of the Helicopter Panel, 3 July 1943.
109. Ibid., Minute from the Chief of Research and Development, 15 July 1943.
110. Ibid., Minute by the Deputy Director of Research, Development and Technology, 20 January 1944.
111. Ibid., Minute from the Director of Scientific Research, 20 July 1943.
112. Ibid., Minute from the Deputy Director Scientific Research, 20 July 1943.
113. Ibid.
114. G.E. Walker, 'Activities of Weir, Hafner and Bristol 1933–1960', in R.A.C. Brie (ed.), *A History of British Rotorcraft 1866–1965* (Yeovil: Westland Helicopters, 1968), p. 74.
115. Ibid.
116. Ibid.
117. R. Hafner, 'British Rotorcraft', *Journal of the Royal Aeronautical Society*, Vol. 70, Part 1, January 1966, p. 238.
118. R. Hafner, 'Four Decades of Rotating Wing Activity 1928–1965', in R.A.C. Brie (ed.), *A History of British Rotorcraft 1866–1965* (Yeovil: Westland Helicopters, 1968), p. 39.
119. Ibid.
120. A. McClements, 'Review of British Helicopter Activities 1943–1946', in R.A.C. Brie (ed.), *A History of British Rotorcraft 1866–1965* (Yeovil: Westland Helicopters, 1968), p. 106.
121. K. Watson, 'Activities of Weir, Cierva and Saunders-Roe 1933–1962', in R.A.C. Brie (ed.) *A History of British Rotorcraft 1866–1965* (Yeovil: Westland Helicopters, 1968), p. 57.
122. Ibid.
123. J. Shapiro, 'Cierva Autogiro Company 1943–1951', in R.A.C. Brie (ed.) *A History of British Rotorcraft 1866–1965* (Yeovil: Westland Helicopters, 1968), p. 86.
124. USNA, Air Corps and Army Air Forces Library Collection, 'Memorandum from Major Tappan to General Chidlaw', 28 May 1943, File No. 452.1.
125. USNA, War Production Board Collection, 'The Helicopter and its Future' by Grover Loening, Chairman of the Helicopter Committee of the National Advisory Committee for Aeronautics, 3 December 1943, File No. 314.248.
126. Watson, 'Activities of Weir, Cierva and Saunders-Roe', p. 57.
127. Shapiro, 'Cierva Autogiro Company', p. 86.
128. Ibid., p. 87.
129. A. McClements, 'A Review of British Helicopter Activities', p. 106.
130. Walker, 'Activities of Weir, Hafner and Bristol', p. 74.
131. This refers to a core, or dominant, design. See P.P. Saviotti and A. Trickett, 'The Evolution of Helicopter Technology, 1940–1986' (Mimeo, University of Manchester, 1987), p. 7.
132. E.W. Rawlins and W.J. Sambito, *Marines and Helicopters, 1946–1962* (Washington, DC: US Marine Corps History and Museums Division, 1976), p. 4.

3

Establishing a British Helicopter Industry, 1945–47

Between 1945 and 1947 no helicopters were produced in the UK. However, this period was crucial for it established the basic framework of assumptions and structures under which helicopter procurement was to be conducted until 1960. The government department responsible for implementing UK helicopter industrial and procurement policy – the MAP, replaced in October 1945 by the Ministry of Supply (MoS) – laid down basic policy parameters that were to endure until 1960. The policy assumption was that government financial support for R&D in industry and a 'buy-British' purchasing commitment would enable the UK to become self-sufficient in helicopter design and manufacture. The two-year period was also instrumental in galvanising the assumptions and technological strategies of the firms entering the helicopter market. On the basis of MAP/MoS policy, British firms were led to perceive considerable benefits from in-house research and development. Westland, however, elected instead to enter the market through licensed production. And finally, by 1947, two distinct sets of procurement procedures and processes had emerged: one in which indigenous helicopter R&D was conducted and another set affecting Westland as a licensed producer. These 'twin-track' procurement arrangements formed a second long-term determinant of UK helicopter R&D and production.

BRITISH GOVERNMENT HELICOPTER POLICY, FIRMS' RATIONALES FOR MARKET ENTRY AND COMPANY STRATEGIES, 1945–47

Premises of Post-1945 MAP/MoS Helicopter Industrial Policy

By mid-1945, the MAP formulated the basic tenets of post-war UK government helicopter industrial policy. It was a policy characterised by a remarkable degree of consistency until 1960. On 1 May 1945, the Director of Scientific Research stated that henceforth,

> the Policy of this Ministry [MAP] is to undertake research at our Establishments and stimulate interest of aircraft firms on Helicopters as

> we believe there are potential fields, civil and military, for this type of aircraft. To this end we are planning a comprehensive programme including the setting up of a research group at RAE to deal with the difficulties and complex aerodynamic problems associated with rotary-wing aircraft.[1]

Rather than continued reliance on American production technology, the MAP's new objective was 'to establish and foster a strong [indigenous] helicopter industry with the design and production capacity to cater for all home markets and bid for [potential future] export markets'.[2]

This signalled a fundamental shift from wartime planning assumptions. During 1945, it was not even considered as a long-term option that Britain should fulfil any post-war helicopter production requirements from US manufacturing. Instead, indigenous sourcing and policies to create a domestic industry were assumed to be a resumption of 'normalised' industrial strategy as the UK returned to peacetime conditions. Throughout late 1945 and early 1946, while the MAP aircraft procurement functions were transferred to the Ministry of Supply, a more detailed rationale underpinning the new policy became clear.

The first driver was UK government perceptions of the post-war prospects for the aircraft industry *in toto* compared with the prognosis of a large-scale decline in production output. As early as 1943, discussions had been initiated between various government departments to consider the post-war future of the aircraft industry. To adapt to the anticipated decline in the demand for production aircraft, 1943 Treasury estimates had been that the output of the industry would be reduced by 90 per cent of its 1942 production levels after the termination of hostilities.[3] By 1945, however, the political decision had been made that no government measures should be introduced to alter the existing structure of the aircraft industry.[4] Instead, because the scale of wartime manufacture had transformed the pre-war aircraft industry into a major employer and producer, the impending decline in demand had created pressures for government intervention 'to maintain employment and, hopefully, the profitability of a strategically and economically vital sector'.[5] Against this general imperative, the encouragement of firms to enter the helicopter field was part of a broader strategy to support and fund R&D in British industry to compensate for reductions in fixed-wing manufacture.

The second policy driver was the perceived need to 'catch up' with wartime technological advances in both the USA and Germany:

> The pace of wartime production had been such as to prevent extensive [UK] research and development; in addition, virtually all military transport production had been centred in the United States. Thus compared to American firms, the industry was not prepared for commercial production.[6]

By 1945, British officials were aware that concentrating resources on bomber and fighter production 'meant that at the end of the war very few advanced projects were under development... and we were falling behind in the science of aerodynamics'.[7] Throughout 1945, intelligence reports were detailing the extent of German scientific and industrial innovation in jet aircraft, variable wing-sweep research and rocketry.[8] On this basis, British defence technology policy was to be premised on a broad research and development approach in areas neglected during wartime. Enunciated formally, the *Statement Relating to Defence*[9] of February 1946, the first 'principle' of supply and provision of defence equipment was to be 'concentration on research', since 'scientific progress... is so rapid that safety lies far more in the maintenance of an adequate organisation for pure and applied research than in the building up of stocks of obsolescent equipment'.[10]

As a relatively new technology, government was keen for indigenous helicopter R&D to be subsumed in the broader R&D programme as an area for investigation by industry. Moreover, Britain's 'gap' in helicopter development had been a product of *de facto* reliance on US production after 1940. Officials assumed, therefore, that helicopters should be incorporated in the programme of aircraft development for possible civil and military markets[11] as 'basic knowledge on helicopters... [was]... more limited in the United Kingdom than elsewhere at the end of the war, and much ground had to be made up'.[12]

A third cluster of factors driving policy were MAP predictions about potential civil and military helicopter markets. By 1945, on the military side, Sikorsky helicopters obtained under wartime agreements were in service or entering service in the USA and Britain.[13] This procurement indicated to officials that future military demand would want to replace Sikorsky types already in service. In terms of potential civil demand for helicopters, evidence presented to the Ministry suggested considerable market opportunities for British firms. After 1943, the Brabazon Committee had been tasked by the Cabinet to plan a programme of aircraft designs that would form the basis of civil production at the end of the war, and to suggest firms that should be invited to submit tender designs.[14] By early 1945, MAP officials were themselves advising the Brabazon Committee of preliminary specifications for future civil helicopter types. Under these circumstances, the officials were eager to encourage British aircraft manufacturers to exploit these potential opportunities and to compete with American firms for domestic and export markets which 'can be expected to develop in the coming years'.[15] Because future projects would be in an environment of 'speculative costs of a magnitude which few aircraft firms would be able to meet from their own resources,'[16] Ministry attention was also focusing on potential mechanisms to channel government support and finance into the industry.

The final factor driving policy was the MoS's perception of the relative ease with which British companies could 'catch up' with American wartime helicopter advances. Officials did recognise the wartime lead that American firms had obtained in helicopter production. In 1945, for example, Andrew

McClements – later to become the Assistant Director, Research and Development (Helicopters) at the Ministry of Supply – noted that

> ... we [in Britain] are far behind the Americans in this branch of Aeronautical Engineering, as is borne out by the fact that only two British prototypes at present under construction are likely to have any production future, whereas the Americans have about 16 types flying and at least 2 in limited production.[17]

However, the dominant view at the Ministry reflected the prevalent assumption after 1942 that '... generally speaking, the fundamental design knowledge on rotating wing aircraft [in the UK] is at least as good if not better than that in the USA'.[18] Though the grounds for 'official opinion' were not stated overtly, this complacency appears to have been based on the Ministry's technological judgement and assurances made by industry. As a result, an active policy of supporting domestic projects was considered attractive because of the view that British firms could enter production and compete with US firms on the basis of their technological know-how.[19] Consequently, by mid-1945, the MAP/MoS had formulated its rationale for a programme of indigenous helicopter development on the basis of officials' estimates of potential future military and civil requirements, and on the assumption that UK firms were at the state of the art in helicopter design.

Aircraft Firms: Rationales for and Approaches to Market Entry

After 1945, four British firms were engaged in helicopter development. Three – the Bristol Aeroplane Company, which established its Helicopter Department in 1944, Fairey Aviation, which started helicopter work in late 1945, and Westland Aircraft, which commenced helicopter activities in early 1947 – were fixed-wing aircraft manufacturers for whom helicopters formed a new commercial venture. For Cierva, the pre-war autogiro manufacturer and the post-war arm of Weir helicopter activities, rotary-wing aircraft had been the core business. In each case, corporate assumptions about the commercial potential of post-war helicopter markets were instrumental in their decision to enter or remain in the field.

Mirroring MoS concerns, a primary reason for market entry was diversification. Cierva considered helicopter development a natural continuation of its pre-war business and an extension of work on the W.9.[20] In contrast, Fairey, Bristol and Westland all saw the helicopter field as a mechanism for adjusting to the anticipated post-war decline in demand for military fixed-wing production. During the war, Fairey Aviation had mass-produced a range of aircraft including the Battle, the Swordfish, the Fulmar, the Albacore and the Firefly. Though Fairey emerged from the war with orders for the Firefly, the company Board were concerned about the longer-term production demand. In the Bristol Aeroplane Company's case, the prospect of declining fixed-wing markets led to a broader strategy of diversification of which helicopter development was only a part:

> To keep its assembly lines and work-people busy, it [Bristol] began producing motor cars, prefabricated houses, plastics and marine craft, while developing new types of military and civil aircraft to meet anticipated post-war requirements.[21]

Similar considerations influenced the Board of Westland. Westland's major activity during the war had been the production of naval fixed-wing aircraft for the Admiralty. By 1945,

> at the termination of hostilities consideration was given to extending its naval interests; but apart from the Wyvern, the company was unsuccessful in obtaining Admiralty contracts of the kind which had been so useful in the past. Another possibility was to continue the high-altitude fighter line, and produce a jet-powered successor to the Welkin, but here again no government contracts were forthcoming.[22]

With shrinking fixed-wing orders, entry to the helicopter field was to form a component of the company's broader diversification strategy that included the formation of Westland Engineers (light engineering), production agreements with Richard Wilcox Limited of Canada (building materials) and Westland's acquisition of the United Balance Company (building materials).[23]

Firms were also attracted to helicopter work because of their perception of market potential, both military and civil. On the military side, all were aware of the technological advances in US industry and Royal Navy orders from Sikorsky, both of which indicated the likelihood of continued and growing service interest in helicopters.[24] The firms were also aware of the MoS policy that emphasised support for indigenous helicopter R&D to support future service requirements. What appeared to be the prospect of firm civil requirements from the influential Brabazon Committee, coupled with the government's policy of supporting R&D and underwriting transport aircraft development, provided added incentives for market entry. In short, the company boards shared the perception that

> by the time the war had ended, the brief period of service of these aircraft [helicopters] had given an indication of the usefulness of this unique type of flying machine. There was good reason to believe that the helicopter would be needed on an ever-increasing scale for military applications, and for numerous jobs in the civil field.[25]

A final factor was the availability of expertise. Throughout the war, the core of Britain's helicopter and autogiro design teams had been dispersed and redeployed in support of the war effort. By 1945, these qualified scientists and engineers (QSEs), released from 'wartime occupations', were actively seeking employment in the helicopter development field.[26] Moreover, though indigenous helicopter work had effectively ceased after 1940, individual designers had obtained access to developments in the USA. This access proved to be attractive for British aircraft manufacturers considering the helicopter market. Hafner and other pre-war helicopter/rotary-wing designers, for example, who had been recruited earlier by Bristol, had obtained test experience of the Sikorsky R-4 while at the Airborne Forces Experimental Establishment.[27] Likewise, Fairey recruited Dr J.A.J. Bennett partly on the basis of his wartime role in monitoring Sikorsky developments.[28] Finally, Westland was able to engage O. Fitzwilliams, formerly Director of the Rotary Wing Section at the Airborne Forces Experimental Establishment, to head their new helicopter unit.[29] To add to the attraction of this available manpower, the MAP actively encouraged the firms to exploit this know-how to compete with American firms in helicopter development.[30]

Bristol, Cierva and Fairey's decisions to engage in in-house 'all-British' development reflected a number of considerations. First, they shared the assumption that future markets for production helicopters would primarily be public sector markets: domestic military orders and civil requirements from the major civil operators under public ownership such as British European Airways (BEA) and the British Overseas Airways Corporation (BOAC). Second, under the general parameters of government policy, their perception was that they would enjoy protection from overseas firms when future British civil and military helicopter requirements were to emerge. As far as military aircraft were concerned, government policy after 1945 was to 'buy British'. Incorporated into the 1945 Civil Aviation Act, it was axiomatic that 'it is the Government's general policy to require the Corporations to use British aircraft'.[31] On this basis, Cierva, Bristol and Fairey had good grounds to commence in-house helicopter development.

A stated tenet of MAP/MoS policy was that government financial support would also be forthcoming for R&D. Indeed, government policy had already assumed that few aircraft firms would be capable of meeting R&D costs from their own resources. On the civil aviation side, the Permanent Secretary of the Ministry of Civil Aviation pointed out in 1946 with regard to R&D that

> The Government decided . . . that the interests of British air transport throughout the world warranted the placing of Government orders in anticipation of the needs of the operators.[32]

On the military side, the 1946 Defence White Paper had explicitly stated the government's commitment to aircraft R&D as a primary defence objective. In view of these policy developments, firms were attracted to in-house helicopter development because of the prospect of receiving government funding to offset R&D outlays. Whereas Cierva, Bristol and

Fairey recognised that private venture capital would be necessary to initiate helicopter projects, a major incentive for in-house R&D was the perceived likelihood of substantial MoS R&D funding subsequently.

The firms also shared the MoS assessment that design and fundamental knowledge on rotating wing aircraft in the UK was comparable to that in the USA. This, coupled with the prospect of protectionist government procurement policies and R&D subsidies, outweighed any perceptions of benefits from possible licensed production arrangements with American firms. To illustrate this point, in early 1946 the Fairey Board had been offered a manufacturing license by Sikorsky which it turned down because of its perception of greater benefits from following the in-house indigenous route.[33]

By contrast, a different set of considerations shaped Westland's decision to adopt a licensed production approach in 1947. First, Westland Aircraft Chairman Mr (later Sir Eric) Mensforth had inspected Sikorsky's R-4 in the USA in 1944 and monitored their subsequent initiatives. He was impressed by the design and the stage of development. Mensforth and the Westland Board recognised that, by 1947, Sikorsky had made incremental improvements to the R-4/R-5 concept which were significantly in advance of indigenous British alternatives.[34] Second, by 1947:

> ...Westland built helicopters to Sikorsky designs partly because they did not have adequate staff or facilities to do anything else, in view of the Wyvern commitment.[35]

And third, the Westland Board were influenced by their analysis of the relative state of US and British helicopter development capabilities

> A fundamental fact was that not a single British helicopter existed at that time and active projects could be counted on the fingers of one hand. To have developed a new rotor head, transmission and control system would have been a lengthy and costly task, with no guarantee of ultimate success... Another factor borne in mind was the large number of patents applicable to rotor heads and helicopter transmission and control systems that were already held by the United States.[36]

More important was Westland's assessment of market potential: by negotiating a production licence, the company would be able to enter manufacture and achieve sales more quickly than was possible through in-house development.[37] In the event, Westland signed a licensed production agreement with Sikorsky on 10 January 1947 for the production in the UK of the four-seater S-51 helicopter – a refined and developed variant of the wartime R-5 originally intended for the US civil market. The agreement allowed Westland to manufacture the S-51 and market it anywhere in the world except the US and Canada.[38] It also left Westland free to develop, modify, re-engine and otherwise improve the basic Sikorsky design so that it was not compelled to lag behind its US licenser.[39] Though no direct evidence has emerged on this point, the generosity of the licence appears to reflect Sikorsky concerns after 1945 over a potential decline in domestic helicopter demand[40] as part of the massive US cutbacks in military aircraft procurement, and recognition that MoS protectionist policies meant that a licensed agreement was the only way for Sikorsky to penetrate the British helicopter market.

Firms and Technological Strategies, 1945–47

The 1945 to 1947 period was also important because the British firms established what were to be their longer-term technological approaches to helicopter design and development. In formulating their technological strategies, the firms had a considerable degree of latitude because of the absence of specific military and civil requirements and specifications on which to fix design. During this time, Sikorsky helicopters obtained under wartime arrangements from the US were meeting existing military requirements. Immediate orders were also unlikely in 1945 because UK government procurement policy was to rely on the massive stocks of wartime fixed-wing aircraft in the short-term, rather than purchase new aircraft.[41] Moreover, when the Brabazon Committee finally reported in November 1945, the outline civil helicopter specifications that emerged were general in nature: ‘a 4-seater helicopter for development purposes, a 10-seater helicopter for charter and aerodrome-city services and a helicopter for crop spraying’.[42] With this degree of design flexibility, each firm formulated a distinct and differing design strategy.

The Westland licensed production approach was the most conservative in technological terms in that it involved replicating manufacturing drawings of the ‘conventional’ configuration developed by Sikorsky. The Sikorsky S-51 design had been flight tested in the USA during February 1946 and had subsequently entered production. Rather than embarking on fundamental design work, Westland’s technical activities after January 1947 were to ‘anglicise’ Sikorsky ‘Extract-Sheet’ drawings and technical data and immediately prepare tools and jigs for manufacture.[43] In entering the market via the S-51 licensed production route, Westland had a negligible input into the design parameters of the helicopter. Instead, they were replicating a four-seater helicopter with a take-off weight of 2,663 kg (5,870 lb). While the value-added component of Westland’s licensed production until 1960 was to increase with subsequent agreements with Sikorsky, the core of the firm’s overall technological strategy remained constant.

At the Bristol Aeroplane Company, the Helicopter Department’s design team adopted a strategy of designing and developing helicopters in-house that conformed to the ‘conventional’ configuration established by Sikorsky. With the Type 171 project, initiated in 1944, Hafner’s objective was to 'refine' the basic design incorporated in the Sikorsky R-4 and R-5 helicopters with a project that combined:

1. the basic configuration that had been established by Sikorsky,
2. the main rotor and its controls that had been demonstrated successfully by the Hafner Gyroplane, and
3. the know-how of the Bristol Aeroplane Co. on aircraft structures.[44]

The Type 171 (later named the 'Sycamore') was designed to share broad performance characteristics already achieved by Sikorsky in the S-51. Like the S-51, the Type 171 was a four-seater and intended for utility roles. Weighing some 2,540 kg (5,600 lb), it was also of similar dimensions and capacity to the S-51 which Westland was to manufacture and produce. In effect, therefore, the Type 171 represented an 'all-British' version of the configuration under licensed production at Westland.

By late 1945, the Brabazon Committee had signalled the potential civil requirement for a ten-seater helicopter for charter and aerodrome-city transport. Bristol's response was to design a twin-engine tandem-rotor helicopter, designated Type 173, with a maximum take-off weight of 4,808 kg (10,600 lb), or twice that of the Type 171. Hafner's approach in the Type 173 design was to incorporate two of the tested Type 171 engine and rotor systems but operating them in reverse directions. Importantly, Bristol's technical approach was to adapt the Sikorsky configuration and apply developed components through a 'building-block' process. Like Westland, Bristol's technological strategy, well established by 1947, was to characterise the firm's design and development approach until 1960.

After June 1945, the Fairey Helicopter Division's technological strategy was the most radical. Dr J.A.J. Bennett, now the Chief Designer at Fairey, advocated the development of compound helicopters. The objective was to combine the 'advantages of both the helicopter and the autogiro while trying to minimise the effects of their disadvantages'.[45] Bennett's compound approach was to incorporate two independent systems in the aircraft, one for hovering and vertical take-off (the helicopter function), and one for forward flight. Vertical take-off and hovering was to be provided by a centrally-mounted main rotor; in forward flight, the power to the main rotor would be disengaged and propulsion then provided by horizontally-mounted propellers attached on stub wings. In theoretical terms, Fairey's attraction[46] to this configuration was that it dispensed with the need for the counter-torque tail-rotor selected by Sikorsky as a means to provide stability when hovering, on the grounds that in forward flight the 'conventional' tail-rotor contributed little but extra weight.

Fairey's assumption was that their design solution also offered three further practical benefits over contending configurations.[47] The first was enhanced safety: in the event of engine failure, the main rotor would automatically act as an autogiro, negating the need for pilot correction. Second, because the rotor had no propulsive function in flight, the rotor system and flight control were predicted to be comparatively simple. And third, lower vibration was anticipated as well as a decreased probability of blade stall, which theoretically permitted higher forward speeds. The Helicopter Division's only development project between 1945 and 1947 was the 'Gyrodyne', first announced in April 1946. As a four/five-seater, weighing 2,177 kg (4,800 lb), and being a utility type, the Gyrodyne was a potential competitor to the Bristol and Westland types. In configuration terms, the Gyrodyne was representative of Fairey's design strategy until 1960.

Cierva adopted a most eclectic strategy. Its W.9 experimental project had been abandoned by 1945 on technical grounds because of the limited utility of tail-jet thrust to counteract torque.[48] Later, between 1945 and 1947 the firm's activities were limited to two projects. In late 1944, design was commenced of a heavy lift multi-rotor helicopter designated the 'Air Horse'. A three-rotor design with a planned maximum take-off weight of 6,804 kg (15,000 lb), the Air Horse was the world's biggest helicopter then under development. In stark contrast to the Air Horse, Cierva's other project, the W.14 'Skeeter', conformed to the basic Sikorsky configuration but was of a much lower all-up-weight than the S-51, Bristol Type 171 or Fairey Gyrodyne. Intended as a light, two-seater helicopter with a maximum take-off weight of 549 kg (1,210 lb), the project commenced during 1947.

By 1947, the market entry and long-term technological strategies of the major firms that were to comprise the British helicopter industry until 1960 had been established. The significance of the technological approaches for patterns of helicopter R&D and production was to become clear after 1947. The choice of market entry strategies – Westland's licensed-production approach in contrast to the firms adopting in-house and indigenous R&D – was, however, to have more immediate implications between 1945 and 1947.

PARALLEL PROCUREMENT PROCESSES, 1945–47

Westland's 1947 entry into the UK helicopter market with a Sikorsky licence had one particularly important effect: this was to create two distinct and parallel helicopter procurement processes in the UK that were to endure until 1960. The first process affected Bristol, Fairey and Cierva, the firms who had elected to conduct in-house design and development under the tenets of MoS industrial and procurement policy. The second affected Westland as the only manufacturer of non-indigenous helicopter technology.

The 'Indigenous Procurement Process'[49]

Bristol, Fairey and Cierva had made three core assumptions on entering the post-war helicopter field. The first was that while the use of company private venture capital was essential to enter the market, government R&D funding would subsequently be forthcoming. The second was that domestic military and public-sector civil helicopter markets were likely to be considerable. The third was that, under the tenets of MoS industrial policy, their programmes would enjoy protection from non-national technological competition in these markets. By 1947, the firms' assumptions were operating within what had become a highly complex procurement process involving numerous government ministries and a plethora of committees – in shorthand the 'Indigenous Procurement Process'. This process was to prove vital because it determined the scale and scope of government R&D expenditure, the size of domestic military and civil helicopter markets and, indirectly, the innovation incentive structure the firms confronted in terms of their core market entry assumptions.

After 1947, no less than seven government ministries, supplemented by both intra- and inter-departmental committees, had a role in 'indigenous' helicopter procurement. The interaction of these ministries – the Ministry of Supply, the Ministry of Defence, the Ministry of Civil Aviation, the Air Ministry, the War Office, the Admiralty and HM Treasury – defined the environment affecting the 'indigenous' industry's core assumptions about government R&D funding and prospective markets. The essential elements of this process are summarised below.

On 29 October 1945, Prime Minister Attlee had announced that the procurement functions of the wartime Ministries of Aircraft Production and Supply would be merged under a new Ministry of Supply. The new Department was to assume responsibility for all research, development and procurement for the Army and Royal Air Force, and for research, development, and procurement of aircraft, electronics and guided weapons for the Royal Navy. To meet these responsibilities, under a Chief Scientist, the MoS was divided into several major sections: the Controller of Munitions being concerned with the development of equipment for the Army; a Directorate-General of Atomic Weapons, a Controller of Guided Weapons and Electronics and, finally, a Controller of Supplies (Air) responsible for aircraft development and supply. Beneath the Controller of Supplies (Air) were two Principal Directors for Technical Development and for Scientific Research. Under them were Directors of Research and Development, respectively, for Aircraft, Engines, Armaments, Instruments, Communications, Equipment and Guided Weapons.[50]

The MoS, within the remit of the Controller of Supplies (Air), assumed four main functions concerning the development and procurement of helicopters and aircraft more generally.[51] First, the MoS was to act as the procurement agency for the three Services and the Ministry of Civil Aviation, drawing up specifications and negotiating contracts for production aircraft. The choice of production aircraft and the costs of production were borne on the Vote of the individual Services and civil operators so, in its first role, the MoS acted as a technical adviser and purchasing agent. Secondly, the Ministry was directly responsible for implementing the government's research and development programme for military and civil aircraft. In this respect: 'The cost of research and design up to the stage of the prototypes [was] borne on the Vote of the Ministry of Supply'.[52] In terms of embarking on a new R&D project, the 'formal' procedure began with an Operational Requirement (OR) formulated by the Air Ministry or the Admiralty.[53] It was recognised, however, that

> in practice the Operational Requirement may spring from or be influenced by suggestions by the aircraft constructors or the Ministry of Supply as well as by purely military [or civil] requirement.[54]

In implementing an R&D programme, it is important to note that MoS R&D funding in industry was extensive, where the building of models and prototype building was concerned, since the Ministry's own research establishments did not construct either aircraft or aero engines. Thirdly, the MoS was responsible for running and operating these government aeronautical research establishments, such as the Royal Aircraft Establishment (RAE) at Farnborough. Finally, the Ministry was tasked to act as the sponsoring Department for the aircraft industry within Whitehall.

The Ministry's functional responsibilities, coupled with the broader policy directives under which it operated, defined the MoS approach to indigenous aircraft R&D and production. A combination of the MoS role as the aircraft industry's sponsoring department and the policy parameters set *inter alia* by the 1946 *Statement Relating to Defence*, which defined government policies of 'catching-up' and focusing of industrial resources on R&D, created imperatives at the Ministry for extensive development funding in industry and 'buy-British' purchasing policies.[55] In sum, protecting and supporting UK indigenous aviation technology was a central factor underpinning the MoS approach after 1945.

It was against this broader background and assumptions that MoS helicopter policy operated until 1960. The MoS interface with those firms adopting the 'indigenous' helicopter design and development route was exercised through a small cadre of MoS officials. Between 1945 and late 1947, as a new and emerging area of technology and industrial activity, 'indigenous' helicopter projects had come within the general remit of the MoS Principal Directors for Technical Development and Scientific Research.[56] However, as a 'solid tribute to the rising importance of the helicopter',[57] all helicopter R&D was placed under a Directorate of Research and Development (Helicopters) during December 1947. Functionally, the Directorate was directly under the Principal Directors of Technical Development and Scientific Research and headed by a Deputy Director Research and Development (Helicopters) (see Figure 1).

The remit of the Directorate of Research and Development (Helicopters) was wide-reaching. Mirroring the overall functions of the MoS in microcosm, the Directorate's terms of reference were broad: formulation and implementation of MoS helicopter R&D policy for industry; 'supervision and coordination of rotary-wing research at [government research] Establishments'; administration and service provision for the MoS Rotating Wing Committee; liaison with other branches of the MoS with helicopter interests; and provision of the main official 'channel of exchange of helicopter information'.[58] This specialist helicopter branch remained relatively unchanged in its structure and role until 1960. From the outset, the branch was small in number. Between 1947 and 1949 its staff consisted of three individuals[59] – a Deputy Director (Captain Liptrot), an Experimental Officer (Bristol Type 171, Bristol Type 173) and an RAF Squadron Leader (Air Horse, Skeeter and miscellaneous R&D) – a very small group compared with the total MoS non-industrial staff of 21,000 personnel.[60] Moreover, between 1949 and 1959 – a period during which the MoS was to sponsor numerous helicopter airframe and engine programmes – staffing levels in the Directorate never exceeded five officials in total.[61]

Figure 1: Outline Organisation of the MoS (Air), 1947

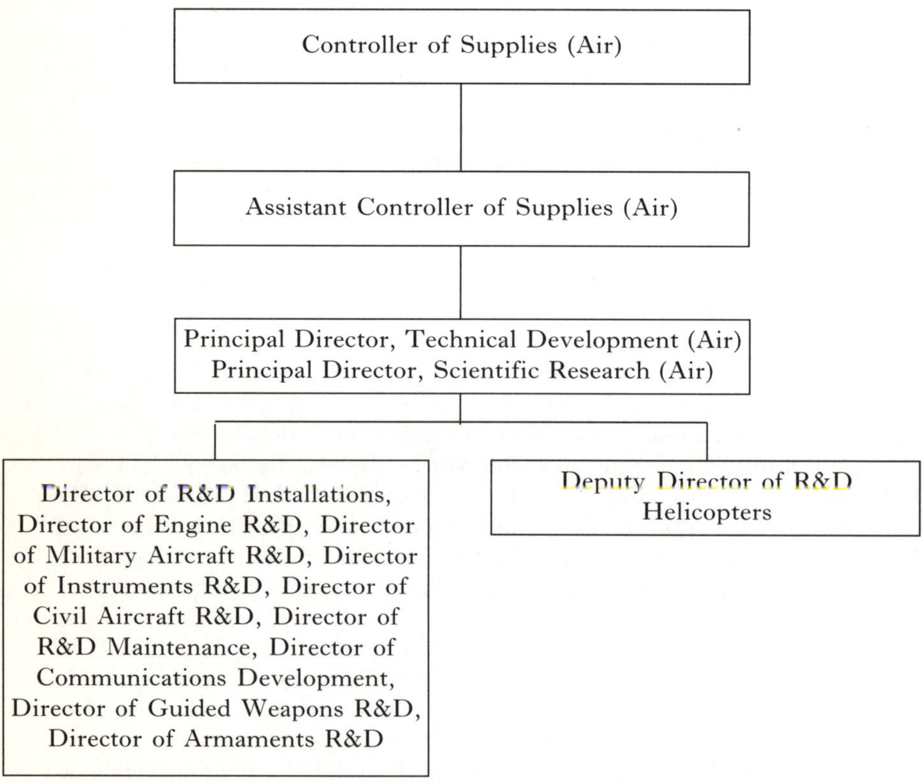

Source: Adapted from AVIA 55/90, Ministry of Supply (Air) Quarterly Notes issued by the Army Assistant to DMARD, December 1947.

The MoS as a whole, and the Directorate of Research and Development (Helicopters) in particular, shared the same assumptions and objectives as firms entering the post-war helicopter industry through the 'indigenous' development route – namely, the provision of government R&D funding for projects in industry, 'buy-British' policies for production helicopters and the expectation of large-scale service and civil markets. However, though funded from the MoS Vote, decisions which concerned the *scale* of MoS R&D expenditure on helicopter programmes in industry were largely beyond the Ministry's control. As the locus of government technological expertise, the MoS had some control over R&D resource allocation, but in its function as an intermediary ministry between the aircraft industry and the armed services and civil operators, MoS influence over the formulation of *user requirements and the scale of production orders* was limited by the functional responsibilities of other government departments.

Decisions affecting the scale of MoS aircraft R&D funding for 'indigenous' helicopter projects as a proportion of the total MoS aircraft R&D Vote were determined and defined by two other ministries: the Ministry of Defence (MoD) and the Ministry of Civil Aviation (MCA). The *Central Organisation for Defence*[62] White Paper of 1946 had led to the creation of the MoD.[63] The primary roles of the MoD were

> ...the apportionment of available resources between the three Services in accordance with the strategic policy laid down by the Defence Committee, framing general policy to govern research and development and the correlation of production of programmes, and settling questions of general administration on which a common policy for the three services was desirable.[64]

As far as the second of these functions was concerned – framing policy for military R&D – responsibility resided in the MoD's Defence Research Policy Committee (DRPC). Composed of staff officers responsible for formulating requirements for the three services, scientific advisers to the service departments and scientists involved in the development of new equipment,[65] the DRPC's terms of reference were 'to advise the Minister of Defence and the Chiefs of Staff on matters connected with the formulation of scientific policy in the defence field'.[66] Specifically, the Committee's role was to

> ...consider all major questions which require joint consultation, examine the research and development programmes of the Admiralty and the Ministry of Supply and advise on priorities, with the object of ensuring the best use of the resources available in scientific manpower, materials and money. The Committee will take into account work being carried out by Civil Departments and by industry.[67]

The DRPC was not granted formal executive powers, but tasked instead to 'advise' on research and development priorities. It had, therefore, considerable influence on R&D resource allocation decisions within the MoS. Once military requirements had been generated for aircraft development by the Services, the MoS itself or suggestions from industry, DRPC endorsement had to be sought by the MoS after which the DRPC included 'the [R&D] project in the [overall aircraft R&D] programme at a particular importance and priority rating'.[68] The DRPC effectively established relative military aircraft R&D priorities and expenditure levels in the context of the overall MoS R&D programme. The DRPC consequently had a central role in dictating levels of MoS expenditure on helicopter programmes in industry intended for domestic military markets.

DRPC decisions did not take place in a vacuum. The Committee's priority ratings for competing military R&D projects were influenced by priorities in the operational requirements branches of the individual Service Ministries. Fundamental to DRPC priority ratings for a particular project was the question whether or not it was linked to a specific service requirement. This distinction, whether or not a service Operational Requirement existed, led to a project's classification as either 'Research' or 'Development'. 'Research', or those projects concerned with the process of creating scientific capital, were defined as

> all that work, much of it of a very theoretical and fundamental nature, which [was] not directly specific to meeting immediate service requirements . . . [which] invariably involve building prototypes or flying models and hence the placing of projects with firms.[69]

'Development' status was assigned to projects for which formal operational requirements had been produced. While substantively the same technical activity as research – design work, construction of models and prototype aircraft[70] – the existence of an Operational Requirement was the defining and determining characteristic of a development programme. Against these categories, the principle underlying DRPC funding allocation policy was to concentrate resources on 'Development' work.

The Ministry of Civil Aviation also had a pivotal role in MoS R&D resource allocation. Created in October 1944, the MCA remit was to formulate short- and long-term civil aviation policy. In its procurement function, the Ministry was responsible, *inter alia*, for conveying to the MoS the immediate civil aircraft production requirements of the two nationalised airlines that provided all domestic and overseas air transport services – British European Airways (BEA) and the British Overseas Airways Corporation (BOAC) – and for formulating longer-term research and development policy for civil aviation. At the formation of the MCA

> it was decided . . . that, while responsibility for the design and production of civil aircraft, equally with that for military aircraft, would remain

> with the Minister of Aircraft Production [and subsequently the Minister of Supply], the Ministry of Civil Aviation would have direct access to him on equal terms with the Secretary of State for Air and the First Lord of the Admiralty, in order to ensure a fair share of the available resources for civil aviation.[71]

The MCA Transport Aircraft Requirements Committee (TARC) was responsible for defining civil aircraft priorities, which in turn governed MoS allocation of resources for civil aircraft R&D in industry. Like the DRPC, the TARC had no executive powers but did have the important role of translating the requirements of the civil operators into relative priority ratings for MoS R&D expenditure in industry.[72] Decisions within the MCA, therefore, were to be a further determinant of the level of MoS industrial R&D sponsorship for firms undertaking 'all-British' helicopter projects.

The final department of state with functional responsibilities for MoS R&D expenditure was HM Treasury.[73] The Treasury's primary preoccupations were the aggregate size of the MoS aircraft R&D Vote[74] and the scrutiny of financial aspects of research, development and subsequent production programmes.[75] In practice, Treasury involvement in the MoS aircraft R&D programme was limited primarily to assessing and endorsing the overall MoS Estimate, rather than detailed oversight on a project-by-project basis.[76] In the case of DRPC decisions, for example, Treasury officials were not represented on the Committee itself, though the Treasury received meeting agendas and, if it 'had any reason to think that any particular project was not going according to plan or required fresh appraisement by the [DRP] Committee, [they were] at liberty to ask for discussion on it'.[77] Treasury involvement thus added a further tier to the process of helicopter R&D funding-allocation decisions.

By 1947, therefore, intricate bureaucratic procedures had been set in place that were to dictate the level of MoS R&D funding for 'indigenous' helicopter programmes which are summarised in Appendix 2. The 'Indigenous Procurement Process' was further complicated, however, by separate procedures governing military and civil aircraft production requirements. While MoS industrial and procurement policy was to support and fund national programmes, decisions relating to operational requirements and the scale of production required by military and civil operators were the domain of the armed service ministries and the commercial air transport companies. Whereas aircraft R&D costs were borne on the MoS Vote, expenditure on orders for production in quantity was borne on the service and civil aviation ministries' votes.[78] In turn, the procurement procedures relating to each of these 'user' ministries were complex in themselves.

After 1937, when the Fleet Air Arm was separated from the RAF, the Admiralty had acquired control over the selection of aircraft and associated equipment for the Royal Navy.[79] Within the Admiralty, specific branches were concerned not only with the formulation of operational requirements in conjunction with MoS officials but also with defining RN unit production requirements. Coordination of RN aircraft requirements with those of the Air Ministry and branches within the MoS was conducted loosely through a series of inter-departmental committees including the Sea/Air Warfare Committee. Likewise, specialist branches existed in the Air Ministry to generate RAF aircraft operational requirements and production demands. In the case of the Air Ministry, Air Council authorisation was required for the placing of production orders which were then transferred to and implemented by the MoS.

Procedures for processing War Office aircraft requirements were fundamentally different. They stemmed from the division of functional responsibilities established between the Army and the RAF in 1917.[80] As far as Army aircraft requirements were concerned

> the War Office [had] – in effect – no direct relations with the Ministry of Supply; its requirements for aircraft [were] put to the Air Ministry and by them to the Ministry of Supply. Moreover, production aircraft [were] ordered by the Air Ministry and the Air Ministry [did] not recover the costs from the War Office.[81]

All Army aircraft production requirements were paid for, purchased by and operated by the RAF. Under these arrangements, the primary channel for War Office aircraft requirements to the MoS was through the Air Ministry via the inter-departmental Land/Air Warfare Committee and its various sub committees.[82] Finally, civil aircraft production requirements were generated by branches within the Ministry of Civil Aviation after consultation with the nationalised airlines and then transferred directly to the MoS. With all MCA production orders, Treasury authorisation was required and each production programme in industry was subjected to annual Treasury scrutiny. A synthesis of the procedures as they related to production decisions is summarised in Appendix 3.

After 1945, firms adopting the in-house and indigenous route to helicopter manufacture had assumed this approach would provide for government R&D funding, substantial domestic military and civil orders, and market protection from non-national competition. Against these assumptions, intricate bureaucratic procedures had emerged by 1947 that would dictate the extent to which each of the firms' market entry assumptions would be realised. These institutional arrangements making up the 'Indigenous Procurement Process' remained largely unchanged until 1960.

The 'Licensed Production Procurement Process'

Westland was the only British firm electing to enter the post-war helicopter field via a licensed production strategy. The Westland Board were also unique in terms of their market entry rationale. Westland's first assumption was that by exploiting the wartime lead established by Sikorsky it would be able to compete for domestic military and civil helicopter production orders more quickly than its UK rivals. In effect, the licensed approach was seen as a mechanism to 'leap-frog' over indigenous British R&D programmes. The second assumption was that licensed production of proven American designs using the firm's private venture capital would remove the need for costly, potentially lengthy and technologically risky design and development. By adopting this strategy, the Westland Board had elected in *de facto* terms to circumvent the procedures and assumptions of both MoS helicopter industrial policy and its domestic rivals. By 1947, against this backdrop, Westland's activities were to be located under entirely different bureaucratic arrangements: in shorthand the 'Licensed Production Procurement Process'.

In bureaucratic terms, the 'Licensed-Production Procurement Process' was far less complex than the 'Indigenous Procurement Process'. By circumventing in-house R&D and employing private venture capital, Westland was not subject to the sophisticated procedures that dictated MoS funding provision for design and development in industry. Instead, the main determinants of R&D inputs for Westland's activities were those which had already been conducted by Sikorsky, and more fundamentally, the incentives for innovation provided in the USA. In addition, Westland's technical approach was entirely separate from inputs dictated by the various UK government ministries with resource allocation functions for indigenous helicopter R&D projects.

Westland, as a helicopter manufacturer with commercial interests in potential UK public sector military and civil markets, was subject to government bureaucratic procedures for production and purchasing. There were, however, deviations from the 'Indigenous Procurement Process' in this sphere. The first was that, as a licensed producer, Westland had not elected to conduct 'Development' based on domestic service or civil requirements.[83] Because the firm was not developing equipment on the basis of military or civil operational requirements, its manufacturing activities were not linked to the complex procurement procedures established between the MoS and the Service ministries and MCA to translate 'Development' programmes into production aircraft.[84] The second difference concerned the role of the Treasury. As Westland had adopted licensed production through private-venture investment rather than with government R&D funding, the firm's technical activities were immune from Treasury scrutiny. Instead, Westland only had to seek Treasury authorisation for any dollar expenditure incurred in obtaining helicopters, or indeed anything else from Sikorsky, and royalty payments on licences because currency exchange controls had been put in place after 1945. Consequently, by 1947 there were fundamental and significant procedural differences between the 'Licensed Production Procurement Process' summarised in Appendix 4, and production arrangements for 'all-British' MoS-sponsored projects.

SUMMARY

Between 1945 and 1947, no helicopters were produced in the UK. Nevertheless, the period was significant in three other respects. First, it marked the amortisation of the post-war helicopter industrial and procurement strategy of Britain's primary aircraft procurement agency, the MoS. Second, it was a period in which the firms entering or re-entering the UK helicopter field defined, established, formulated and consolidated their commercial and technological strategies. On the one hand, a series of assumptions led Bristol, Cierva and Fairey to perceive significant long-term benefits from in-house and indigenous helicopter R&D; on the other, the Westland Board had identified potential gains through the licensed production route to market entry. Third, and as a consequence of these events, two parallel helicopter procurement procedures and processes had emerged by 1947.

Because of these important trends within the UK there has been little focus on parallel helicopter developments in the USA between 1945 and 1947. By way of a summary, however, little had changed by 1947 in terms of the post-1940 US technological lead over British firms. During April 1947, during an internal MoS review of relative industrial capabilities, officials were forced to concede that

> a cursory examination of helicopter development in Britain, will inevitably lead one to the conclusion that the British industry is a long way behind that of the United States, as indeed it is, if actual production of helicopters be the only criterion ... comparison with American progress is bound to appear unfavourable to this country.[85]

As subsequent chapters show, this US technological lead in helicopter design and manufacture established in wartime after 1947, coupled with the effects of the UK 'twin track' procurement processes, were to become two primary determinants of Westland's subsequent licensed production success and the comparative failure of 'all-British' MoS-sponsored projects.

NOTES

1. PRO AVIA 15/954, Minute from the Director of Scientific Research, Ministry of Aircraft Production, 1 May 1945.
2. PRO AVIA 65/6, Note on the MoS Helicopter R&D Programme with Special Emphasis on the Civil Transport Role, MoS Air 2(a), 17 October 1953.
3. This is developed in more detail in T. Geiger, '"The Next War is Bound to Come": Defence Production Policy, Supply Departments and Defence Contractors in Britain, 1945-57', in H. Mercer, N. Rollings and J.D. Tomlinson (eds), *The Labour Governments and Private Industry: The Experience of 1945 to 1951* (Edinburgh: Edinburgh University Press, 1992), p. 97.
4. Ibid.

5. K. Hayward, *Government and British Civil Aerospace: A Case Study in Post-War Technology Policy* (Manchester: Manchester University Press, 1983), p. 13.
6. W.P. Snyder, *The Politics of British Defence Policy, 1951–1961* (Princeton: Princeton University Press, 1963), p. 331.
7. The Supply of Military Aircraft, *Cmd. 9388* (London: HMSO, 1955), p. 3.
8. D. Wood, *Project Cancelled: The Disaster of Britain's Abandoned Aircraft Projects* (London: Tri-Service Press, 1986), p. 8.
9. Statement Relating to Defence, 1947, *Cmd. 7042* (London: HMSO, 1947).
10. Ibid.
11. H. Self, 'The Status of Civil Aviation in 1946', *Journal of the Royal Aeronautical Society*, September 1946, p. 759.
12. Second Report with Evidence taken before Subcommittee E of the Select Committee on Estimates of Session 1956–7, The Supply of Military Aircraft, *HCP 34* (London: HMSO, 1956), p. vii.
13. D.W. Wragg, *Helicopters at War: A Pictorial History* (London: Robert Hale, 1983), p. 47.
14. Self, 'The Status of Civil Aviation', p. 759.
15. PRO AVIA 65/6, Note on the MoS Helicopter R&D Programme with Special Emphasis on the Civil Transport Role, MoS Air 2(a), 17 October 1953.
16. Ibid.
17. A. McClements, 'A Review of British Helicopter Activities 1943–1946', in R.A.C. Brie (ed.), *A History of British Rotorcraft, 1866–1965* (Yeovil: Westland Helicopters, 1968), p. 103.
18. Ibid., p. 103.
19. See, for example, PRO AVIA 55/90, A Review of British, American, French and Russian Helicopters, ADI (Tech.) Paper 3/47, 29 April 1947.
20. For a more expansive discussion of this point see W.J. Reader, *The Weir Group: A Centenary History* (London: Weidenfeld & Nicolson, 1971).
21. J.W.R. Taylor and M.F. Allward, *Westland 50* (London: Ian Allan, 1965), p. 158.
22. Ibid., p. 105.
23. Ibid., p. 96.
24. L.B. Bryson, F.E. Heenan and C.A. Johnson, 'Helicopters in the Royal Navy', *Royal Aeronautical Society Journal*, Vol. 76, August 1972, p. 470.
25. Taylor and Allward, *Westland 50*, p. 106.
26. See, for example, G.E. Walker, 'Activities of Weir, Hafner and Bristol 1933–1960', in R.A.C. Brie (ed.), *A History of British Rotorcraft, 1866–1965* (Yeovil: Westland Helicopters, 1968), p. 74.
27. See C.H. Barnes, *Bristol Aircraft since 1910* (London: Putnam, 1988), p. 361.
28. For a more general discussion see H.A. Taylor, *Fairey Aircraft since 1915* (London: Putnam, 1974), p. 390.
29. O. Fitzwilliams, 'Westland Helicopter Activities 1946–60', in R.A.C. Brie (ed.), *A History of British Rotorcraft, 1866–1965* (Yeovil: Westland Helicopters, 1968), p. 117.
30. PRO AVIA 65/6, Note on the MoS Helicopter R&D Programme with Special Emphasis on the Civil Transport Role, MoS Air 2(a), 17 October 1953.
31. Self, 'The Status of Civil Aviation', p. 759.
32. Ibid.
33. Wood, *Project Cancelled*, p. 110.
34. These developments are discussed expansively in Sir Eric Mensforth's autobiography: E. Mensforth, *Family Engineers* (London: Ward Lock, 1981).
35. Fitzwilliams, 'Westland Helicopter Activities', p. 117.

36. Taylor and Allward, *Westland 50*, pp. 106-7.
37. Mensforth, *Family Engineers.*
38. Taylor and Allward, *Westland 50*, pp. 106–7.
39. Ibid.
40. I am grateful to Norman Polmar for this observation. For more details on Sikorsky's helicopter orders in the immediate post-war period, see M. Allen, *Military Helicopter Doctrines of the Major Powers, 1945–1992: Making Decisions about Air–Land Warfare* (London: Greenwood Press, 1993), p. 3.
41. P.A. Towle, *Pilots and Rebels: The Use of Aircraft in Unconventional Warfare, 1918–1988* (London: Brassey's, 1989), p. 126.
42. Self, 'The Status of Civil Aviation', p. 759.
43. Fitzwilliams, 'Westland Helicopter Activities', p. 115.
44. R. Hafner, 'British Rotorcraft', *Journal of the Royal Aeronautical Society*, Vol. 70, Part 1, January 1966, p. 237.
45. E.J. Everett-Heath, *British Military Helicopters* (London: Arms & Armour, 1986), p.58.
46. For a more expansive discussion see J.A.J. Bennett, 'Rotorcraft Achievements' in R.A.C. Brie (ed.), *A History of British Rotorcraft, 1866–1965* (Yeovil: Westland Helicopters, 1968), pp. 81-3.
47. Ibid.
48. See Chapter 2.
49. This Section avoids a detailed description of the origins of the administrative structures under which British aircraft projects were conducted because these matters have been discussed extensively elsewhere. See, for example, S.R. Twigge, *The Early Development of Guided Weapons in the United Kingdom 1940–1960* (Reading: Harwood, 1993), pp. 81–125; and, F.M.G. Willson, 'Defence Organisation – 1958 Style', *Public Administration*, Winter 1958, pp. 385–90.
50. For a discussion of the internal organization of the Ministry of Supply see: Third Report from the Select Committee on Estimates, Expenditure on Research and Development, Session 1946–47, *HCP 132–1* (London: HMSO, 1947), p. 9.
51. For a more general discussion see Snyder, *The Politics of British Defence Policy*, pp. 145–7.
52. Third Report from the Select Committee on Estimates, 1946–47, *HCP 132–I*, p. 12.
53. Second Report from the Select Committee on Estimates, 1956–57, *HCP 34*, p. xviii, Para. 72.
54. Ibid.
55. Statement Relating to Defence, 1947, *Cmd 7042*, (London: HMSO, 1947).
56. PRO AVIA 55/90, Ministry of Supply (Air) Quarterly Note Issued by the Army Assistant to DMARD, December 1947.
57. Ibid.
58. PRO AVIA 65/723, The Work of AR/H, 17 July 1959.
59. Ibid.
60. On 1 April 1948, the MoS non-industrial staffing level, including those engaged in production, development and research work, was 21,000 personnel. These figures are derived from: Statement Relating to Defence, 1948, *Cmd 7327* (London: HMSO, February 1948), p. 12.
61. Ibid.
62. Central Organizations for Defence, *Cmd 6923* (London: HMSO, October 1946).
63. For a more detailed discussion of the formation of the MoD, see for example: M. Edmonds, 'Central Organizations of Defence in Great Britain', in M. Edmonds (ed.), *Central Organizations of Defence* (London: Francis Pinter, 1985), pp.

85–107; M. Howard, *The Central Organisation for Defence* (London: RUSI, 1970); F.A. Johnson, *Defence by Ministry: The British Ministry of Defence, 1944–1974* (London: Duckworth, 1980); and M.D. Hobkirk, *The Politics of Defence Budgeting: A Study of Organisation and Defence Resource Allocation in the United Kingdom and the United States* (London: Macmillan, 1984).
64. Edmonds, *Central Organizations*, p. 88.
65. Third Report from the Select Committee on Estimates, 1946–47, *HCP 132–I.*, p. 12.
66. Ibid.
67. Ibid.
68. Second Report from the Select Committee on Estimates, 1956–57, *HCP 34*, p. xix, Para. 73.
69. The Supply of Military Aircraft, *Cmd 9388* (London: HMSO, 1955) p. 9.
70. Ibid., pp. 9–10.
71. H. Self, 'The Status of Civil Aviation', p. 729.
72. For a more expansive discussion of the role of the TARC, see, for example, K. Hayward, *Government and British Civil Aerospace*, p. 35.
73. For a more expansive discussion of overall Treasury activities, see, for example, S. Beer, *Treasury Control* (Oxford: Oxford University Press, 1956).
74. PRO T 225/606(1), Machinery for the Control of Defence Research and Development Expenditure, 4 November 1957.
75. PRO T 225/606(1), Defence Research Policy Committee, 13 July 1955.
76. PRO T 225/606(1), Internal Memorandum, 9 November 1954.
77. Ibid.
78. Third Report from the Select Committee on Estimates, 1946–47, *HCP 132–I*, p. 12.
79. For a detailed discussion of this point, see for example, J. Dowling, *RAF Helicopters: The First Twenty Years* (London: HMSO, 1992), pp. 16–17.
80. Ibid.
81. PRO AVIA 65/6, Memorandum from AS Air 2 to AA/DMARD, 9 February 1953.
82. PRO WO 32/11857, Land/Air Warfare Subcommittee: First Meeting, 12 November 1946.
83. The Supply of Military Aircraft, *Cmd 9388*, p. 10.
84. These detailed procedures were established in the Third Report from the Select Committee on Estimates, 1946–47, *HCP 132–I*, p. 10.
85. PRO AVIA 55/90, A Review of British, American, French and Russian Helicopters, ADI (Tech.) Paper 3/47, 24 April 1947.

4

Helicopter Policy, 1947–50

The 1947 to 1950 period was to be significant in two key respects. On the one hand, despite competition from MoS-sponsored R&D programmes and 'buy-British' procurement policies, Westland licensed-produced technology was unique in obtaining domestic UK helicopter orders. On the other hand, and largely separate from Westland's licensed-manufacturing activities, constraints were to affect innovation on MoS-sponsored 'all-British' projects at Bristol, Cierva and Fairey. These trends had two sources: first, the linkage of the US technological lead, technology transfer from Sikorsky and bureaucratic factors in the 'Licensed Production Procurement Process' provided crucial facilitators for Westland's success in winning orders; and second, the 'Indigenous Procurement Process' affecting MoS-sponsored projects generated severe barriers to 'all-British' helicopter innovation. The outcome by 1950 was not only the first phase of Westland's market dominance through its licensed-production strategy, but also the technical and commercial failure of 'all-British' projects against which Westland was not a direct competitor.

AN OVERVIEW OF FIRMS AND PROJECTS, 1947–50

Between 1947 and 1950, UK helicopter industrial efforts comprised four firms and six projects. The Bristol, Cierva, Fairey and Westland helicopter teams each consolidated the programmes[1] and design approaches they had initiated after 1945.[2] More important for longer-term trends in R&D and production, the post-1947 projects fell into discrete categories in terms of all-up-weight; categories that affected both potential operational roles for the projects and the degree of competition between them. The two Cierva projects were each located in potential market niches as both the 'Large' three-rotor 'Air Horse' (6,804 kg auw) and the 'Micro' 'Skeeter' (549 kg auw) were effectively immune from rival UK projects. Similarly, in developing the tandem-rotor Type 173 (4,808 kg auw) Bristol was not confronted with a direct British competitor on grounds of size and all-up-weight. After 1947, the 'Small' helicopter class, however, contained three contending projects – the compound configuration Fairey Gyrodyne (2,177 kg auw), Bristol's Type 171 (2,540 kg auw) and the Westland licensed-produced S-51 (2,663 kg auw) – and it was in this market segment that Westland was to win production orders. Westland's commercial success with the S-51 project accounted for all UK helicopter manufacturing output by 1950, a foundation which marked the first phase in the firm's subsequent market dominance.

WESTLAND PRODUCTION ORDERS, THE US TECHNOLOGICAL LEAD AND 'THE LICENSED PRODUCTION PROCUREMENT PROCESS', 1947–50

By 1950, Westland had obtained S-51 orders from the Royal Navy and the Royal Air Force in the face of direct competition from the 'all-British' Bristol Type 171 and Fairey Gyrodyne projects. Though MoS policy was to 'foster' indigenous R&D and encourage procurement of 'all-British' production technology, Westland was able to circumvent these protectionist barriers because of two factors: access to the US Sikorsky design and manufacturing lead through the process of technology transfer gave Westland a production edge over 'all-British' alternatives; and the 'Licensed Production Procurement Process' enabled the firm to circumvent the protectionist barriers that MoS helicopter industrial policy implied.

UK Service Requirements and Westland S-51 Production Orders

By late 1944, the RN had cancelled its wartime order for 250 Sikorsky R-5 helicopters. The cancellation reflected the Admiralty's view that with a diminishing threat to Atlantic shipping lanes and an end to hostilities in sight, the R-5 bulk purchase was of limited operational utility.[3] The residual order for 25 Sikorsky R-4s, however, was continued under the provisions of the Lend-Lease scheme. After 1944, these helicopters were used by the RN experimentally to assess the suitability of the helicopter *per se* in search and rescue (SAR) roles.[4] Early post-war R-4 trials were land-based and, by 1947, when pilot training and operating procedures had been established, sea trials were initiated. While the helicopter demonstrated a longer-term operational potential, the Admiralty's assessment was that the sea trials were unsuccessful, primarily because of the unsatisfactory performance of the R-4.[5] At the same time, Admiralty officials also evaluated longer-term aviation requirements and became convinced that whereas in future the helicopter's primary role would be SAR, its potential as an anti-submarine warfare (ASW) system was considerable.[6] Given helicopters' SAR and ASW potential and the limitations of the Sikorsky R-4, the RN had concluded by 1947 that 'all that was needed was [a larger] aircraft with the necessary weight carrying ability'[7] to perform these roles.

By March 1948, the Admiralty had formulated its longer-term helicopter requirements. Because of the limited all-up-weight of the R-4s in service the

Admiralty's decision was 'to regard them as a wasting asset in the expectation that we [the RN] would be allowed to obtain British built helicopters in their place',[8] and access to helicopters with greater lift was stated as vital to longer-term RN aviation interests.[9] The enthusiasm of the Admiralty for heavier-lift was indicated in correspondence to Treasury officials during March 1948:

> Apart from their other uses in Naval Aviation, light helicopters fulfil an important role in the field of current research and development in providing air co-operation for trials of new types of anti-aircraft and other weapons, the importance of which needs no emphasis.[10]

In mid-1948, and in the absence of an 'all-British' alternative, the Admiralty became 'anxious' to take 'advantage of the opportunity' to obtain six 'British-built helicopters known as the Westland Sikorsky S-51' by the first quarter of 1949,[11] initially for research purposes. Treasury authorisation was forthcoming and production orders were placed with Westland on 5 April 1948.[12] Later, during May 1948, a meeting was held between Admiralty, Treasury, MoD and MoS officials to consider the Naval Aviation Programme for 1949/1950.[13] At the meeting:

> The Admiralty representative emphasised that the need for helicopters was urgent in connection with trials which have been given the highest priority. It was left to the Admiralty and the Ministry of Supply to decide whether the order should be for the Bristol [Type 171] or the [Westland] Sikorsky type.[14]

Treasury authority for a further six helicopters was granted in May, and by late July 1948, with MoS approval, the Admiralty decided that 'as it appears unlikely that the Bristol 171 would be tested and cleared technically in time for production and deliveries to be made in 1949–50 we propose that a further 6 Westland Sikorsky S-51 should be ordered'.[15] By late 1948, therefore, some eighteen months after entering the helicopter field and despite indigenous competition from the MoS-backed Bristol Type 171, Westland had succeeded in securing production orders for twelve licensed-built Sikorsky S-51s.

Air Ministry orders followed a similar pattern. Like the RN, the RAF had obtained Sikorsky R-4s from the US in 1944 under Lend-Lease[16] that later replaced the Avro-built Cierva C.30 and C.40 Rota autogiros of No. 529 Squadron. The Sikorsky R-4s were later supplied to a newly established RAF Helicopter Training School near Andover in early 1945.[17] At this stage, the Helicopter Training School's primary function was to train army air observation post (AOP) pilots to fly helicopters.[18] By 1947, however, 'the RAF considered that they had exhausted the development possibilities of the R-4 . . . and reluctantly concluded that they could not be used operationally',[19] partly because the task of maintaining the helicopters was hampered by the lack of spare parts which had to be ordered from the

USA. In late 1947, the then redundant RAF R-4s were either transferred to the RN for SAR work or allotted to the army for AOP experimental work with Flight No. 657 AOP Squadron that had been formed in May 1947. In *de facto* terms, therefore, by mid-1947 the RAF had ceased helicopter operations. In contrast to the Admiralty, however, Air Ministry officials had concluded the RAF had no identifiable single service role for the helicopter. Though the RAF was left with a 'toe hold' in the AOP role, a function that had been largely assumed by the Army at Andover, 'the RAF's [operational] policy ... became in 1948 one of waiting for [helicopter] tasks to arise'.[20] In the interim, the Air Council's procurement policy was that any purchase of helicopters had to wait until RAF service-specific requirements had been identified and suitable production models had emerged from industry.

March 1949 marked a major reversal of RAF helicopter policy. On 8 March, a signal from the Commander-in-Chief in Malaya was dispatched to the Chiefs of Staff urgently requesting helicopters for casualty evacuation[21] in the ongoing communist-inspired insurrection. According to the signal, Malayan operations had been hampered severely because of difficulties in ground transportation of wounded troops in jungle terrain.[22] Stressing the immediacy of the requirement, the Commander-in-Chief requested production models of available British helicopter types to be operational in Malaya by autumn 1949 at the latest. In response, Air Ministry and MoS officials evaluated the potential of the Bristol Type 171, the Fairey Gyrodyne and the Westland S-51, grading each type according to performance, suitability, availability and cost. In the event, speed of response was to be the primary criterion and only the last 'was able to get reasonably close to the deadline of Autumn 1949'.[23] Initially, orders for three S-51s were placed with Westland and a ground crew training programme at the manufacturers was initiated.[24] Like earlier S-51 RN procurement and despite competition from 'all-British' MoS-sponsored alternatives, Westland again succeeded in winning service orders.

There were two reasons for Westland's success. The first was that, as a licensed producer, Westland acquired the US lead in helicopter airframe design and production through a process of technology transfer which, in the late 1940s, enabled the firm to out-compete British projects on the primary criterion of availability. Second, it reflected a miscalculation on the part of Westland's UK competitors: rather than 'buy indigenous' principles, the reality was that between 1947 and 1950 the 'Licensed Production Procurement Process' militated against the protectionism anticipated by Bristol, Cierva and Fairey for UK Service markets.

The US Lead, Technology Transfer and Westland Production Orders

The primary criterion for UK service procurement of Westland S-51 helicopters in preference to the Bristol and Fairey 'indigenous' alternatives was lead-time and, therefore, availability. Admiralty orders with Westland after 1947 were based on the urgency of RN testing requirements and the absence of 'all-British' helicopter alternatives, while Air Ministry orders in place of the Bristol Type 171 and the Fairey Gyrodyne related to the immediacy of the RAF's requirements in Malaya. Westland's ability to manufacture helicopters ahead of its UK competitors was premised on a two-stage process. First, Sikorsky and the US helicopter industry as a whole had maintained the wartime technological lead over British developments. Second, access to Sikorsky know-how through the S-51 license enabled Westland to assimilate this lead and enter production well ahead of rival UK MoS-sponsored projects.

By 1947, continuation of the US lead in helicopter design and production was based on important innovation incentives. In industrial terms, despite a short-term decline in manufacturing output during late 1945,[25] US efforts remained considerable to the extent that more than 70 American firms were designing or developing helicopters in 1947.[26] In this respect, the scale of the US industry – measured by the number of helicopter firms – dwarfed Britain's four post-war helicopter market entrants.

On the demand side, American wartime developments had fostered civil interest to the extent that 'government agencies were deluged with inquiries about setting up short-haul helicopter passenger services; even the Greyhound bus company filed an application to start inter-city [heli]copter runs'.[27] A manifestation of this commercial interest was a further 58 Sikorsky civil production orders by 1948. In contrast to the situation in Britain between 1945 and 1948, post-war US military helicopter orders remained extensive: the US Navy had placed orders for 93 Sikorsky production helicopters with US firms,[28] and both the US Marine Corps[29] and US Coast Guard were initiating major helicopter procurement programmes. By the end of the war the USAAF had already acquired over 400 R-4 and R-6 helicopters. After 1945 the USAAF became the United States Air Force (USAF), marking a complete separation from the US Army. Though the USAF nominally retained responsibility for procuring aircraft for close air support of ground forces, it concentrated almost exclusively on strategic aerial warfare. To compensate for deficiencies in USAF close air support aircraft, the independent Tactical Air Command was established in 1946 to allow the US army to procure aircraft for its own aviation units. Significantly, in terms of rotary-wing production orders, the USAF did not object to army acquisition of helicopters because 'helicopters did not appear to pose a threat to the air force's exclusive control of [fixed wing] airpower missions'.[30] Between 1945 and 1948, this independence enabled the Tactical Air Command to place orders for 50 production helicopters with US firms.[31]

Moreover, on the R&D side, US government agencies were committed to development funding and production orders in industry. After 1945, the US Navy's Bureau of Aeronautics (BuAer), for example, had implemented a development strategy of improving existing helicopter components and eliminating unknown areas of design and construction through funding of industry.[32] Likewise, the US Marine Corps was already formulating longer-term plans for pilot training and the release of $11m for helicopter procurement.[33] Consequently, the immediate post-war US helicopter field was characterised by growing production demand, R&D support from government agencies and a consolidating industrial infrastructure.

By 1947, these innovation incentives were reflected in US advances in helicopter R&D, manufacturing techniques and production output. Sikorsky's development approach after 1945 had been to make incremental improvements in component reliability and increase the all-up-weight of proven wartime designs.[34] By refining wartime R-5 prototypes, including the introduction of dual controls, nosewheel undercarriage and rotor-blade improvements, Sikorsky began scale manufacture of the 4-seater S-51 during August 1946 with both civil and military variants.[35] During late 1946, the key indicator of Sikorsky's lead over comparable indigenous UK Bristol Type 171 and Fairey Gyrodyne projects was their respective phases in the development cycle. Whereas the Sikorsky S-51 was in quantity production, the Bristol Type 171 was undergoing basic prototype testing and the Fairey Gyrodyne was still at an early design stage.[36] The first technological precursor to Westland's S-51 licensed-production decision of early 1947, but also its subsequent ability to win UK service production orders, was Sikorsky's post-war extension of its wartime lead over British design and development capabilities. The second stage was the process of technology transfer and assimilation through Westland's licensed production strategy. After 1947, the S-51 licence enabled Westland to access Sikorsky know-how that had been derived, in turn, from substantial US government R&D backing, accumulated manufacturing process expertise, and incrementally refined and operationally proven production technology.

The impact of Westland's licensed approach on relative production lead-times becomes apparent when key development phases on the Westland S-51, Bristol Type 171 and Fairey Gyrodyne are compared.[37] In early 1947, when the Bristol and Fairey teams were preoccupied with basic design and prototype testing, Westland were already preparing for the manufacture of established Sikorsky production technology. By May 1947, Westland had received six S-51s from Sikorsky for demonstration trials as well as S-51 drawings. At this stage, ground running tests on the Bristol Type 171 and Fairey Gyrodyne had revealed the need for further design modifications. By 5 October 1948, Westland had achieved first flight of its S-51 production prototype and hand tooling for a production batch of 30 S-51s was initiated in November. Over this period, both Bristol and Fairey undertook further prototype testing. In January 1949, Westland transferred a specimen S-51 to the RN for three-month trials. Conversely, throughout 1949, development problems and new engine installation forced Bristol to conduct further redesign on the Type 171. Similarly, a prototype crash on

17 April 1949 caused by rotor-head fatigue failure led to the suspension of Gyrodyne development and lengthy crash investigation.

The relative development challenges are highlighted by contemporary accounts of the three firms' activities. On the one hand, after January 1947, the Westland helicopter team began 'anglicising' Sikorsky technical drawings.[38] 'Anglicising' essentially involved creating 'Extract Sheets' of the Sikorsky design to conform with available British materials and components. Whereas 'the anglicising...was very extensive, every part of the helicopter being in some respect...different from the American original,'[39] the basic technical task was to adapt and re-engine a production-proven Sikorsky layout. On the other hand, Bristol and Fairey were conducting major and ongoing development of unproven and experimental rotor technology, airframe layout and basic components.[40] Consequently, these fundamental differences in technical activities, each involving radically different levels of technological risk, proved to be a primary facilitator of Westland's ability to enter scale manufacture ahead of competing UK projects.

'Licensed Production Procurement Process' and Westland Orders

The US technological lead, transferred to Westland in a single package under the terms of the 1947 licence, explains how the firm was able to produce helicopters in advance of 'indigenous' British helicopter projects. The firm's opportunity to obtain production orders, however, related to a further set of factors. The Westland Board's rationale for selecting licensed production in favour of in-house R&D was two-fold. On the one hand, it was assumed that harnessing the US technological lead in helicopters provided a mechanism for entering manufacture before its UK competitors and getting 'down to the business of selling helicopters more quickly than would otherwise have been possible'.[41] The second was that as '[UK] Service [helicopter] requirements in effect described already existing American aircraft,'[42] the Board judged that licensed designs were unlikely to encounter protectionism in competition for UK public sector orders. In the event, Westland's second assumption was to prove correct because specific characteristics of its licensed production strategy circumvented potential barriers to UK public sector markets from the government agencies with powers of veto on 'buy-national' grounds: the service ministries, HM Treasury and the MoS.

For Admiralty and Air Ministry officials, the MoS industrial policy emphasising 'buy-indigenous' was secondary to the service ministries' urgent operational helicopter requirements. During 1948, when the Admiralty specified its desire to purchase 'British-built' helicopters,[43] early service release overrode considerations of helicopter design origin. Likewise, the Air Ministry's preoccupations in March 1949 were lead-time and performance rather than the design source of available British helicopter production. Consequently, the primacy of operational considerations meant that the service ministries posed no protectionist barriers to Westland licensed-produced technology.

A potentially more serious organisational impediment to Westland receiving helicopter orders was HM Treasury. Treasury objectives, in addition to overseeing public expenditure *per se*, were to minimise dollar foreign exchange expenditure on balance-of-payments grounds. Importantly, key features of Westland's licensed production undermined potential Treasury objections to the services' bids for S-51 procurement. The first was that

> [Westland's] introduction in January 1947 of the S-51 was a wholly private venture which involved the Company in licensing arrangements, experimental manufacture and redesign to British standards, flight development and tooling, to the extent of £260,000 before any orders were received or any recovery of this outlay could be begun.[44]

By relying on the firm's own capital to cover licence costs and its in-house technical expertise, Westland was able to produce the S-51 in Britain without recourse to UK public expenditure, thereby circumventing any Treasury opposition on balance-of-payments criteria. Of more significance were the financial implications for the Treasury in the event that it chose to reject service proposals for Westland S-51 purchases. Without an 'all-British' alternative in the operational time-scale dictated by the services, the Treasury was confronted with the choice between 'buy-Westland' or incur dollar expenditure on imported off-the-shelf US production helicopters. In its 1948 bid for six Westland-built S-51s, for example, the Admiralty options were either to purchase S-51s from Westland or to request authorisation for $50,000 from the Treasury for imported spares to maintain the RN's fleet of Sikorsky R-4s.[45] Confronted with these alternatives, the Treasury officials were keen to endorse orders with Westland precisely because they would avoid dollar expenditure.

The most serious bureaucratic barrier remaining was the MoS in its functions of providing technical advice to the services, placing production contracts and, most importantly, implementing its policy of 'buy indigenous' helicopters. Ironically, given longer-term procurement trends, the MoS perception between 1947 and 1950 was that licensed-produced S-51s posed no significant commercial threat to the ministry-sponsored 'all-British' programmes at Bristol, Fairey and Cierva. Until 1950, MoS officials viewed Westland's helicopter manufacturing as a short-term 'production capacity,'[46] catering for immediate service requirements in the interim until 'indigenous' types became available. Ministry officials' confidence in 'indigenous' helicopter programmes and the 'stop-gap' nature of Westland S-51 orders were apparent in an MoS internal review of 1950 which concluded that:

> technically we [MoS-sponsored R&D programmes] are holding our own and in certain cases taking the lead, e.g. in the Bristol 171 we had under

> development a machine which we considered to be more refined and better engineered than any other in the same class; in the Bristol 173 we were developing the only twin-engined machine in the world.[47]

MoS perceptions of a limited Westland threat to 'indigenous' helicopter programmes were also reinforced by their assessments of Westland's longer-term status as an aircraft firm. During August 1950, the MoS reviewed the future size and shape of the UK aircraft industry[48] as a whole against its objective of keeping 'in being a healthy and efficient industry and maintain it at a level of activity sufficient to provide an adequate industrial base for expansion in emergency'.[49] Early conclusions were that financial constraints precluded government support 'to maintain all the existing design capacity in the airframe industry'[50] and that all aircraft firms should be assigned either 'chosen' or 'non-chosen'[51] status. Under this two-tier system, 'chosen' firms were to form the nucleus of companies with 'essential design units'[52] and would be eligible for government R&D funding. 'Non-chosen' firms, in contrast, were to be 'non-essential' units and precluded from bidding for development funding; they would focus instead on manufacturing and subcontract work.

Whereas Bristol, Fairey and eleven other aircraft firms were given 'chosen' status, the MoS evaluation was that on the basis of its design capability Westland should be placed in the 'non-chosen' category. Though the 'two-tier' classification was subsequently revised during the Korean War rearmament process, it was indicative of MoS perceptions that the longer-term design capability and viability of Westland *per se* was limited, and that, by default, the firm consequently posed a potential, though constrained, long-term threat to 'indigenous' MoS-sponsored helicopter development. In the interim, this perception undermined potential MoS objections to 'stop-gap' purchasing of Westland S-51s against the Ministry's broader helicopter industrial policy. With no objections posed by the MoS, therefore, Westland had circumvented the final bureaucratic hurdle to winning vital orders.

BARRIERS TO 'ALL-BRITISH' HELICOPTER INNOVATION

The US wartime lead, the mechanisms of technology transfer and the 'Licensed Production Procurement Process' affecting Westland's helicopter activities help to explain the firm's success in gaining *manufacturing* orders. However, these formed only one element of overall UK helicopter *R&D and production* between 1947 and 1950. At the most general level, post-war UK public expenditure priorities militated against R&D investment in 'all-British' helicopter projects on the scale that American industry had enjoyed throughout the early and mid-1940s, and from which Westland had benefited as a licensed producer. The objective of the Attlee government throughout the late 1940s was to rebuild the British economy as quickly as possible after the war and honour election pledges to introduce a comprehensive welfare system. Military aircraft procurement was low on the list of spending priorities, in part because the government introduced a defence policy premised on there being no likelihood of war in the near future, but also because of policies 'aimed at a speedy reduction in defence spending from 25 per cent to approximately 5 per cent of GNP'.[53]

The second, and more direct element dictating overall UK helicopter R&D and production was a series of constraints affecting innovation on MoS-sponsored indigenous projects that arose principally from the 'Indigenous Procurement Process'. After 1945, those UK firms that adopted the in-house helicopter R&D route and the MoS shared three core assumptions: that large-scale government R&D funding would be forthcoming, that domestic public civil and military markets would be sizeable and that 'buy-British' procurement policies would protect indigenous programmes from non-national competition. The reality between 1947 and 1950, however, was that deficiencies in the 'Indigenous Procurement Process' had the opposite results: organisational factors undermined expectations of large-scale MoS R&D industrial sponsorship, limited the potential scale of UK production markets and, with the placing of service orders with Westland, undermined assumptions by Bristol, Cierva and Fairey about a protected domestic helicopter market. These factors had adverse implications for 'all-British' helicopter innovation because, starved of government R&D support and orders, the firms were reluctant to invest their own finance and technical resources to force the pace of 'indigenous' projects. These factors were significant because they not only retarded 'all-British' programmes but also indirectly enhanced Westland's UK market position as a licensed manufacturer.

Constraints Affecting 'All-British' Projects: The MoS Perspective

Problems affecting 'indigenous' UK helicopter programmes between 1945 and 1950 were alluded to after the award of S-51 production contracts in an internal MoS review, dated 6 February 1953, conducted by the MoS Assistant Director of Research and Development (Helicopters) (ADRD/H).[54] The review claimed that indigenous helicopter projects had 'not shown up well' compared with both US efforts and Westland licensed production after 1945 because,

> on the one hand, neither MoS nor the British industry has had sufficient support from the Services, the [civil] Corporations and the [Defence Research Policy Committee] to make the helicopter sufficiently attractive to give it priority; on the other hand, the services, disappointed at the slow rate of development progress have not been willing to give us such support.[55]

Central to the ADRD/H's thesis was that 'all-British' helicopter R&D

projects had been affected by a lack of priority caused by bureaucratic arrangements for 'indigenous' procurement. The first deficiency identified was that the Army, as 'the branch of the Services most interested in the helicopter,'[56] was precluded from having its helicopter requirements sanctioned by the MoS because of the reluctance of the Air Ministry and the Defence Research Policy Committee to endorse MoS expenditure on development and production. The second was that, while 'the [military and civil] users might have shown more initiatives', the MoS and the helicopter industry could also 'be criticised for not forcing the pace of development'[57] through the provision of more extensive funding and resources. The review concluded that

> ...if the technical advances offered [between 1945 and 1950] had been exploited less slowly, the users would have been much more confident in ordering our machines. Orders would have stimulated the industry and the rate of development would have been further increased.[58]

The implications, according to the ADRD/H, were two-fold. On the one hand, the lack of innovation incentives for 'all-British' projects clearly benefited Westland as a licensed producer: without either development funding or orders, indigenous projects failed to meet service requirements 'in a reasonable time' so that the users had to look 'elsewhere for alternative equipment which exists, and can be produced in a reasonable time'.[59] This was predictably the Westland S-51. On the other hand, a lack of development priority, coupled with Westland production contracts, had meant that

> the fact that our services are not using our [indigenous MoS-sponsored] equipment renders our chances of selling our equipment in a competitive market remote ... since our equipment is not being flown intensively, we do not acquire that experience which can only come with usage; our designs are therefore seriously handicapped.[60]

Despite earlier MoS complacency about 'stop-gap' production orders with Westland, 1953 marked their *post de facto* analysis that problems in the 'Indigenous Procurement Process' had retarded indigenous helicopter development whilst simultaneously – and unintentionally – enhancing Westland licensed production. However, the ADRD/H's review provided the MoS perspective into what were more extensive and serious bureaucratic constraints on 'all-British' helicopter innovation between 1945 and 1950.[61]

The UK firms entering the post-war helicopter field via in-house R&D had accepted that speculative projects and private venture investment were necessary precursors to market entry. During July 1945, for example, Cierva unilaterally issued a brochure for the firm's W.11 helicopter, later to become the 'Air Horse' project.[62] Similarly, Bristol Aircraft Company's recruitment of Hafner and their initiation of the Type 171 project had been a speculative venture rather than a direct response to an existing civil or military requirement. Furthermore, the Fairey Gyrodyne was developed initially with private venture capital based on the firm's calculations of the longer-term sales potential. Each Bristol, Cierva and Fairey project was 'designed with the MoS in view as a potential customer'.[63] Though the firms accepted that their own funds were required to 'pump-prime' their projects, they also confidently assumed that large-scale government R&D funding would eventually be provided under MoS industrial policy.

With the remit of 'fostering' indigenous helicopter technology and aware of industry's expectations of public R&D support and production orders, the institutional logic of MoS officials was reflected in two strategies after 1945. The first, in the bureaucratic role of the government's 'technical adviser', was to generate helicopter specifications formulated on what MoS officials assumed would be the future domestic helicopter needs of the armed service ministries and civil aviation. This was achieved by writing 'Outline User Requirements' around the Ministry's own predictions of the technical and performance characteristics of the designs and projects initiated unilaterally by Bristol, Cierva and Fairey. The second, given the Ministry's latitude to initiate and fund basic research, was to place 'Experimental' contracts with these firms for the projects that they had already set in train. The assumptions of MoS policy were that by formulating 'Outline User Requirements' and providing 'Experimental' funding they would stimulate development in the helicopter industry and encourage subsequent service and civil operational requirements. These in turn would lead to authorisation for MoS 'Development' funding after DRPC and TARC endorsement and, ultimately, generate service and civil production orders.

The first of these strategies was evident in MoS initiatives after 1945. In their advisory capacity, MoS officials influenced the Brabazon Committee in formulating post-war civil helicopter requirements during early 1946. They succeeded in securing the inclusion of three 'Outline User Requirements' in the Brabazon Programme that were explicitly written to conform with 'indigenous' helicopter design proposals from industry.[64] These requirements included a 'four-seater' helicopter (Civil Aircraft Operational Requirement CAOR.1/46) covering both the Bristol Type 171 and the Fairey Gyrodyne projects, a '10-seater' helicopter (CAOR.2/46) describing Bristol's Type 173 proposals and a 'Crop Spraying Type' (CAOR.3/46) conforming to the Cierva W.11 'Air Horse' design.[65] Subsequently, MoS officials attempted to coordinate these outline civil requirements with their own estimates of likely military helicopter interests to increase service ministry awareness of these 'indigenous' projects. In formulating MoS 'Experimental Specification' E.20/45 to cover the Bristol Type 171 and the Fairey Gyrodyne, the MoS Deputy Director of Research and Development (Helicopters) 'deliberately chose the particular size, performance etc.,' of the specification with his assessment of potential service requirements 'in view'.[66] Likewise, on receipt of Bristol's brochure for the 10-seater Type 173, the MoS forwarded the proposals to the Air Ministry Director of Operational Requirements (DOR) 'asking him whether a military version of this type [was] required'.[67] Finally, for the MoS 'Experimental Specification' E.19/46 covering the Cierva W.11 'Air Horse' development, during 1946 the Deputy Director of Research and Development (Helicopters)

> ...visualised this type as of military value, since it is the flying equivalent of a 2½ ton lorry with a range of 100/150 miles. [He] asked DOR if he [had] any Air Staff requirement for such a type.[68]

The MoS support to industry also extended to 'Experimental' funding contracts. Under the 'Indigenous Procurement Process', the MoS had latitude to place 'Experimental' helicopter contracts without direct recourse to the DRPC and the TARC. Without firm military requirements on which to sanction more extensive 'Development' contracts, the MoS Deputy Directorate of Research and Development (Helicopters) succeeded in releasing project funding after 1946 because

> At that time official interest in the helicopter by the service users, was practically non-existent; there was, however, some civil user interest. Hence, MoS was able to finance the design and construction of [the] 3 types of research helicopter, the size and performance of which were related to the possible needs of the civil user.[69]

After 1946, therefore, momentum behind existing indigenous British helicopter R&D projects came from two sources. Bristol, Cierva and Fairey entered the field via in-house development on a speculative private-venture basis in anticipation of government financial support and promising domestic public-sector markets. The MoS, with its policies of sponsoring and fostering 'indigenous' R&D-formulated specifications, allocated experimental resources to helicopter projects and attempted to generate service and civil interest as a means of 'pushing' this 'all-British' helicopter technology. The bureaucratic procedures affecting MoS-sponsored 'all-British' projects, however, meant that decisions affecting the *extent* of military and civil demand, and thus the *scale* of MoS R&D funding, were the domain of the service ministries via the DRPC and the commercial airlines through the MCA and the TARC. Between 1946 and 1950, as the subsequent sections demonstrate, a lack of production demand for MoS-sponsored projects by these agencies undermined 'Development' status and funding for 'all-British' projects in industry.

Institutional Logic of the Admiralty and RN Helicopter Demand

Between 1947 and 1950, the RN was the largest UK purchaser and operator of helicopters. In three key respects, however, Admiralty procurement decisions undermined demand and the release of MoS R&D resources for 'all-British' helicopter programmes.

The first factor was the availability of US-designed technology, both imported and sourced from Westland, which fulfilled immediate Admiralty helicopter requirements. Between 1945 and 1948 the Sikorsky R-4s obtained directly from the US under wartime agreements had satisfied the RN's testing requirement. Subsequently, the RN's more stringent specifications were covered by production contracts for Westland licensed variants of the S-51. The net effect was that there were few incentives for the Admiralty to press the DRPC to release large-scale MoS 'Development' funding for the alternative 'all-British' Bristol Type 171 and Fairey Gyrodyne programmes, as its short-term demand was already catered for.[70] Moreover, the RN's policy approach to MoS-sponsored 'indigenous' programmes was set against its overall aircraft development concerns.[71] The opportunity to obtain *'British-built'* helicopters from Westland provided a convenient mechanism for sourcing production technology from a domestic firm, while simultaneously avoiding the need to endorse 'all-British' helicopter R&D projects that would inevitably compete with MoS expenditure elsewhere on the Naval aircraft programme.

The second factor militating against Admiralty pressure for the release of MoS 'Development' funding for 'indigenous' programmes was the specific nature of RN helicopter requirements. The experimental purposes for which the RN wanted helicopters during the period effectively limited Admiralty interest to the Westland S-51, the Bristol Type 171 and the Fairey Gyrodyne. That is, the primary objective of RN helicopter procurement between 1947 and 1950 was to obtain a helicopter of similar size and characteristics to the Sikorsky R-4 but with a marginally larger all-up-weight based on RN assessments of the feasibility of ship-borne helicopter operations. The result was that the three remaining UK programmes – the much larger Cierva 'Air Horse', the Bristol Type 173 and the 'micro' Cierva Skeeter – were all deprived of any support or operational requirements from the Admiralty that might have facilitated their being granted 'Development' status in terms of MoS project sponsorship. After 1947, the MoS had thus sponsored and supported three helicopter programmes, which, by 1950, had been of no immediate operational interest to the armed service agency responsible for procuring the majority of British production helicopters.

The third factor undermining the release of large-scale MoS R&D funding for 'all-British' projects was the Admiralty's perception of the importance of the helicopter *per se* relative to overall RN aviation requirements. Despite the growing Admiralty enthusiasm for helicopters, they remained a marginal component of naval aviation. By financial year 1950–51, helicopters accounted for only 3.6 per cent of RN aircraft on order by number, and approximately 3.8 per cent of predicted expenditure.[72] Moreover, helicopter procurement was in direct competition with high-priority 'combat aircraft types' including the Sea Fury Mk II single-seat night fighter, the Sea Hornet

Mk 20 strike fighter and the Firefly Mk 5 anti-submarine aircraft.[73] Given its influence on allocation decisions affecting scarce aviation development resources, the Admiralty's priority was to advocate MoS R&D priority expenditure on these front-line fixed-wing aircraft, rather than on 'indigenous' helicopter programmes for which it had no requirement.

Consequently, through 'pump-prime' 'Experimental' funding, MoS policy was to 'push' indigenous UK helicopter designs. However, the availability of American production technology both through import and via Westland licensed manufacture meant that the Admiralty had no production demand for 'all-British' projects. The net effect was that Admiralty procurement decisions deprived the 'all-British' projects of development priority and funding.

War Office and Air Ministry Inter-Service Rivalry, 1945–50

While the ADRD/H's 1953 report alluded to problems in translating army helicopter requirements into MoS funding on indigenous helicopter R&D, the analysis failed to elucidate the complex bureaucratic relations and differing organisational objectives of the Air Ministry and the War Office between 1945 and 1950. The reality was that interservice rivalry between these ministries became a central factor in undermining both the core assumptions of MoS helicopter industrial policy and the market expectations of British firms adopting the 'in-house' route to helicopter development. Unlike the post-war procurement arrangements in America whereby the US Army had already placed sizeable helicopter orders, procedures governing British Army access to helicopters throughout the 1940s and 1950s contributed to a situation where 'the country which had utilized air power most intensively and imaginatively ... had become technologically conservative'.[74]

As early as 1940, War Office officials had recognised, like the US Army Air Forces, the potential of rotary-winged aircraft for tactical roles. In correspondence with the Air Ministry Operational Requirements Branch during December 1940, the War Office commented that '... the [British] General Staff feel that an aircraft working on the helicopter principle might be of great military value'.[75] However, after indigenous British helicopter work was abandoned in 1940, army wartime interest was limited to the operational potential of the Hafner Rotachute project at the AFEE.

By 1945, renewed War Office interest in helicopters was stimulated by US technical advances, the Royal Navy's experience with Sikorsky R-4s, and the perceived potential of the new projects at Bristol, Cierva and Fairey. Enthusiasm was reinforced by a 1945 War Office study of possible helicopter applications in the Army Medical Service[76] that found that the technical characteristics of the helicopter offered smooth transportation and an ability to operate in bad weather conditions. It concluded that 'it appears possible that the helicopter may very largely supersede normal methods of transportation for the graver type of casualties'.[77] In addition to a medical-specific role, subsequent investigations also indicated that helicopters could, in theory, supplement or replace the load-carrying military transport vehicle and other means of battlefield transportation.[78] By late 1945, War Office officials had concluded that:

> ...the Army probably has a very much larger number of tactical applications for the helicopter than any other Service, [and] any...definition which can now be given of these tactical applications is obviously essential towards the preparation of suitable specifications, both for those types of helicopters which it is now considered practical to build and for other more advanced development.[79]

During August 1945 the War Office identified five generic helicopter types that would meet all foreseeable army requirements (Figure 2). Because MoS 'Experimental Contracts' at Bristol and Cierva had been placed with future civil requirements in mind, War Office concerns were to formalise its size and performance requirements as early as possible so that the projects could be modified technically to account for any future manufacture of 'suitable' army variants.[80] By October 1945, more detailed specifications for types 'A' and 'B' had been formulated around the Bristol Type 171 and Fairey Gyrodyne projects and the War Office assumed that Cierva's 'Air Horse' project would enable development of an experimental machine of the Type 'C' by early 1946. Finally, the War Office recommended that the 'Midget' (Type D) and the 'Ultra-Large' (Type E) 'should be made the subject of design studies at an early stage'.[81] Consequently, by late 1945, preliminary War Office requirements were in place for a spectrum of helicopter types; with the exception of types D and E, they had been written to conform to 'all-British' R&D projects already covered by MoS 'Experimental Contracts'. *Prima facie*, therefore, precisely the interest and potential demand anticipated in MoS industrial policy was evident in War Office deliberations.

Procedures for 'indigenous' helicopter procurement meant that the translation of army outline requirements to 'Development' status and then production orders for MoS-sponsored projects were entirely dependent on the Air Ministry and DRPC. In *de facto* terms, the War Office had no direct contact with the MoS. Instead, the bureaucratic procedures were that the War Office's only channel for its helicopter requirements was through the Air Ministry via the inter-service Land/Air Warfare Committee (L/AWC). Thereafter, when the Air Ministry received army R&D demands, they were evaluated by the DRPC and, if endorsed, assigned 'Development' status. Only then were the requirements transferred to the MoS at a DRPC-designated priority rating on which 'Development' funding allocations could be based. Throughout this process, the division of R&D funding liability between the Air Ministry and the MoS was that:

Figure 2: War Office Helicopter Requirements, August 1945

Type A (Small)
AUW of 3,200 lb
2-seater (occasionally 4)
Cruise speed of at least 100 mph
Tasks: Artillery observation, reconnaissance, inter-communications and staff journeys; adaptable for the carriage of at least one stretcher; suitable for short distance cable laying.
Services: Royal Artillery, Royal Armoured Corps, Signals, General Staff and Royal Army Medical Corps.

Type B (Medium)
AUW of 6,000 lb
5/6-seater
Minimum cruising speed of 85 mph
Tasks: General transportation of Commanders and Staff. Transportation of light equipment, cable laying and repair of air-laid cable. Air ambulance (adaptable for attendant and at least three stretcher cases).
Services: General Staff, Signals, Royal Army Medical Corps, Airborne Forces and Royal Engineers.

Type C (Large)
AUW of 12,000 lb
Load of 30 cwt or 12–16 persons
Acceptable speed of 85 mph
Tasks: General transportation of cargo or personnel. Acceptable as air ambulance.
Services: Airborne Forces, Royal Army Medical Corps and RASC

Type D (Midget)
Single-seater
Acceptable cruising speed of 75 mph
Tasks: Duties of all kinds including reconnaissance. A primary factor for this machine is ease of maintenance and cheapness of production.
Services: All arms, Signals, Royal Armoured Corps.

Type E (Ultra-Large)
Load transporter or flying crane
5-ton payload
Tasks: Moving equipment, vehicles and guns across obstacles. Marriage of bridging and other equipment.
Services: Royal Engineers, Royal Armoured Corps, RASC and Airborne Forces.

Source: PRO AVIA 55/90, A Study of the Potential Applications of Helicopters to Army Roles Part II issued by the Army Assistant to the Director of Military Aircraft Research and Development, 11 August 1945.

> The cost of research and design up to the stage of the prototypes [was] borne on the Vote of the Ministry of Supply. The cost of any orders for production in quantity for field trials or for re-equipment [was] borne on the ... Air Vote. The Ministry of Supply place[d] the contracts for the manufacture and recover[ed] the cost from the Air Ministry.[82]

For production contracts to meet army requirements, therefore, the aircraft were ordered and funded from the Air Ministry Vote; the Air Ministry, however, did not recover these procurement costs from the War Office.[83] Crucially, Air Ministry decisions were the central determinant that dictated production orders and the development priority assigned to army helicopter requirements.

In stark contrast to the War Office, very different considerations shaped Air Ministry perceptions of the operational utility of helicopters after 1945. The emerging Cold War galvanised Air Ministry operating concepts, doctrine and procurement priorities. The overriding operational priority was the 'strategic' use of air power: the Air Staff 'wanted to concentrate [resources] on deterring direct aggression by the Soviet Union . . . For this, jet aircraft were needed rather than World War II fighter bombers.[84] Against this doctrinal imperative, transport aircraft *per se* were assigned relatively low status and the Air Ministry were reluctant to divert scarce development and procurement resources to 'tactical' aircraft to support army requirements. In short, Air Staff policy after 1945 was that

> the production of offensive aircraft inevitably took precedence over helicopter development and there could be no question of risking funds on helicopter projects before they had been proven successful by industry.[85]

A further factor shaping Air Ministry attitudes, with the exception of limited Sikorsky R-4 trials until 1948, was the RAF's failure to identify any single service helicopter role for itself prior to the urgent Malayan requirement in 1950. On this basis, the Air Ministry approach between 1945 and 1950 was 'one of waiting for tasks to arise, . . . Bids had therefore to be not only exclusively appropriate to helicopters but also to have clear priority over other air operational demands'.[86]

Finally, Air Ministry officials were sceptical about the utility of helicopters against cost-efficiency and technical criteria. The Air Council's view was that

> . . . in general, the types of helicopters at present available do not, as a means of transport, compare favourably with fixed-wing aircraft on the several counts of initial cost, range and load carrying capacity. They consider[ed] that wherever a fixed-wing aircraft can be used, it should be used, in preference to the helicopter.[87]

The dominant Air Ministry perception at the time was that helicopters were 'the most expensive form of mechanical transport in existence' and that 'the extreme vulnerability of the helicopter [was] a further point to be taken into account'[88] when compared with the relative utility of fixed-wing aircraft.

The divergence of War Office and Air Ministry views of the relative utility of the helicopter, coupled with the different ministries' functional responsibilities in the 'Indigenous Procurement Process', had direct implications for the production demand and MoS R&D funding levels for indigenous programmes between 1945 and 1950. Given the RAF's operational priorities and institutional logic, Air Ministry incentives frustrated War Office helicopter R&D requirements because endorsement leading to MoS 'Development' funding for helicopter projects would inevitably compete with MoS expenditure on fixed-wing programmes. The period was certainly characterised by Air Ministry procrastination in processing army helicopter R&D demands. The outline requirements for the five generic helicopter types were formulated by the War Office in August 1945, but it was well over a year before the Air Ministry transferred three – types A, B and C – to the MoS. For MoS officials eager to dovetail potential army requirements with the projects in British industry, this Air Ministry delay was a source of evident frustration. Between August 1945 and September 1946, the MoS Deputy Director of Aircraft Research and Development (DDARD) tried to elicit military specifications and requirements from the Air Ministry, but without success. When the Air Ministry Director of Operational Research finally passed the War Office outline requirements in September 1946, the MoS DDARD's response was that for 'Type A'

> there is no difficulty whatever in meeting the requirement . . . indeed, the basic aircraft are already building in the Bristol [Type 171] and the Fairey 'Gyrodyne'. In laying down these types I deliberately chose them of such size, load carrying capacity etc. as to make them meet your requirements. In the absence of any guidance from you I used the latest available requirements of A.2/45 and A.4/45.[89]

For Types B (Medium) and C (Large), the DDARD indicated that the MoS 'can easily design and develop [the former] to Specification E.20/45', and the Cierva 'Air Horse' 'would give you [the Air Ministry] a flying crane or transport type'.[90] Consequently, by early September 1946, the MoS were confident of meeting War Office helicopter demands with 'indigenous' projects already in receipt of 'Experimental' contracts. MoS frustration about Air Ministry processing of War Office helicopter requirements at this stage was evident in the DDARD's barbed comments to the Air Ministry. In respect of the air observation post (AOP) type, the DDARD wrote, 'I informed you of this [the technical characteristic of the projects] as long ago as 2 February 1946 when I asked you for your requirements'.[91]

This pattern was indicative of subsequent Air Ministry processing of War

Office requirements between 1946 and 1950. The War Office would convey its helicopter requirements to the Air Ministry via the L/AWC and the Air Ministry response was to return them to the L/AWC for further 'clarification'. Though the Air Ministry finally produced Operational Requirement OR 232 for the AOP helicopter (Type A) in January 1947, the Air Ministry simultaneously returned the requirements for types B and C to the L/AWC with a request for the War Office to 'define its needs more precisely'.[92] Later in 1947, army requirements for the Ultra-Large helicopter that had partially been written around the Cierva 'Air Horse' were again referred back to the L/AWC 'for a more detailed specification of requirements'.[93] Throughout this period, the MoS was not only deprived of detailed military specifications on which to base the 'Experimental' projects under way at British firms, but also lacked authorisation for the release of extensive 'Development' funding that firm service requirements could have generated.

The Air Council's view, that helicopter R&D was of marginal importance compared to fixed-wing aircraft development, generated a second impediment. This was the situation when War Office helicopter requirements were finally formulated. Air Ministry interest was to convey them to the MoS via the DRPC with the lowest possible priority rating. This occurred between 1945 and 1950, primarily because the Air Ministry monopoly of technical expertise enabled it to influence DRPC ratings for helicopter projects in relation to MoS aircraft R&D expenditure elsewhere. A primary example of this trend was OR 232 issued by the Air Ministry in January 1947 that was then endorsed by the DRPC but with minimal priority status. The result in December 1947, after DRPC recommendations for R&D savings measures after its assessment of all aircraft R&D projects on a priority basis, was that 'the economic situation . . . caused all projected military versions of British helicopter designs to be stopped'.[94] The Air Ministry response to the DRPC's recommendations was to withdraw its endorsement of the Bristol and Fairey projects and 'wait until a suitable helicopter had been produced to meet civil needs and buy it "off the shelf" if necessary'.[95] In *de facto* terms, therefore, between December 1947 and the urgent requirement in Malaya for production helicopters in 1950, the Air Ministry had little demand for MoS helicopter R&D expenditure and industrial development relevant to army requirements.

The final impediment to financial support and orders for 'indigenous' projects before 1950 was Air Ministry reluctance to incur expenditure on helicopter production from its own procurement budget. After December 1947, the economy measures that had effectively halted any potential Air Ministry development support applied also to Air Ministry purchasing policy to the extent that fixed-wing production aircraft had precedence over helicopter development, and funding on helicopter projects would only be considered after projects had been manufactured for civil markets.[96] Inter-service rivalry between the War Office and the Air Ministry between 1945 and 1950 was significant because it undermined production demand – and thus indirectly, 'Development' status – for the 'all-British' helicopter projects under MoS 'Experimental' sponsorship.

The comparative failure of the army to have its helicopter requests actioned by the Air Ministry raised the supplementary issue of why the War Office did not adopt a more proactive strategy. Clearly, the Air Ministry's reluctance to support helicopter R&D and production '...no doubt contributed to the feelings of frustration evident at the War Office, where the slowness of helicopter development was the target of some criticism'.[97] Moreover, the War Office certainly did not 'regard the present situation [with respect to helicopter procurement] as satisfactory',[98] especially in respect of the low Air Ministry development priority for helicopter programmes. The primary constraints precluding the War Office from achieving its helicopter goals were two-fold. On the one hand, War Office officials were relatively new to the aircraft procurement process and no army aviation organisation existed to pose a credible alternative to the RAF.[99] On the other, because 'the RAF contained most of the technical expertise, it was difficult to press an army requirement without it being blinded by science'.[100]

Consequently, the bureaucratic objectives and procurement relations between the Air Ministry and the War Office between 1945 and 1950 reduced the priority of 'all-British' helicopter R&D projects. These factors, coupled with the Admiralty's approach to helicopter procurement, meant that the level of MoS R&D funding and scale of production contracts were left to demands generated by the UK civil helicopter market.

MCA and Civil Helicopter Requirements

In the absence of military requirements, the 1946 MoS 'Outline User Requirements' described what MoS officials assumed would satisfy future UK civil helicopter demand. After 1946, the translation of the Bristol Type 171 and Type 173, the Fairey Gyrodyne and the Cierva 'Air Horse' – around which the requirements had been written – into high-priority MoS 'Development' status was dependent on the extent to which civil production orders actually emerged. The reality was that a combination of limited civil-user demand for the MoS-sponsored projects coupled with the availability of US helicopter production technology constituted the final factor that undermined MoS policy objectives.

Between 1946 and 1950, in the small-to-medium helicopter class limited operator interest *per se*, and ready access to American production technology, undermined domestic UK civil demand for the Bristol Type 171 and the Fairey Gyrodyne programmes. During early 1945, after he had returned from Washington for duty with the (then) Ministry of Aircraft Production,[101] R.A.C. Brie had produced formal proposals that the Supply Ministry and the Post Office should sponsor an experimental mail service in the London area using Sikorsky YR-4 helicopters already imported from America.[102] In stark contrast to the already sizeable and growing civil helicopter requirements emerging in the USA, UK enthusiasm at this stage was limited. As Brie himself pointed out:

> In 1946 I endeavoured to arouse the interest of BOAC and BEA in the helicopter's potential for civil use, but success only came about through a chance conversation I had with Mr. Garro Jones, MP, and his influence with Lord Listowel, the Postmaster General. This resulted in the Post Office expressing a willingness financially to sponsor a series of mail carrying experiments.[103]

Without an indigenous British helicopter design in production, the MoS decided that to stimulate potential future demand BEA should take operational responsibility for three Sikorsky S-51 and two Bell 47 helicopters, which would be imported directly from the USA.[104] On 1 July 1947, the BEA Helicopter Experimental Unit was established, and because of Westland's S-51 licence arrangement with Sikorsky, was located at Yeovil with a staff of pilots and maintenance engineers.[105] Subsequently, a series of experimental mail services were established first in the West Country (January/February 1948) and then in East Anglia (June/November 1948). Later, on 1 June 1950, and with the same aircraft inventory, BEA commenced the world's first scheduled helicopter passenger service between Liverpool and Cardiff.[106]

The initial purchase of the Sikorsky and Bell helicopters 'was made with the confident expectation that British twin engine equipment ... would become available in five years or so'.[107] However, at the same time, operation of these US helicopters reduced the priority accorded to the Bristol and Fairey projects in the short term. Because immediate BEA experimental and operational requirements had been met, the need for investment in British alternatives in train with industry was negated. Consequently, in the small-to-medium helicopter class, limited civil interest, coupled with a lack of service orders, meant that the 'all-British' helicopter projects were again reliant on MoS 'Experimental' funding and private venture capital for development between 1945 and 1950.

In the heavy-lift helicopter sector, the explanation for the manufacturers' failure to attract large-scale government development investment had a different source. Despite the absence of US and domestic competition, only limited commercial interest emerged for the Cierva W.11 'Air Horse' project. By September 1945, some early enthusiasm was generated and Cierva designs were revised after tentative enquiries from Pest Control Limited of Cambridge who saw the 'Air Horse' as a vehicle with the potential to disperse liquid crop spray more effectively than by ground vehicles.[108] After liaison between the firm and the MCA, the original Cierva MoS Experimental Specification was adapted and issued on 28 June 1946 as Civil Aviation Operational Requirement CAOR.3/46.[109] Shortly afterwards, during July 1946, the British Colonial Office also took an interest in the project for possible overseas use and the MoS issued a development contract for one machine to MoS Specification E.19/46 which had been formulated around CAOR.3/46.[110] As early development was conducted, a second prototype, to Specification E.10/48, was ordered by the MoS during early 1947.[111] The major problem, however, was that despite MoS attempts to 'push' the Cierva design, there was very little demand in relation to the spectrum of fixed-wing civil programmes on which the MCA could justify pressing for the release of large-scale development funding.

The 'Priority Problem' for 'all-British' Helicopter Innovation, 1945–50

Consequently, the differing institutional logics of the bureaucracies involved in the 'Indigenous Procurement Process' and the availability of Westland-built variants of US Sikorsky technology created constraints for 'all-British' projects. The MoS assessment, reflected in the ADRD/H's 1953 Review, was that 'all-British' projects had been undermined by a lack of support from the service ministries and the MCA. Conversely, from the perspective of the service ministries and the MCA, the MoS was sponsoring 'all-British' helicopter projects to which they, for a variety of reasons, assigned low development priority and had limited production demand.

The net outcome was a 'priority problem' for MoS-sponsored helicopter projects in three key respects. First, rather than the release of large-scale MoS 'Development' funding to force the pace of development, the lack of production demand and development priority undermined MoS investment on 'indigenous' programmes. Second, without this MoS development support and domestic production orders, both of which were core market entry expectations of firms adopting the in-house route, the firms themselves were reluctant to risk their own capital to stimulate more rapid project innovation. Third, Westland was an indirect beneficiary because the factors retarding 'indigenous' UK helicopter development enhanced the firm's relative position because of its own reliance on the significant innovation incentives provided in the USA to Sikorsky.

The impact of the resource problems affecting MoS helicopter project expenditure between 1945 and 1950 is illustrated by a number of statistical indicators. The first was MoS helicopter R&D industrial funding as a proportion of total MoS aircraft R&D funding (Table 7). Between the financial years 1946–47 and 1950–51, MoS helicopter funding was negligible in comparison with its total aircraft R&D budget, remaining below 1 per cent of the total expenditure in each year. In terms of absolute expenditure the situation confronting official funding for 'indigenous' R&D projects was in marked contrast to the indirect R&D investment that Westland received as a licensed producer. Instead, through the technology transfer process, Westland benefited from:

> ...the intention of the American services (notably the Army and the Navy) to integrate the helicopter into their fighting equipment on a major scale...As a result large sums of money [were] made available for helicopter research, development and production.[112]

Table 7: MoS Helicopter R&D Industrial Expenditure Relative to Total MoS Aircraft R&D Industrial Expenditure (£000), 1945–46 to 1950–51

	1945–46	*1946–47*	*1947–48*	*1948–49*	*1949–50*	*1950–51*
Total MoS Helicopter R&D Expenditure	0	115	180	127	280	192
Total MoS Aircraft R&D Expenditure	14,112	17,305	20,466	24,954	33,226	28,859
MoS Helicopter R&D Expenditure as a Proportion of MoS Aircraft R&D Expenditure (%)	0	0.7	0.9	0.5	0.8	0.7

Source: PRO AVIA 65/6, Statistics for Parliamentary Question 10264, Extra-Mural Research and Development Expenditure on Rotating-Wing Aircraft, 1954.
Note: Current prices.

The second indicator of limited investment related to MoS helicopter R&D funding on a project-by-project basis (Table 8). Despite Fairey's initial expectation of extensive MoS support after 1946, in practice the lack of service and civil endorsement for the Gyrodyne project resulted in limited MoS funding until financial year 1949–50. Though the Bristol Type 171 programme intended to improve and refine the basic Sikorsky R-5/S-51 design configuration, cumulative financial MoS input amounted only to some £456,000 between 1945–46 and 1950–51. While the Bristol Type 171 project was the major recipient of MoS project funding, actual expenditure was insignificant compared with cumulative US government R&D funding at Sikorsky after 1942. An indication of the funding crisis affecting 'all-British' projects was MoS concern over its own limited investment compared with the innovation incentives in the USA where 'the helicopter industry [had] received a good deal of support and encouragement from both military and civil requirements'.[113] Again, and in contrast to 'indigenous' UK programmes, it was US government investment and incentives that Westland received and benefited from through its licensed production strategy.

There were also adverse down-stream effects on the investment behaviour of those firms conducting in-house 'indigenous' helicopter R&D. Denied official backing and support for their projects, Bristol, Cierva and Fairey were provided with disincentives to risk private venture capital to force the pace of development on their helicopter programmes. The trend that had become apparent to MoS officials by 1950 was summarised in the MoS Under Secretary (Air) observation that:

> ... there was a definite feeling among firms that development was not leading to any orders being placed and this tended to discourage firms from putting much effort into helicopter development.[114]

Table 8: MoS Extra-Mural Expenditure on Rotary-Wing Aircraft Projects, 1945–46 to 1950–51 (£000).

Description	*Spec.*	*Company*	*Contract*	*45/46*	*46/47*	*47/48*	*48/49*	*49/50*	*50/51*
Small Ramjet	E.148	Bevan	2079	–	–	–	4	–	–
Sycamore Mk 1 and 2	E.20/45 E.34/46	Bristol	5490	–	95	98	93	58	36
Sycamore Mk 3 and 4	E.34/46 A.9/49	Bristol	2505	–	–	–	–	18	58
Type 173 Mk 1	E.4/47	Bristol	1597	–	–	–	–	60	80
Air Horse	E.19/46	Cierva	6941	–	20	92	25	81	27
Crop Sprayer	E.10/48	Cierva	2875	–	–	–	5	5	11
Gyrodyne	E.16/47	Fairey	2102 7270	–	–	–	–	58	–
Skeeter	A.13/49	Saro	4087	–	–	–	–	–	–
Helicopter Engines	–	–	–	–	–	–	–	–	–
TOTAL				0	115	190	127	280	212

Source: PRO AVIA 65/6, Statement of Expenditure on Rotary-Wing Aircraft, 10 May 1954.
Note: Current prices.

The implications in terms of the firms' investment behaviour created serious impediments to innovation on 'all-British' helicopter programmes. The first was the ability of firms to retain key design staff. According to MoS scrutinies, small-scale official support and the limited prospect of production orders contributed to a 'general lack of progress' that was creating 'depression [in industry] and the tendency for specialist staff to go abroad'.[115] In the helicopter industry itself there was also a growing reluctance to deploy scarce technical resources on helicopter projects. In correspondence with the MoS, the Bristol Aeroplane Company Board, for example, argued that

> the success of the helicopter in the USA can be attributed entirely to the keen backing it has received from the armed services. In this country support has been lukewarm and the future shows little more

> promise ... [For Bristol, therefore] ... questions as to whether a valuable technical team is being employed to the best advantage inevitably arises.[116]

The second set of innovation barriers concerned project development resources. With limited MoS R&D funding and little incentive for private investment, prototype construction and testing on 'indigenous' programmes was severely constrained. With the available funding, the number of development prototypes was limited: there were two prototypes on the Cierva 'Air Horse' project, two for the Fairey Gyrodyne project, while Bristol could sustain only three for the Type 171 development. The firms' perceptions were that the failure of the MoS to support more development prototypes was adversely affecting the speed of innovation and development. Industry's concern was that

> undoubtedly the most important thing in the development of any helicopter is the rapid build-up of flying time. The helicopter as a machine is relatively new, and although the basic theories of aerofoils are employed in the rotor system, much fundamental data on resonance etc. will have to be gathered over the years before the design of any new helicopter can be accepted from the drawing board, as is the case with normal fixed-wing aircraft today. The problems can only be resolved by intensive and continuous flying aimed at achieving reasonable component lives running into at least 1000 hours, on a number of machines. You may ask where this is leading, but it is really making a case for ensuring that a reasonably large number of research aircraft are made and when made flown hard and continuously until the desired results are achieved ... [Currently] with small numbers [of research prototypes] available for research and endurance flying, the build-up of the background hours so essential to the establishment of a reliable helicopter, must be inevitably slow.[117]

On the Fairey Gyrodyne and the Cierva 'Air Horse' projects, the limited provision of funds for prototype development had more serious implications which ultimately contributed to project cancellations. On 17 April 1949, the crash of one of the two Gyrodyne prototypes due to component fatigue led to extensive MoS investigations, after which the 'programme was effectively cancelled'[118] by Fairey. Similarly, after only 80 hours flying time, the first 'Air Horse' prototype experienced rotor blade disintegration, leading to the death of three test personnel. Under MoS pressure, Cierva elected to abandon the project.[119] In each case, limited MoS and private venture investment were instrumental in generating problematical technical development and poor project performance, and contributed to the firms' decisions not to continue further development.

An equally serious development impediment affected the helicopters' power-plants. In the absence of large-scale helicopter production orders the major British aero-engine manufacturers were unwilling to enter the helicopter engine field. The smallness of the market 'inhibited the engine manufacturers in applying the same intensity of effort to this type of engine [helicopter] as to the corresponding fixed-wing type'.[120] The result was that between 1945 and 1950 British helicopter designers were forced to rely on engine technology originally designed for fixed-wing aircraft. Reliance on converted aeroplane engines – the Alvis Leonides, De Havilland Gipsy Major and Gipsy Queen, and the Cirrus Bombardier – meant 'reasonably reliable' power-plants were available and incorporated into helicopters, but the engines 'were never really satisfactory power plants for rotary wing aircraft'.[121] The primary limitation was that helicopter designers required engines that operated under more exacting conditions. Average power-output requirements for helicopters were 30% to 40% greater than that of the same engine in a fixed-wing aircraft. The result was that additional strain was placed on the engines and their reduced performance tended to limit payload. In the case of the twin-rotor Bristol Type 173, for example, development was slowed down because the Alvis Leonides had insufficient power to hover after one engine failure.[122]

Analysis of the factors affecting 'all-British' helicopter projects between 1947 and 1950, therefore, points to a series of constraints on innovation. In contrast to the benefits that accrued to Westland through its licensed production strategy, 'indigenous' MoS-sponsored R&D projects were afflicted by a lack of production demand and development priority. Moreover, indicators suggest that the interaction of the availability of American production technology and Westland's location in the British helicopter market on the one hand, and bureaucratic barriers generated by the 'Indigenous Procurement Process' on the other, militated against public and private sector investment and retarded development rates on 'all-British' projects.

SUMMARY AND CONCLUSIONS

Between 1947 and 1950, important determinants dictated patterns of UK helicopter R&D and production. Despite competition from 'indigenous' UK government-sponsored helicopter projects, Westland-licensed production technology was unique in obtaining UK helicopter production orders. In turn, the success of this licensed produced technology was accounted for by a number of factors. First, with extensive government support the US helicopter industry had maintained its wartime lead over British helicopter capabilities. Second, through the process of technology transfer, Westland accessed this lead through the firm's licensed production strategy. And third, the absence of 'all-British' competition and the nature of Westland's approach to licensed production enabled the firm to circumvent potential protectionist barriers in the 'Licensed Production Procurement Process'.

The variables explaining Westland orders were only one element in a more complex picture. The comparative failure of 'indigenous' British helicopter projects, whether in direct competition with Westland technology or not, reflected the mismatch between design and development and user needs, and impediments in the 'Indigenous Procurement Process'. The availability of both off-the-shelf and licensed-production helicopters of US design and the bureaucratic relations between the Air Ministry and the War Office created a situation where the MoS was effectively attempting to 'push' development on programmes for which there was very limited domestic demand. This impeded 'all-British' helicopter development.

1950 would be the first post-war watershed. On the one hand, Westland sought to consolidate its market position through new licensed production arrangements with Sikorsky. On the other, with revised policies the MoS sought to gain the initiative.

NOTES

1. This chapter deliberately avoids a highly descriptive treatment of technical development of the UK helicopter projects in train between 1947 and 1950 for two reasons. First, detailed accounts have already emerged and this approach risks excessive repetition. Secondly, while day-to-day activities provide insight into programme development, for the sake of clarity the chapter considers only those technical factors that formed central variables dictating patterns of R&D and production during the period. For the sake of completeness, references to key texts describing these events are highlighted in subsequent notes in this section. A summary of the main characteristics for all UK helicopter projects initiated between 1945 and 1960 is contained in Appendix 1.
2. The most comprehensive technical accounts of the Bristol projects during the period include: C.H. Barnes, *Bristol Aircraft since 1910* (London: Putnam, 1988); E.J. Everett-Heath, *British Military Helicopters* (London: Arms & Armour Press, 1986), pp. 41–51; and R. Hafner, 'British Rotorcraft', *Journal of the Royal Aeronautical Society*, Vol. 70, Part 1, January 1966, pp. 235–42. The major Ministry of Supply technical files covering these events are: PRO AVIA 53/21, Bristol Helicopter Company: Supply of Sycamore (1948–52); PRO AVIA 54/163–54/174, Bristol Helicopter Spec. 34/46; PRO AVIA 54/626-54/627, B171 Helicopter; PRO AVIA 54/680–54/683, B171 Helicopter; PRO AVIA 54/395, Army Version of B4/46 Helicopter Spec. No. A9/49; PRO AVIA 65/1311, B173: Design and Performance (1947–55); and PRO AVIA 65/8, B173 Development Programme (undated). For the most comprehensive descriptions of the technical development of the Cierva projects between 1947 and 1950 see: P. London, *Saunders and Saro Aircraft since 1917* (London: Putnam, 1988), pp. 236–63; Everett-Heath, *British Military Helicopters*, pp. 29–40; K. Watson, 'Activities of Weir, Cierva and Saunders-Roe, 1933–1962', in R.A.C. Brie (ed.), *A History of British Rotorcraft 1866–1965* (Yeovil: Westland Helicopters, 1968), pp. 51–63; and D. Wood, *Project Cancelled: The Disaster of Britain's Abandoned Aircraft Projects* (London: Tri-Service Press, 1990), pp. 95–9. The accuracy of these technical accounts is confirmed in Ministry of Supply files: PRO AVIA 54/631, Development of the W.11 Helicopter (1947–56); PRO AVIA 54/1065, W.11; BEA Requirements (1948–49); PRO AVIA 54/1123, W.11; BEA Requirements

(1950–51); PRO AVIA 54/397, Small Helicopter for Air Observation Spec. No. A13/49; and PRO AVIA 54/541–54/544, A13/49 Skeeter. For a day-to-day account of Fairey Gyrodyne development between 1947 and 1950 see: H.A. Taylor, *Fairey Aircraft since 1915* (London: Putnam, 1974); R. Sturtivant, *British Research and Development Aircraft: Seventy Years at the Leading Edge* (Yeovil: Haynes, 1990), pp. 184–85; and Everett-Heath, *British Military Helicopters*, pp. 58–61. The relevant Ministry of Supply files are: PRO AVIA 54/1321, Fairey Jet-Engined Helicopters: Policy (1947–48); and PRO AVIA 54/1380, VTO (Fairey): Policy (1946–48). Relevant technical descriptions of the Westland S-51 programme during the period are: O. Fitzwilliams, 'Westland Helicopter Activities 1946–60', in R.A.C. Brie (ed.), *A History of British Rotorcraft 1866–1965* (Yeovil: Westland Helicopters, 1968), pp. 115–23; and J.W.R. Taylor, and M.F. Allward, *Westland 50* (London: Ian Allen, 1965). Relevant Ministry of Supply files that substantiate these accounts are: PRO AVIA 53/32, Supply of Dragonfly; PRO AVIA 55/176, Helicopters for CASEVAC: Production of the Dragonfly Helicopter (1949–53); PRO AVIA 54/1972, S-51 Spec. S.14/48: General Design (1944–50); and PRO AVIA 55/163, Dragonfly Production Requirements (1948–53). Admiralty files include PRO ADM 264/34, Dragonfly HR1 Aircraft: Pilots' Notes (1950).

3. For a more extensive discussion, see I.C. Cheeseman, 'Rotary Wing Aircraft', in F. Gregory, M. Imber and J. Simpson (eds), *Perspectives Upon British Defence Policy, 1945–1970* (Southampton: Southampton University Press, 1978), pp. 192–3.
4. For more detail of these trials see D.W. Wragg, *Helicopters at War: A Pictorial History* (London: Robert Hale, 1983), p. 47.
5. L.B. Bryson, F.E. Heenan and C.A. Johnson, 'Helicopters in the Royal Navy', *Royal Aeronautical Society Journal*, Vol. 6, August 1972, p. 471. See also: PRO ADM 1/20428, Requirements for Helicopters in the Royal Navy (1946–47).
6. Ibid. The development of this debate is contained in PRO ADM 1/20936, Joint Paper on Sea and Air Aspects of Fleet Defence Against Submarines (1947).
7. Ibid.
8. PRO T 225/1101, Letter from the Air Branch (Admiralty) to HM Treasury, 20 March 1948.
9. Ibid.
10. Ibid.
11. Ibid.
12. Ibid., Letter from HM Treasury to the Air Branch, Admiralty, 5 April 1948.
13. Ibid., Naval Aircraft Programme, 1949/50: Note of a Meeting held in the Treasury, 19 May 1948.
14. Ibid.
15. Ibid., Letter from the Admiralty Air Branch to HM Treasury, 28 July 1948.
16. For more details see Royal Air Force, 'Rotary Wings in the RAF', *The Aeroplane and Astronautics*, 18 March 1960, pp. 336–7.
17. Wragg, *Helicopters at War*, p. 35.
18. Royal Air Force, 'Rotary Wings', p. 337.
19. J. Dowling, *RAF Helicopters: The First Twenty Years* (London: HMSO, 1992), p. 6.
20. Ibid., p. 20.
21. P.A. Towle, 'The RAF and the Malayan Insurgency', *Air Clues*, Vol. 43, No. 8, August 1989, p. 289.
22. Ibid.
23. Everett-Heath, *British Military Helicopters*, p. 43.
24. Dowling, *RAF Helicopters*, p. 27.
25. By late 1945 a number of wartime helicopter production orders, notably the UK Admiralty order for 250 Sikorsky R-5s, were cancelled. However, deliveries were

such that the USAAF was still acquiring what were to amount to over 400 Sikorsky R-4 and R-6 helicopters. For more details see M. Allen, *Military Helicopter Doctrines of the Major Powers, 1945–1992* (London: Greenwood Press, 1993), p. 3.

26. See, for example, W.R. Young, *The Helicopter* (Virginia: Time Life Books, 1982), p. 99.
27. Ibid.
28. N. Polmar and F.D. Kennedy, *Military Helicopters of the World: Military Rotary-Wing Aircraft since 1917* (London: Arms and Armour Press, 1981), p. 285.
29. E.W. Rawlins and J. Sambito, *Marines and Helicopters, 1946–1962* (Washington, DC: US Marine Corps, History and Museums Division, 1976), p. 14.
30. Allen, *Military Helicopter Doctrines*, pp. 3–4.
31. Ibid., p. 3.
32. Rawlins and Sambito, *Marines and Helicopters*, p. 4.
33. Ibid., p. 14.
34. For a more extensive analysis see M.R.H. Uttley, 'British Helicopter Production, 1945–1960: A Case Study of Technology Transfer and Market Dominance', *Science and Public Policy*, Vol. 18, No. 4, August 1991, p. 239; and R. Worcester, *Roots of British Air Policy* (London: Hodder & Stoughton, 1966), p. 180.
35. K. Munson, *Helicopters and Other Rotorcraft since 1907* (London: Blandford Press, 1968), p. 124.
36. See Everett-Heath, *British Military Helicopters*, pp. 42–58.
37. Development chronologies compiled from Everett-Heath, *British Military Helicopters*, and O. Fitzwilliams, 'Westland Helicopter Activities', pp. 115–24.
38. Fitzwilliams, 'Westland Helicopter Activities', p. 115.
39. Ibid.
40. See for example G.E. Walker, 'Activities of Weir, Hafner and Bristol, 1933–1960', in R.A.C. Brie (ed.), *A History of British Rotorcraft, 1866–1965* (Yeovil: Westland Helicopters, 1968), pp. 74–5.
41. Taylor and Allward, *Westland 50*, pp. 106–7.
42. Fitzwilliams, 'Westland Helicopter Activities', p. 117.
43. PRO T 225/1101, Letter from the Air Branch (Admiralty) to HM Treasury, 20 March 1948.
44. PRO AVIA 65/6, Westland Aircraft Limited, Memorandum on Helicopter Design and Development, 14 September 1953, p. 2.
45. PRO T 225/1101, Letter from the Admiralty Air Branch to HM Treasury, 20 March 1948.
46. PRO AVIA 65/602, Minute by AS/Air 2, Ministry of Supply, 27 October 1950.
47. PRO AVIA 65/6, The Helicopter and its Potential, by the Ministry of Supply ADRD/H, 6 February 1953.
48. PRO AVIA 65/602, Minute by US (Air), Ministry of Supply, 4 October 1950. See also the documents contained in PRO T 225/511, Defence Programme: Production Priorities (1951–1955).
49. PRO AVIA 65/602, Letter from the MoS to Westland Aircraft Ltd., 20 October 1950.
50. Ibid.
51. PRO AVIA 65/602, Minute from US (Air), Ministry of Supply, 27 October 1950.
52. PRO AVIA 65/602, Letter from the MoS to Westland Aircraft Ltd., 20 October 1950.
53. M. Edmonds, 'Central Organisations of Defence in Britain, 1945–85: The Federal-Unification Debate', in M. Edmonds (ed.), *The Defence Equation: British Military Systems Policy, Planning and Performance* (London: Brassey's, 1986), p. 62.
54. PRO AVIA 65/6, The Helicopter and its Potential, by the Ministry of Supply ADRD/H, 6 February 1953.

55. Ibid., p. 1.
56. Ibid.
57. Ibid.
58. Ibid.
59. Ibid.
60. Ibid.
61. See M.R.H. Uttley, 'British Helicopter Developments, 1945–1960: Government Technology Policy in a Changing Defence Environment', in R. Coopey, M.R.H. Uttley and G. Spinardi (eds), *Defence Science and Technology: Adjusting to Change* (Reading: Harwood, 1993), pp. 125–41.
62. Sturtivant, *British Research and Development Aircraft*, p. 176.
63. A. McClements, 'A Review of British Helicopter Activities, 1943–1946', in R.A.C. Brie (ed.), *A History of British Rotorcraft, 1866–1965* (Yeovil: Westland Helicopters, 1968), p. 107.
64. PRO AVIA 15/2245, Minute from the MoS Director of Defence Research and Development (Performance), 16 August 1946.
65. Ibid.
66. Ibid.
67. Ibid.
68. Ibid.
69. PRO AVIA 65/6, The Helicopter and its Potential, by the Ministry of Supply ADRD/H, 6 February 1953.
70. This point is developed further in PRO AVIA 65/6, The Helicopter and its Potential, by the Ministry of Supply ADRD/H, 6 February 1953.
71. For more details see the collection of documents in: PRO T 225/1101, Fleet Air Arm: Provision of Aircraft (1946–49); PRO T 225/1102, Fleet Air Arm: Provision of Aircraft (1949–51); and PRO ADM 1/21827, Analysis of Future Development of Naval Aviation (1950).
72. Statistics derived from PRO T 225/1101, Letter from the Air Branch, Admiralty, to HM Treasury, 20 January 1949. The Admiralty proposals to HM Treasury for the Naval Aviation Programme were for 499 aircraft units, of which 18 were helicopters. The provisional total cost estimate of the bid was £14,196,975, of which £533,250 was to be for the purchase of helicopters. All figures in contemporary prices.
73. Ibid.
74. P.A. Towle, *Pilots and Rebels: The Use of Aircraft in Unconventional Warfare, 1918–1988* (London: Brassey's, 1989), p. 126.
75. PRO AVIA 15/954, Minute from Lieutenant-Colonel J. Stephenson, General Staff, to the Air Ministry Operational Requirements Branch, 10 December 1940.
76. PRO AVIA 55/90, A Study of the Potential Applications of Helicopters to Army Roles Part II by Army Assistant to DMARD, 11 October 1943.
77. Ibid.
78. Ibid., The Helicopter's Place in the Military Transport Organisation by Brigadier G.S. Hatton, 30 September 1948.
79. Ibid., A Study of the Potential Applications of Helicopters to Army Roles Part II by Army Assistant to DMARD, 11 August 1945.
80. Ibid.
81. Ibid.
82. Third Report from the Select Committee on Estimates, Expenditure on Research and Development, Session 1946–47, *HCP 132–I* (London: HMSO, 1947), p. 275.
83. PRO AVIA 65/6, Memorandum from AS Air 2 to AA/DMARD, 9 February 1953.
84. Towle, *Pilots and Rebels*, p. 126.
85. Dowling, *RAF Helicopters*, p. 102.

86. Ibid., p. 20.
87. PRO AIR 2/15149, Draft Letter from the Air Ministry to the War Office, March 1953.
88. Ibid., Draft Letter from the Air Ministry to the Under Secretary of State, War Office, 4 July 1953.
89. PRO AVIA 15/2245, Letter from the MoS DDRD to the Air Ministry DOR, 11 September 1946.
90. Ibid.
91. Ibid.
92. Dowling, *RAF Helicopters*, p. 99.
93. Ibid., p. 101.
94. PRO AVIA 55/90, Ministry of Supply (Air) Quarterly Notes Issued by the Army Assistant to DMARD, December 1947.
95. Ibid.
96. Dowling, *RAF Helicopters*, p.102.
97. Ibid., p. 101.
98. PRO AVIA 65/6, Memorandum from A.S./Air 2 to AA/DMARD, 9 February 1953.
99. R.A. Norman-Walker, 'The Formation of the AAC, 1955–1957', *Army Air Corps Journal*, 1982, p. 9.
100. Ibid.
101. R.A.C. Brie, 'BEA Helicopter Experimental Unit 1947–1954', in R.A.C. Brie (ed.), *A History of British Rotorcraft 1866–1965* (Yeovil: Westland Helicopters, 1968), p. 47.
102. Ibid.
103. Ibid.
104. G.S. Hislop, 'Helicopter Activities of Fairey, Westland and British European Airways, 1947–1965', in R.A.C. Brie (ed.), *A History of British Rotorcraft 1866–1965* (Yeovil: Westland Helicopters, 1968), p. 125.
105. Brie, 'BEA Helicopter Unit', p. 47.
106. For more detail see Everett-Heath, *British Military Helicopters*, p. 74.
107. E. Pribram, 'British Helicopter Engines 1945–1965', in R.A.C. Brie (ed.), *A History of British Rotorcraft 1866–1965* (Yeovil: Westland Helicopters, 1968), p. 100.
108. Sturtivant, *British Research and Development Aircraft*, p. 176.
109. Ibid.
110. Ibid.
111. Ibid., p. 177.
112. PRO AVIA 65/6, The Helicopter and its Potential, by the Ministry of Supply ADRD/H, 6 February 1953.
113. Ibid., Comments by the Ministry of Supply US (Air) at a Meeting held on 30 June 1953 in the House of Commons to discuss Development and Production of Helicopters in the United Kingdom, 30 June 1953.
114. Ibid.
115. Ibid., The Helicopter and Its Potential, by the Ministry of Supply ADRD/H, 6 February 1953.
116. Ibid., Letter to the MoS Under Secretary (Air) from the Aircraft Division, The Bristol Aeroplane Company, 13 April 1953.
117. Ibid.
118. Sturtivant, *British Research and Development Aircraft*, p. 185.
119. Ibid., p. 177.
120. Pribram, 'British Helicopter Engines', p. 99.
121. Ibid.
122. Walker, 'Activities of Weir, Hafner and Bristol', p. 75.

5

Helicopter Developments, 1950–55

Between 1950 and 1955, UK helicopter R&D and production entered a new and qualitatively different phase. Seeking to maintain its competitive edge, the Westland Board signed a second licensed-production agreement with Sikorsky in 1950 for manufacture of the larger S-55 helicopter. Westland viewed the agreement not only as a means to win production orders in the short term but also as a mechanism to assimilate Sikorsky know-how and generate its own 'in-house' R&D capability. Conversely, reacting to the growing gulf between British and American helicopter production output and the commercial threat to 'all-British' projects posed by Westland, the MoS adopted a radical and high-risk policy during 1950 that was designed to 'leap-frog' the US lead. The underlying factors affecting UK helicopter R&D and production, however, reflected remarkable continuity with the immediate post-war period. By 1955, the position was that further orders for Westland were issued whereas MoS-sponsored 'indigenous' helicopter projects experienced commercial setbacks and failures. Crucially, Westland had further consolidated its commercial hold in, and dominance over, the UK helicopter sector.

FIRMS AND PROJECTS, 1950–55

During 1950, the Hunting Percival company established a Helicopter Division[1] because of the firm's technical estimate of the potential aerodynamic and commercial future of jet-driven helicopters.[2] In conjunction with the engine firm D. Napier & Son, Percival began rotor-tip helicopter development on the assumption that, with MoS development support, the jet-drive concept could lead to cheaper and mechanically simpler helicopters than the 'conventional' Sikorsky configuration.[3] By January 1951, Cierva had closed as an independent company and its facilities, designs and technical staff had been acquired by Saunders-Roe (Saro). Cierva's market exit reflected commercial necessity: following the 'Air Horse' crash and with orders for only three MoS-financed 'Skeeter' prototypes the firm had inadequate resources to continue helicopter development.[4] Saro's decision to take over Cierva reflected in part its decision to diversify from waterborne aviation projects, but also Saro's need to acquire Cierva's premises at Eastleigh for subcontract work on the Vickers Viscount wing-building programme.[5] The take-over was sanctioned by the MoS on the strict understanding that Saro would complete the existing Skeeter contracts covered by Specification A.13.49.[6] After 1951, therefore, with Cierva's exit the restructured British helicopter industry comprised the five teams at Bristol, Fairey, Saro, Percival and Westland.

Between 1950 and 1955, the UK helicopter industry carried out eleven prototype development or production projects. Five – the Bristol Type 171 and Type 173, the Saro 'Skeeter' and 'Air Horse', and the Westland S-51 – were projects commenced before 1950. The remaining six were new additions to Britain's catalogue of post-war helicopter programmes. Development on four of the new projects – the Percival 'P.74' initiated in 1950, the Fairey 'Jet Gyrodyne' and 'Rotodyne', and the Fairey 'Ultra-Light' – was sponsored by the MoS. Two projects, the Westland S-55 and the Westland 'Widgeon' were commenced on a private venture basis.

The array of projects formed discrete design niches as each firm consolidated its technical strategy.[7] Fairey's technical approach after 1950 was to advance the Gyrodyne compound configuration and investigate rotor-tip blade-propulsion applications. Not overtly intended for production, the Jet Gyrodyne[8] project, initiated in 1949, experimented with tip-jets in the remaining Gyrodyne prototype. After 1950, the Rotodyne[9] project built on the Jet Gyrodyne concept in the form of a large compound design capable of vertical take-off. The Ultra-Light project,[10] initiated in 1954, applied the rotor tip-drive approach to the development of a small helicopter design. Bristol's technical focus[11] was to apply the established Sikorsky configuration in its mechanically-driven Type 171 and Type 173 designs, while the Saro approach was to develop further the Skeeter concept.[12] Initiated in 1950, the Percival P.74 project,[13] conducted in conjunction with Napier's development of the 'Oryx' engine,[14] represented an attempt to develop the single-rotor tip-jet-drive concept. Finally, Westland consolidated production of the S-51, extended licensed production in 1951 to include the Sikorsky S-55 and applied Sikorsky component designs in its in-house Widgeon project during 1954.[15]

The spectrum of projects also formed discrete market segments in terms of all-up-weight (auw), which had implications both for potential operational roles and also the degree of potential domestic UK market competition. As experimental prototypes, the Fairey Jet Gyrodyne (2,722 kg auw) and the Percival P.74 (3,515 kg auw) were not overtly in competition for short-term production markets. However, the 'heavy-lift' sector contained two contenders in the Bristol Type 173 (6,124 kg auw) and Fairey Rotodyne (14,969 kg auw) projects. At the other extreme, the 'micro' class contained two rival projects in the Saro Skeeter (1,043 kg auw) and the Fairey Ultra-Light (817 kg auw). Bristol's Type 171 project (2,449 kg auw) presented the Westland S-51 (2,663 kg auw) with potential competition. In electing to produce the larger Sikorsky S-55 (3,402 kg auw) under licence, however, Westland had entered a market segment effectively immune from domestic competition on weight grounds.

The final factor distinguishing UK helicopter projects remained the differing market expectations and commercial strategies of the helicopter firms themselves. Throughout the early 1950s, Bristol, Fairey, Saro and Percival continued to share the core assumptions implied in stated MoS helicopter industrial policy: that large-scale MoS R&D support would soon be forthcoming; that domestic civil and military production markets would be sizeable; and that 'buy-British' procurement policies would ultimately protect their programmes from non-nationally sourced equipment. In the interim, these firms were also keen to work on small-scale R&D contracts already provided by the MoS to keep their helicopter design teams in being. Conversely, Westland was again unique in assuming that licensed production could provide a commercial edge. After winning initial S-51 contracts, the Westland Board recognised that 'the usefulness and economies of the helicopter would increase in direct proportion to its size'[16] and in November 1950 concluded a second licensed agreement for the eight-seat Sikorsky S-55. Despite the protectionist tenets of MoS industrial policy, Westland calculated that by risking venture capital to acquire the US Sikorsky manufacturing lead it would again secure UK orders. On this assumption, the firm was proven correct.

BRITISH HELICOPTER PRODUCTION, 1950–55

Despite the spectrum of MoS-sponsored helicopter R&D projects, Westland had by 1955 further consolidated its dominance of British helicopter production. Westland's earlier Admiralty S-51 orders in 1948 had been important because they provided the crucial entry point into UK service markets. The firm consolidated these initial contracts and by late 1953, when production was discontinued, cumulative S-51 manufacture was 139 units and net sales of £7m, of which £1.75m was from exports.[17] Westland had modified the basic Sikorsky design to include a number of variants: the Mk 1 for air-sea rescue (13 built for the RN), the Mk 2 for casualty evacuation (4 built for the RAF), the all-metal-blade Mk 3 (58 built), the Mk 4 (12 built for the RAF), the Mk 5 upgrade, the Mk 1A (commercial variant of which 47 were built) and the Mk 2A (commercial variant of which 5 were built).[18] In operational terms, the S-51 was deployed extensively by the RN,[19] and the RAF in Malaya,[20] and it was exported to the Belgian Congo (3), Ceylon (2), Egypt (2), France (9), Iraq (2), Italy (3), Japan (5), Thailand (3) and Yugoslavia (10).[21]

After project development delays, the Bristol Type 171 did ultimately enter production as a competitor to the Westland S-51. During 1949, Bristol began manufacturing a batch of 15 aircraft, 13 of which were retained by the MoS for testing and development work. Between 1950 and 1953, the firm's output was limited to small-scale contracts for a number of Type 171 variants: the HC Mk 10 (8 built), the Mk 3A (2 built for BEA), the Mk 4 (5 built); the HC Mk 10 (1 built for RAF casualty evacuation), the HC Mk 11 (4 built for the Army); the HC Mk 12 (4 built for the RAF), and the HC Mk 13 (2 built for the RAF).[22] It was not until April 1953, however, some nine years after Hafner had commenced Type 171 design, that the standard HR Mk 14 variant entered service with the RAF.[23]

Though an 'all-British' MoS-sponsored competitor to Westland-built S-51s had emerged, the Bristol Type 171 'was never able to make a significant breakthrough into the world helicopter market and in particular to challenge the supremacy built up by the contemporary Sikorsky S-55'.[24] More important was the fact that during November 1950, Westland had gained access to this 'supremacy' with the second Sikorsky licence agreement. By November 1951 the Admiralty obtained Treasury authorisation to place an initial order for ten Westland-built S-55s, and Air Ministry orders for Westland soon followed. The significance of these orders were two-fold. First, as the MoS-sponsored Bristol Type 171 was emerging as a competitor to the S-51, Westland had secured contracts for what was a more advanced class of helicopter measured by performance, all-up-weight and operational potential. Second, Westland had again circumvented protectionist MoS industrial policies and obtained contracts that later paved the way for 308 S-55 orders, or some 30 per cent of total UK helicopter production output between 1945 and 1960.[25]

UK Service Helicopter Requirements and Westland S-55 Production Orders

Like Westland's S-51 contracts in the late-1940s, the primary impetus for S-55 procurement came from the Admiralty. By 1950, the RN still envisaged two primary roles for the helicopter. The first was search and rescue (SAR), which had led to Westland S-51 orders in 1948. Admiralty trials indicated that the S-51 helicopter offered considerable improvements over the Sea Otter amphibious fixed-wing aircraft for search and rescue at sea, and by 1949 the RN had reformed No. 705 Squadron to train pilots to command detached SAR flights from aircraft carriers and land-based air stations.[26] The Squadron was initially equipped with twelve Westland S-51 Mk.1s, designated the 'Dragonfly' in production form, and throughout 1951 these helicopters were deployed on the aircraft carrier *Indomitable*.[27] Later in the year, Admiralty enthusiasm for helicopter-borne SAR was reflected in Westland's receipt of a three-year contract to build 72 S-51s for delivery by March 1954.[28]

By 1951, a combination of new operational demands and technological opportunity led to a shift in Admiralty SAR helicopter requirements. As part of its fixed-wing aircraft procurement programme, the RN had placed production orders for the three-seater Firefly Mk 7,[29] which were to have a knock-on effect for RN SAR helicopter requirements. Confronted with greater helicopter lift requirements, the Admiralty Air Branch had concluded by November 1951 that

> the usefulness of the [Westland S.51] Dragonfly as a search and rescue aircraft is . . . limited as it can only rescue one man at a time, whereas one [helicopter] capable of rescuing a crew of three will be required when Firefly 7 and other 3-seater aircraft come into service.[30]

Technological opportunity was provided by the operational performance of the Sikorsky S-55, already under licensed production at Westland. The Admiralty were aware that the larger eight-seat American-built S-55 was being deployed for casualty evacuation in the Korean War.[31] Citing this proven performance and the lack of a British-designed alternative, the Admiralty informed HM Treasury on 28 November 1951 that it wished to replace part of its existing S-51 contract with orders for Westland-built S-55s in the SAR role.[32]

The second helicopter role envisaged by the Admiralty was anti-submarine warfare (ASW). As early as November 1946, officials had recognised not only the potential mobility and flexibility of helicopters compared with existing ship-borne ASW systems but also their immunity from sea-based weapons such as homing torpedoes.[33] Moreover, it was realised that, being airborne, helicopters could circumvent the major limitation of ship-borne sonar – namely 'ships own noise' – or detection interference caused by the speed and mechanical noise from the ship.[34] By 1951, Admiralty intelligence indicated that the Soviet Union was adapting German wartime U-boat designs and investigating nuclear propulsion methods, both of which indicated Soviet development of a stealthy submarine capability.[35] In response, the Admiralty formed the Helicopter Development Unit at Portland and began monitoring United States ASW developments.

In 1951, American helicopter developments offered a potential solution for Admiralty ASW requirements in the near term. On 28 April 1950, the US Navy had placed specific contracts for the Sikorsky S-55 and deliveries commenced on 27 December 1950.[36] The significance of this S-55 order was that the US Navy had obtained a helicopter with a 'payload [that] made the carrying of "dunking sonar" a practical proposition'.[37] Subsequently, S-55 ASW trials were conducted by the US Navy with a short-range dunking sonar developed by the American EDO Corporation, and designated AN/AQS-1.[38] After the performance trials, Admiralty observers recommended that S-55 ASW 'helicopters should become a naval requirement'.[39] Initially, in the absence of a British airframe or sonar alternative, the Admiralty placed a request to import Sikorsky ASW S-55s under the Mutual Defence Assistance Programme (MDAP)[40] constructed to

US service requirements. The bid was later followed by RN orders for Westland-built S-55 ASW variants with British-developed sonar equipment designed to meet subsequent Admiralty specifications. By January 1952, therefore, despite the spectrum of MoS-sponsored helicopter programmes and the fact that Westland had received 'the strongest assurances from certain Ministry [of Supply] personnel that the Government have no intention of buying this aircraft',[41] the firm won S-55 orders that provided a second crucial toehold in UK service markets.

The first reason for Westland orders, like earlier contracts for the S-51, was that as a licensed producer Westland again acquired the US lead in helicopter design and production through the process of technology transfer. Between 1948 and 1950, US helicopter innovation incentives that had facilitated rapid Sikorsky S-51 development continued. Sikorsky had received US Air Force (USAF) specifications and funding for a 12-seater utility helicopter powered by the proven Pratt & Whitney R-1340 radial piston engine.[42] Against this new military demand, Sikorsky incrementally refined its established configuration, and by 10 November 1949 the larger payload S-55 helicopter achieved first flight.[43] The first US Navy contract for an S-55 variant was placed on 28 April 1950 for the HO4S-1 (observation helicopter for submarine location), and deliveries began on 27 December 1950.[44] On 2 August 1950,[45] Sikorsky received the go-ahead for production of a second series, designated HRS, for US Navy and Marine transport roles. Sikorsky's achievement by 1950 was to place into production a helicopter that allowed the lift of a pilot and eight troops, or a payload that could carry 'dunking sonars' in anti-submarine roles.[46] What Westland had obtained in its licensed-production agreement of November 1950, therefore, was access to a proven system with scope for a number of different roles, developed with extensive official US funding and orders.

The second reason for Westland's initial and subsequent S-55 contracts lay in the organisational goals of the bureaucracies making up the 'Licensed Production Procurement Process'. The Admiralty's primary objective throughout 1951 was early operational entry of S-55 helicopters for ASW. Because Westland were still preparing for S-55 licensed manufacturing, and in the absence of an 'all-British' MoS-sponsored alternative, the Admiralty submitted a bid to import Sikorsky S-55 ASW variants under the MDAP scheme. The MDAP request confronted two immediate problems. First, the US MDAP authorities informed the Admiralty of their reluctance to divert scarce helicopter manufacturing output to the UK because of the US priority of maximising production in support of Korean War operations.[47] Strains on US manufacturing capacity stemmed from the fact that before the outbreak of war in June 1950 the US Services had 105 helicopters on order, but by the end of 1951 the figure had risen to 2,085.[48] Secondly, the US authorities' position was that since Westland had already obtained S-55 licenses from Sikorsky, the RN should use 'potential capacity at Westland'.[49] In the event, the Admiralty

> ...had the greatest difficulty in persuading them [the US MDAP authorities] to accept the bid and they did so only because we [the RN] argued that as the detecting equipment was of American design and manufacture, it was better that we should bid for the aircraft with the operational equipment installed than to bid for the equipment alone and attempt to marry it up with UK built aircraft.[50]

Despite its success in obtaining imported ASW S-55s, an Admiralty requirement for 30 S-55s in the secondary SAR role still remained. Eager to begin procurement, but aware of the potential difficulties in obtaining further US-manufactured helicopters under MDAP, the Admiralty sought Treasury authorisation for a purchase of 30 Westland-built S-55s on 24 November 1951.[51] The Admiralty's proposals were to place contracts for 18 Westland S-55s with a March 1954 delivery date, as a substitute for an equivalent number of S-51 Dragonflies that were already on order, and obtain the balance of 12 S-55s in 1954–55 in lieu of the 12 Dragonflies which were included in the programme for that year. Admiralty estimates were that the S-55 order would be approximately £38,000 per aircraft, or £1,140,000 for 30, exclusive of the costs of spare parts and maintenance repair. Pointing out that the extra cost of the proposal was £534,000 more than an equal number of Dragonflies, the Admiralty argued that these extra costs could be offset elsewhere in the RN programme. Finally, the Admiralty were aware that the order for Westland S-55s might entail dollar expenditure, estimated at $60,000 as a 'guess-estimate', because Westland would have to buy modification parts for engine installation. However, the point was made that the 'project would not fall down because of this' as 'Westland have already been authorised to spend dollars on such engine modification parts as they may have needed for building the 10 they now have in hand.'[52] For the Admiralty, therefore, early entry into service of proven US Sikorsky-designed technology was the main criterion which meant that the RN posed no protectionist barrier to either imported US helicopters or Westland licensed-produced variants.

However, a potentially more serious bureaucratic impediment was HM Treasury. By 28 November 1951, the Treasury responded,[53] suggesting that rather than Westland orders, the Admiralty should submit a further MDAP bid for American-produced S-55s. This response reflected Treasury bureaucratic objectives: with its priority of controlling expenditure, the Treasury recognised that, whereas imported MDAP Sikorsky S-55 would effectively be obtained at zero-cost, domestic S-55 purchases from Westland would be incurred on the Defence Vote. Somewhat paradoxically, given the emphasis of MoS helicopter industrial policy, the Treasury incentive was to advocate that the Admiralty procure imported, rather than British-built, S-55s. The Admiralty's reply to the Treasury on 28 December 1951 was to argue for Westland-sourced S-55s on three grounds. First, officials highlighted potential difficulties because of Korean War strains on US production. Second, Admiralty concerns were that a further request for

S-55s from the US might jeopardise British attempts to obtain American maritime strike aircraft, thereby 'prejudicing this prospective bid and our present happy relations with the UK Military Aid Assistance Group'[54] because the Americans were likely to enquire:

> a) why Westlands were allowed to incur dollar expenditure in obtaining a specimen S.55 and a licence to build them here
> b) who is the prospective customer for the 10 they are now starting as a private venture, involving dollar expenditure on engine modifications, and
> c) why the Navy cannot buy at least these 10 instead of asking the US to provide equivalent aircraft free.[55]

Finally, the Admiralty argued that the scaling-down or cancelling of the existing order for S-51 Dragonflies that an S-55 purchase would imply would have adverse effects on Westland: 'it would, [the Admiralty] suggest, be disheartening for the Firm if we were to reduce our orders for Dragonflies'.[56] The compromise suggested was an RN purchasing authority for Westland's 10 private venture S-55s for delivery commencing in 1952 and an application for US aid for the balance of twenty as a direct End Item (imported from the USA) or, 'better still', by offshore purchase (US payment for development in Britain) from Westland.[57] The Admiralty view was supported by the Ministry of Defence,[58] who pointed out to the Treasury that 'it would be a mistake to bid for the whole 30 [through MDAP] in view of the American reaction when they were approached earlier about the supply of helicopters'.[59]

By 7 January 1952, the Treasury had accepted the Admiralty's compromise but, more importantly, the fact that there was no realistic alternative to Westland orders. Treasury officials conceded that '... the Admiralty has made its case that their chances of getting these 10 helicopters under MDAP are virtually nil since the Americans will point to the fact that these aircraft are being made in the UK already'.[60] Moreover, they recognised that there was little to be gained by pressing for the costs of Westland-built S-55s to be financed by the Americans as an 'offshore' purchase since there was 'no particular reason why they should purchase these helicopters offshore rather than buy any other British-built aircraft in the Air Ministry or Admiralty programmes'.[61] Treasury authorisation was consequently given for an order of 10 Westland-built S-55s and the cancellation of 10 S-51s already in the RN programme, on the assumption that the RN would bid for the remaining 20 S-55s under MDAP.[62] By January 1951, therefore, Westland had effectively circumvented a further potential bureaucratic barrier to UK Service orders.

Under these circumstances the MoS, as the department tasked with fostering 'indigenous' British helicopter technology, could do little to block the Admiralty order. The MoS recognised that its own programme had no project approaching production or delivery that could fulfil what the Admiralty claimed to be urgent requirements for the SAR and ASW roles.

At the same time, this lack of an MoS-sponsored 'all-British' alternative reflected the fact that Admiralty demand for the S-55 was generated by the short-term opportunity provided by the MDAP and Westland-licensed production. Moreover, with limited bureaucratic influence over service purchasing decisions, the MoS could do little to impede the Admiralty orders on 'buy-national' grounds.[63] The consequence was that Westland had succeeded in obtain vital first orders for licensed variants of the S-55.

Having established this crucial market toehold, Westland began after 1950 the process of consolidating its early contracts for the S-55 'Whirlwind'. The first series of Westland-built S-55s equipped with imported American piston engines won 75 orders from the RN and the RAF.[64] Subsequently, Westland was to develop a second series that incorporated British-built piston engines.[65] Like its earlier success with the Sikorsky S-51, after 1950 the combination of exploiting the US helicopter lead and the market entry mechanisms facilitated by the 'Licensed Production Procurement Process' provided the route for Westland's continued domination of British helicopter manufacturing.

THE 'ALL-BRITISH' HELICOPTER PROGRAMME, 1950–55

Westland's manufacturing success was only one factor accounting for overall patterns of UK helicopter R&D and production between 1950 and 1955. In parallel, the second was the ongoing problem for 'all-British' MoS-sponsored helicopter projects arising from limited production demand and R&D investment. At the most general level, the problem after 1950 reflected the same constraints that characterised the 1945 to 1950 period: the short-term availability of helicopter technology of US design origin in the UK market via Westland, the mismatch between MoS-sponsored design and development and user needs, and bureaucratic impediments in the 'Indigenous Procurement Process'. All of these militated against public and private R&D investment and production demand for 'all-British' programmes.

Ministry of Supply Technological Strategy: Policies to Regain the Initiative

In 1949, the MoS conducted its first major internal review of the relative status of helicopter projects in the UK and the USA.[66] The findings in themselves were unsurprising and merely confirmed that British firms were lagging behind American projects measured in production output terms. The significance of the review was that it prompted the MoS to adopt a radical approach that was intended to 'catch-up' with the evident US manufacturing lead and the more immediate commercial threat to MoS-sponsored projects posed by Westland licensed production. What emerged was a major augmentation of MoS helicopter industrial policy:

> It was obvious at that time [1949] that America had acquired so much design, production and operating experience with helicopters using mechanically driven rotors that our chances of regaining the initiative in offering proved equipment in a competitive market were not as good as they could be if we provided alternative methods of rotor propulsion ... which would undoubtedly be required in the future ... It was accordingly decided that our policy would be to include the development and application of jet rotors in our programme. Since the mechanical method of rotor drive would persist because it was best suited for certain operational roles, notably when long endurance was required, no action was taken to curtail development in that field.[67]

The outcome was a twin-track strategy. The MoS would continue to support existing mechanically-driven projects – the Bristol Type 171 and Type 173, and the Saunders-Roe Skeeter project – to satisfy the domestic military and civil demand which officials assumed would emerge in the short-term. In parallel, the MoS would sponsor development of highly experimental 'torqueless rotor' technology on the assumption that British firms could subsequently 'leap-frog' the US lead in 'conventional' helicopter design and capture longer-term domestic and export markets.[68]

The primary drivers for expanding the MoS helicopter programme were two-fold. The first was the technical assessment made by MoS officials of the relative merits of mechanical-drive and torqueless rotor configurations. By 1949, both Fairey Aviation and Percival Aircraft[69] had submitted technical brochures to the MoS outlining torqueless rotor designs with requests for Ministry development support. Fairey's proposal, designated the 'Rotodyne', was a sponsorship bid for a jet-driven version of Bennett's Gyrodyne configuration,[70] whereas, for Percival, government funding for its rotor-tip drive P.74 design was seen as a market-entry mechanism for its newly-established Helicopter Division.[71] In each case, the firms' estimated performance figures pointed to substantial benefits in the torqueless rotor configuration compared to conventional gear-driven helicopters.[72]

In technical terms, the torqueless rotor approach had a number of attractions. Feedback received from the armed services and the Ministry of Civil Aviation (MCA) indicated that the utility of helicopters would be enhanced by increases in size and all-up-weight. At the same time, development problems on the three-rotor Cierva 'Air Horse' led Ministry officials to conclude that lift-capacity could only be extended appreciably using one lifting rotor of the torqueless type. The reasoning here was that torqueless rotors resulted in smaller forces at the blade tips than those from mechanically driven rotors and thus higher power could be generated by torqueless rotors at lower blade stress.[73] In addition, the MoS anticipated that the torqueless rotor approach could facilitate weight savings in the helicopters themselves because it would dispense with the need for the weight penalty of heavy transmission systems, thus allowing larger payloads.[74] Moreover, it was assumed these weight savings would also lead to greater speed and reduced maintenance costs.[75] In theory, therefore, the attraction of the Fairey and Percival proposals was that they appeared to offer the technical means for Britain to 'catch-up' with the evident US production lead.

The second driver for the augmented helicopter programme related to the broader goals of MoS helicopter industrial policy. The MoS recognised that the commercial success of Westland and the implications of the pre-1949 'priority problem' for MoS-sponsored 'indigenous' projects had led to '...a definite feeling among firms that development was not leading to any orders being placed [for 'indigenous' programmes] and this tended to discourage firms putting much effort into development'.[76] In extending sponsorship to include both existing gear-driven projects and torqueless rotor development, the MoS perception was that it 'had promoted what it considered to be a good research programme designed to keep the helicopter industry in being'[77] by signalling the Ministry's commitment to 'all-British' development. By continuing the existing contracts and extending support to cover the Fairey and Percival projects, the assumption was that firms would be encouraged to force the pace of development, and ultimately, 'get ahead of the Americans'.[78]

Between 1949 and 1955, after the formulation of Helicopter Research Specifications for the Fairey Rotodyne and the Percival P.74 and their associated 'Eland' and 'Oryx' engines under development at D. Napier & Son, the MoS programme was to include support for seven 'all-British' helicopter-airframe projects.[79] In key respects, the programme that emerged shared important characteristics with earlier post-war project initiation. For each new project, suggestions had initially emerged from industry with requests for MoS development funding. Eager to support 'indigenous' technology as part of its broader policy remit, the MoS attempted to 'push' the projects through the provision of 'experimental' specifications and contracts. Importantly, therefore, no helicopter project under MoS sponsorship in the augmented programme had been a direct response to formal civil or military helicopter specifications from either the service ministries or the MCA. Instead, the projects reflected the faith of MoS officials in the emergence of production markets and the development capabilities of British firms.

Within its overall policies designed to 'foster and establish a strong helicopter industry...with design and production capability to cater for all home markets,' the MoS assessment was that the revised programme after 1950 meant the British helicopter industry was 'capable of meeting the [production] demands likely to arise'.[80] However, decisions affecting the scale of actual production demand and government R&D funding allocations provided to firms conducting 'all-British' projects resided, under the 'Indigenous Procurement Process', with bureaucracies external to the MoS. What happened between 1950 and 1955 was that the differing objectives and institutional logics of these agencies, coupled with their influence over resource allocation decisions, were to continue to undermine

MoS-sponsored helicopter development. In the meantime, MoS policy faced a new and growing threat: by circumventing the 'Indigenous Procurement Process' and with the aid of technology transfer, Westland began the process of establishing its own in-house helicopter R&D capability in direct competition to the 'indigenous' MoS programme.

Admiralty Helicopter Requirements, 1950–55

The first problem for the MoS programme was a lack of Admiralty demand for 'all-British' helicopter technology. After 1950, the Admiralty had two major helicopter operational requirements: search-and-rescue covered by Naval Aircraft Requirement (NA) 37, and anti-submarine warfare encapsulated in NA 43. In the absence of suitable 'all-British' alternatives by 1951, the Admiralty had procurement plans in train to meet these requirements through a combination of Westland-built S-55s in the SAR role and US S-55s ordered under the MDAP. While immediate RN operational demands were fulfilled, the direct implication of these procurement decisions was to marginalize Admiralty interest in the projects comprising the MoS helicopter programme.

This was evident during September 1952 when the Chiefs of Staff Committee attempted to define and rationalise helicopter requirements for the three services. The Admiralty's position was to reiterate that its immediate helicopter requirements were already met, though it conceded in principle that long-term ASW requirements would probably require a new design or further development of the Bristol Type 173.[81] Given that short-term Admiralty operational demand was satisfied, DRPC authorisation on the latter was restricted to longer-term investigation on the understanding that 'supporting work should be provided with little or no increase in [financial] effort' from the MoS R&D budget.[82] Consequently, the RN's reliance on Westland-built and MDAP S-55s militated against Admiralty pressure for the release of MoS 'Development' funding on 'all-British' projects.

This situation persisted until mid-1953 when the MoS attempted to force the issue of RN demand for 'all-British' helicopter types. On 5 June 1953, amid growing anxiety that its helicopter programme was suffering through limited production orders and in an effort to elicit requirements and development funding,[83] the Minister of Supply wrote to all departments in an attempt to ascertain and coordinate the 'helicopter needs of potential users'.[84] The MoS convened a meeting on 30 June with representatives of the service ministries, the MoD and the MCA.[85] The Admiralty was asked *inter alia* to state its current and potential future R&D and production requirements. Again the Admiralty highlighted its preference for Westland/Sikorsky technology and the mismatch between RN requirements and the MoS helicopter programmes. For its foreseeable SAR requirements (NA 37), the Admiralty reiterated that they could be met adequately by the S-55 Whirlwinds on order from Westland.[86]

In the heavy-lift field, the Admiralty envisaged a role for a 40/50-seat troop transporter of which the Fairey Rotodyne was potentially representative; it did not see it, however, as an Admiralty responsibility. As to the potential of the Bristol Type 173 in the ASW role, the Admiralty's initial position was that it could meet Requirement NA 43 'but the [Type] 173 might be more than the Admiralty required and more expensive than they could afford. The question of using the cheaper WS-55 in this role is being discussed'.[87] Again, despite the spectrum of MoS-sponsored helicopter R&D projects in British industry, the RN's only other interest was limited to the Bristol Type 173, and then as only one alternative for its ASW requirements.

At the end of the meeting, and despite RN reservations over the Bristol Type 173 on cost and performance grounds, a decision was reached that an inter-departmental Admiralty/Air Ministry order be placed for 87 Type 173s, 65 for the former and 22 for the latter. In addition, the MCA had suggested that Bristol Type 173s should be ordered for the good of export markets and that BEA might order a further 10 in order to get them accepted into service. The Admiralty's participation in the joint order for Bristol Type 173s reflected a political compromise. First, the MoS had couched the importance of Type 173 orders in terms of the viability of the British helicopter industry and emphasised helicopter development could be undertaken only if there was more than one user. If the services did not share the costs, it would be uneconomical to develop a large helicopter for civil purposes.[88] Pressure was thus placed on the service ministries and the MCA to place orders to ensure survival of MoS helicopter industrial policy.

Second, and more significant because of the division of funding liability in the 'Indigenous Procurement Process', the Admiralty were in a position to place provisional orders for the developmental Type 173 without incurring risks or costs from its own Vote if the project failed to meet ASW requirements. Because the Bristol Type 173 was still undergoing basic flight-testing, development to the point where the Admiralty could assess the viability of the project against its requirements would be borne by the MoS Vote. In the event, the Admiralty was later to cancel its Bristol Type 173 commitment before incurring costs from its own budget, in favour of a further Westland licensed-produced alternative.

Over a year later during July 1954, the divergence between Admiralty and MoS objectives and priorities had become apparent. By July 1954, the MoS had again reviewed its helicopter programme and concluded that the lack of clear and consistent statements of potential production demand by the services had deprived 'all-British' projects of development funding and manufacturing orders. The Admiralty reaction was revealing and illustrated the gulf between RN and MoS perceptions. In response to the MoS analysis, the Admiralty argued conversely that it had shown serious interest in the helicopter:

> ...the Admiralty arranged a Lend-Lease contract as long ago as 1943 for no less than 250 of the early Sikorsky YR-4 helicopters. The Navy has never given up this interest but has had to rely on anglicised S.51's and S.55's from Westlands and MDAP 'S.55's' from the USA. I do not think that the efforts and successes of the Naval helicopters in Malaya point to a lack of interest any more than does the long established Naval Helicopter School at Gosport which, incidentally, is the only Helicopter School in the United Kingdom. The Admiralty's position has been that no firm in the United Kingdom has appeared capable of making the Naval A/S helicopter staff requirement. Indeed, in the end, the staff requirement had to be tailored to the limitations of the Bristol 173 as soon as Ministry of Supply advice was given that this was considered a practical proposition...[89]

The Admiralty's perspective was clear: it resented the inference that it had not 'taken the helicopter seriously' in both procurement and operational terms. Moreover, the Admiralty was evidently sceptical about the ability of indigenous programmes to meet its requirements and had reluctantly placed orders for the Bristol project only after MoS pressure and in the knowledge and understanding that any development costs would not be incurred from its own budget.

Between 1950 and 1955, therefore, Admiralty operational objectives compounded the lack of demand afflicting the MoS-sponsored helicopter programme. First, while the RN was the major UK purchaser of helicopters, the source of supply was either direct importation or Westland-licensed production. Because RN helicopter demand was satisfied, there was no incentive for the Admiralty either to lobby for the release of MoS 'Development' funds through the DRPC or to place production orders for alternative 'all-British' projects. Second, and equally significant, throughout the period there was a more general mismatch between the 'indigenous' projects making up the MoS helicopter programme and overall RN helicopter requirements. In practice, the MoS were actively supporting R&D work on six projects during a period in which the Admiralty had only partial interest in one, namely the Bristol Type 173. The implication was that MoS policy was an attempt to underwrite projects for which the major UK purchaser of production helicopters had no declared short or long-term need. Between 1950 and 1955, therefore, once deprived of RN support, the military priority assigned to the MoS helicopter programme and the scale of military R&D investment and manufacturing orders was dependent on decisions by the Air Ministry and the War Office.

The War Office, the Air Ministry and Inter-Service Rivalry, 1950–55

Between 1950 and 1955, inter-service rivalry between the War Office and the Air Ministry intensified at the policy level. The effects of differing service institutional logics and the nature of the bureaucratic structure under which military helicopters were procured compounded the problems for the MoS helicopter programme. By default, deficiencies in the War Office/Air Ministry procurement arrangements were to enhance Westland's competitive position in the UK helicopter market, as it had done during the late 1940s.

The adverse implications of inter-service rivalry for the MoS-sponsored helicopter programme were threefold. The first related to the *total number* of production helicopters actually procured by the Air Ministry after 1950. By 1955, the total RAF inventory amounted to fewer than fifty operational helicopters.[90] By way of comparison, the helicopter holdings of the US Marine Corps alone were some 167 units during the same year.[91] The US Army had found heavy-lift helicopters particularly useful during the Korean War. After 1952, with its ability to procure helicopters without reference to the USAF, the US Army set a requirement for twelve helicopter battalions, each with sixty helicopters. By 1955, the US Army had acquired just over 1,200 helicopters.[92] Likewise, Sikorsky's cumulative helicopter production for the US services had reached approximately 1,200 units.[93]

The second concerned the *type* of helicopters procured and operated by the RAF: with the exception of a small number of Bristol Type 171s that were in service by 1955, the bulk of operational helicopters were Westland-built S-51s and S-55s. In the Far East Air Force, for example, which covered Malayan operations, the RAF fleet comprised 20 S-55s, 4 S-51s and 10 Bristol Type 171s. The third was to be found in limited Air Ministry support for 'all-British' projects for which the War Office and MoS were seeking endorsement, which had the effect of undermining government R&D resource allocation. By late 1955, of the spectrum of projects comprising the MoS programme only the Bristol Type 171 project had secured production contracts. A measure of War Office frustrations over existing procurement arrangements was the fact that, by 1955, intense political debate was taking place between the War Office and the Air Ministry over helicopter purchasing at ministerial level.

A major characteristic of the 1950 to 1955 period was inter-service disputes over the scale of RAF helicopter provision for the army, and matters of operational control. On the one hand, despite growing recognition by elements of the Air Ministry that the helicopter was of utility in certain support roles,[94] the Air Ministry's priority was still to concentrate resources on 'front-line' fixed-wing aircraft. On the other hand, perceiving that helicopters offered major improvements in battlefield mobility, the War Office approach was to lobby for additional helicopter resources and argue that the Army should also assume operational control over certain helicopter roles in support of ground missions.[95] However, because of the Air Ministry's *de facto* control, the War Office failed to achieve its objectives and the MoS helicopter programme was consequently deprived of potential production demand, and hence development priority. The Air Ministry did agree, however, to participate in the inter-service procurement of the Bristol Type 173 after the June 1953 meeting convened by the MoS. Like the Admiralty, the bureaucratic mechanisms by which the Bristol Type 173 project was funded meant that the RAF could participate without incurring development costs against its own Vote. For the remaining projects making up the MoS helicopter programme the Air Ministry did little to accommodate army requirements.

The first major issue where differing War Office and Air Ministry priorities had adverse implications was the development of two MoS-sponsored light helicopter projects: the Saro Skeeter and the Fairey Ultra-Light. The War Office wished to acquire a dedicated air observation post (AOP) helicopter, a requirement that had been stated as early as 1945.[96] By 1948, the Air Ministry asked the MoS to keep it informed of Skeeter developments as a possible contender in the AOP role. However, Skeeter prototype development problems occurred in 1948 and

> the Air Ministry was understandably anxious not to commit itself to a production order without convincing evidence that the aircraft would be successful – a reluctance which no doubt contributed to the feelings of frustration evident at the War Office, where the slowness of development was the target of some criticism.[97]

The result was that between 1948 and 1954, the Skeeter project failed to secure military orders; without specific Service endorsement, MoS investment on the project was thus limited to small-scale funding for three prototypes. By November 1952, the War Office had revised its 'Outline User Requirement' for an AOP helicopter that was ultimately forwarded by the Air Ministry to the MoS as OR 319 in July 1953. With an in-service target date of June 1957, MoS contracts were placed with Fairey during 1954 for the Ultra-Light project. Again, however, the relatively low priority assigned to the project was reflected in Fairey receiving funding for only three prototypes. Between 1950 and 1955, therefore, the War Office and the MoS had achieved little in practical terms in generating priority and development funding for an AOP helicopter.

A second and more significant source of bureaucratic friction between the War Office and the Air Ministry was in the heavy-lift and medium-lift helicopter fields. The inability of the War Office to get its helicopter requirements actioned had adverse implications for the MoS-sponsored Fairey Rotodyne and Bristol Type 173 heavy-lift projects. After the Cierva 'Air Horse' prototype crash in 1950, the War Office accepted that no British heavy-lift production helicopter was likely to enter production in the short-term. Aware of the broad parameters of the MoS-sponsored Fairey Rotodyne project, the War Office produced a more detailed requirement calling for a lift capacity of 10,000 lb over a 75–100 mile radius; this was put before the Land/Air Warfare Transport Sub-Committee during August 1951.[98] No large-scale MoS development funding, however, could be released to support the War Office requirement until DRPC endorsement had first been obtained. By October 1952, the DRPC had decided that, in view of R&D costs, it could not approve the heavy-lift requirement. This decision was premised in part on the Air Ministry's reluctance to support the War Office requirement and give it development priority. In this regard, the Vice Chief of the General Staff was reminded in December 1952 that the RAF was '"not really interested" in transport helicopters and would never give them any degree of priority'.[99] Consequently and despite War Office enthusiasm for heavy-lift helicopter development, without Air Ministry and DRPC endorsement the Fairey Rotodyne would have to remain reliant on small-scale MoS prototype funding.

By February 1953, War Office frustrations over the Air Ministry's reluctance to support heavy-lift helicopter development were manifest in a Position Paper prepared by the Deputy Chief of the Imperial General Staff (DCIGS) that was subsequently endorsed by the Executive Committee of the Army Council.[100] The DCIGS argued that heavy-lift helicopter development and procurement was essential in operational terms since

> in view of the increased air threat and the introduction of new weapons, dependence in a future war upon . . . vast numbers of road vehicles is fraught with danger. The only practicable solution to this problem would appear to be the substitution, either wholly or in part, of air supply by helicopter, thus eliminating dependence upon roads and bridges, and introducing far greater flexibility into our maintenance system.[101]

War Office studies had also shown that the helicopter potentially offered an all-weather battlefield capability which was less vulnerable to air attack. To support these claims, the DCIGS pointed out that the US armed services employed cargo helicopters extensively and that American plans were to augment their inventory. In addition, the War Office was aware that the 4 to 5-ton payload Fairey Rotodyne was under development and considered that only large orders could reduce unit costs.[102] Finally, the DCIGS view was that by replacing the existing land-based infrastructure with cargo helicopters, further savings could be generated because the greater speed and load capacity of cargo helicopters would also be accompanied by manpower reductions. Recognising that more analysis of cost, organisational and training arrangements for the introduction of cargo helicopters was necessary to support its case in the face of further Air Ministry hostility, the Executive Committee of the Army Council set up a working party in February 1953 staffed 'taking care that no RAF officers should be included to put a damper on proceedings'.[103]

Despite War Office attempts to force the pace of heavy-lift helicopter development, Air Ministry officials remained antagonistic towards both R&D support and production orders. The Air Ministry position was summarised by the Deputy Chief of the Air Staff (Policy):

> If the army can make a case for it [the heavy-lift helicopter] as a military essential as an alternative vehicle for short distance mobility, it is felt, rather than directing our precious R&D effort, we should buy the development which has already gone on in the USA. It is understood, in this respect, that the Sikorsky S.56, a twenty-passenger transport sponsored by the US Navy Bureau of Aeronautics ... would appeal to the army. Any expense incurred in such a transaction, however, should not be charged against the Air Force Vote.[104]

There were two implications of the Air Ministry position for the Rotodyne project between 1953 and 1955. On the one hand, the project, without Air Council endorsement, was deprived of MoS 'Development' funding that firm military requirements could have facilitated. On the other hand, under existing procurement arrangements whereby all production costs were borne on the Air Ministry Vote, the War Office had no mechanism to bid for either the Rotodyne or American-manufactured alternatives. The Rotodyne thus remained a victim of a lack of production demand and low development priority until 1955.

In late 1952, confronted with the impasse on the Rotodyne, the War Office adopted a second strategy to acquire transport helicopters that was to have implications for the Bristol Type 173 project. The 1952 DRPC meeting, which had rejected War Office heavy-lift proposals, had nevertheless endorsed R&D funding on the Bristol Type 173 project for RAF land-based anti-submarine requirements. On 23 December 1952, the War Office informed the Air Ministry that 'without prejudice to its primary role as an ASW type', the Bristol Type 173 would be suitable in a modified form for Army medium-lift roles.[105] The Army Council claimed that a transport version of the Type 173 could operate with a 3,500 lb payload and a range of 100 miles, both of which would meet Army needs for a medium transport helicopter capability.[106] In addition, the Army Council considered it 'essential' that, parallel to development of the Bristol Type 173, experience should be gained

> ... in the operation in all theatres of ... transport helicopters, e.g. the S.55, as this can be obtained by the Royal Air Force. Only in the light of this experience will it be possible satisfactorily to assess the detailed army requirements to be incorporated in the prototype of the medium transport version of the anti-submarine helicopter.[107]

Internal discussion in the Air Ministry on how to respond to the Army Council indicated the divergence of RAF and Army priorities. The view of the Air Ministry Director of Policy (AS) was that the proposals should be rejected on financial grounds: 'if we were to embark on such a programme as the Army Council wishes [the RAF] might well have to cut other units in the front line'.[108] Moreover, 'the cold fact is that we [the Air Ministry] had no money for these projects and could not meet the WO views without giving up something more important'.[109] The view of the Assistant Chief of the Air Staff (O.R.), was less circumspect:

> The best way to keep casualties low...would be to win the campaign...This means we would have to put all available effort into offensive aircraft and not into frills like helicopters for taking Staff Officers on jaunts and evacuating the odd wounded man...helicopters are luxuries which we cannot afford and should not be considering until more prosperous times return.[110]

Finally, the Air Council's own commitment to the Bristol Type 173 in anti-submarine roles was itself questionable. Air Ministry studies already were underway into whether helicopters or 'potentially cheaper' fixed-wing aircraft should fulfill the ASW requirement. The consensus in the Air Ministry was that if fixed-wing aircraft were adopted, the War Office would be forced to submit their transport requirements to the DRPC[111] without Air Council endorsement.

The Air Council's reply to the War Office was finally drafted in July 1953.[112] The Army Council was informed that the helicopter was an aircraft of 'extreme vulnerability', and 'in its present state [was] the most expensive form of mechanical transport in existence'.[113] Air Council opinion was that it should only be used in circumstances where vertical ascent and descent were essential. Moreover, the Army Council suggestion that S-55s should be introduced in every theatre was rejected as the 'Air Council [did] not see their way to form any helicopter units beyond those already planned'.[114] The implication for the Bristol Type 173 project was that, despite clear Army interest, no Air Ministry development support emerged that could have generated resources or funding. Like the Fairey Rotodyne, therefore, the Bristol Type 173 was a further victim of Air Ministry/War Office inter-service rivalry. The Air Ministry did finally issue OR 325 for a general purpose twin-engined version of the Type 173 in April 1954. Until then, however, the Bristol project based on War Office requirements had effectively been starved of R&D support from its inception.

By late 1953, frustration over the lack of operational helicopter provision from the RAF in support of the Army had become evident at the highest levels in the War Office. On 26 August 1953, the Deputy Chief of the Imperial General Staff informed the Army Council[115] that in his

> correspondence on the subject of helicopters, the Air Ministry have shown unwillingness to proceed any further with introduction at this stage, and moreover, will not confirm officially that they will continue to maintain even the one existing flight of three helicopters under Army operational control.[116]

The DCIGS also listed grave concerns over helicopter procurement arrangements, pointing out that whereas Air Ministry control and funding had worked in the Second World War, it could 'never work efficiently' in peacetime 'under inevitable conditions of financial stringency and separate service estimates'.[117] In this regard:

> it would be far more satisfactory if the Army could assess financial desirability of light aircraft provision in relation to other items of its own equipment, e.g. the desirability of some light aircraft at headquarters for inter-communication in relation to provision of other forms of transport. The army now has no power to make any such comparative assessment or provision.[118]

In addition, the DCIGS argued that the procurement regime meant that the Army was failing 'increasingly to make proper military use of helicopters' already assessed 'at their proper value by the Royal Navy, civil operators and American services', despite the fact that the helicopter would 'probably be of greater comparative value to the Army than to any other service or organisation'.[119] Finally, light aircraft and helicopters for operational use were 'not really of interest'[120] to the RAF; thus, the Air Ministry, with their own difficult problems of financial priorities to resolve, were inevitably averse to making financial provision for a light aircraft organisation flown by army pilots and used entirely for army purposes under army operational control. In conclusion, the DCIGS proposed that 'the only sound solution is that the Army should assume control of its own light aircraft organisation. It is, therefore, proposed that light liaison and Air OP units should become units of the Army.[121]

Army Council acceptance of the DCIGS's analysis precipitated debate at ministerial level. On 25 May 1954, the Secretary of State for War asked the Minister of Defence, Earl Alexander, to arrange an urgent meeting to discuss major changes to the 'existing system'.[122] In the interim, the Secretary of State for War provided the Minister of Defence with a synthesis of the War Office position. The first point was that mobility in contemporary warfare demanded minimising battlefield land vehicles, for which the only solution, 'reflected by present policy in the United States,'[123] was the helicopter. The second was that because of Air Ministry control over procurement, 'progress to date has been disappointing so far as provision of helicopters, statement of staff requirements and progress with research and development are concerned'.[124] Equally, the War Office did 'not believe that it is fair to expect another Department... to devote a good deal of money and effort towards the provision of a service (helicopters) almost exclusively for the benefit of another service';[125] instead, the Army should judge what it could afford to spend on helicopters and the extent to which it could make the necessary savings to fund their acquisition. The Secretary of State for War concluded that the Army should assume certain operational and financial controls over helicopters because he knew

> ...of no precedent where the provision of a vehicle or weapons by one Service exclusively on behalf of another has proved satisfactory. In these days of great financial stringency it is asking too much of the Air Force to give up a squadron of fighters or bombers in order that the army should have an adequate supply of helicopters.[126]

In response, the Minister of Defence arranged a meeting between the three Ministers on 31 May 1954.[127] While the Secretary of State for Air agreed[128] there were important matters to discuss, his comments on the Secretary of State for War's proposals were that 'I think it is sufficient to state that I do not find myself in agreement with either his premise or his conclusions'.[129] What followed the May 1954 meeting was that 'the Army's case effectively passed into suspended animation due to political intransigence, financial stringency, technical difficulties, and resurgent assertions of Royal Air Force prerogatives'.[130] By 1955, the Secretaries of State for War and Air were in protracted discussions about operational and organisational matters concerning the provision of helicopters for army support.[131] Crucially, a net result of this bureaucratic interplay during the 1950 to 1955 period was that the MoS-sponsored helicopter programme had been deprived of both production orders and development priority.

The Ministry of Civil Aviation, BEA and Civil Helicopter Requirements, 1950–55

Before 1950, BEA's operational activities were limited to small-scale experiments with imported US helicopters. In 1947, the BEA Helicopter Unit had been established in Yeovil with Sikorsky S-51s and Bell 47Bs to investigate 'the special problems likely to attend the introduction of passenger-carrying helicopters for civil aviation'.[132] By 1950, however, apart from some 'useful, if not over-publicised mail delivery experiments,'[133] BEA operations had largely stagnated. Throughout 1949 and 1950, night mail and scheduled passenger services were started but these were purely experimental operations 'carried out regardless of cost and clearly uneconomical':[134] using three helicopters and three flights per day, the trial had attracted a total of 821 passengers, or only 48.5 per cent of capacity.[135] Finally, in June 1951, BEA experimented with a London to Birmingham passenger service[136] but this was also uneconomic and, nine months later in March 1952, it was discontinued.

In parallel, other more significant policy developments were to have implications for the MoS helicopter programme. By 1951, after evaluating earlier experimental operations, BEA concluded that commercially viable short-haul helicopter services depended on increased passenger capacity. In response, by October 1951, BEA produced an Outline Requirement for a short/medium-haul helicopter[137] specifying a minimum cruising speed of 130 knots, a passenger capacity of 30 to 40 seats and direct operating costs of 3d per mile.[138] The importance of the BEA requirement was that a clear expression of civil interest had emerged which corresponded broadly with MoS predictions of the size and performance of the MoS-sponsored Fairey Rotodyne project. Equally, and by default, BEA's realisation that large passenger capacity was essential to ensure cost-effective commercial operations meant that, with the possible exception of the medium-lift Bristol Type 173 as an interim design, the state-owned airline had no procurement plans within the range of smaller projects making up the MoS helicopter programme.

Prima facie, the 1951 BEA Outline Requirement covering the Fairey Rotodyne implied prospects for the release of large-scale development support and production orders for a key project in the MoS helicopter programme. Between 1951 and 1954, the reality was that two factors in the 'Indigenous Procurement Process' militated against both. The first was the indirect effect of Air Ministry/War Office inter-service rivalry. In October 1951, both BEA and the MoS recognised that only a joint civil/military requirement for the Rotodyne could generate large-scale 'development' funding from the MoS civil and military aircraft votes. Moreover, they were aware that a joint order offered the prospect of lower final unit costs through economies of scale than if the requirement was limited to BEA alone. Instead, the Air Ministry's reluctance to support War Office heavy-lift helicopter demands limited the aggregate resource allocation from MoS funds to support Rotodyne development relevant to BEA's requirement. Second, confronted with limited service interest and project uncertainties, BEA were reluctant to commit themselves to orders which further marginalized MoS resource allocation for heavy-lift helicopter development.

The impact of these factors in undermining demand for 'all-British' transport helicopter projects is evident in policy developments throughout the period. In October 1951, the BEA Chairman, Lord Douglas, wrote to the Chief of the Air Staff suggesting that BEA and RAF requirements, if any had emerged, should be lined up.[139] By 6 December 1951, and despite the broad similarity of BEA's requirements to the War Office's heavy-lift proposals of August 1951, the Chief of the Air Staff replied that 'no decision had been made on whether the RAF should have a large helicopter'.[140] Attempting to force an Air Ministry decision, the MoS also contacted the Air Ministry on 19 December 1951 and reiterated that the 'best hope' for heavy-lift production helicopters was if the Services and BEA had 'similar' requirements. The Assistant Chief of the Air Staff, reflecting the Air Ministry's concerns over War Office heavy-lift demands, responded that:

> Our [the RAF] heavy lift requirement is still at the discussion stage. With regard to the BEA [Specification], we have yet to decide if such a large machine can be justified. If we agree to sponsor it then the matter is likely to come to a decision in the near future. The project should only be treated as an Air Staff Target with a low degree of importance.[141]

Deprived of military support, BEA after December 1951 was unwilling to place production orders. Without either civil or service endorsement, MoS Rotodyne funding was restricted to small-scale 'experimental' funding on a single prototype at Fairey.[142]

This pattern was characteristic of subsequent policy trends. The DRPC meeting of October 1952 which rejected War Office heavy-lift proposals rendered the Rotodyne project entirely dependent on the MoS civil aircraft experimental Vote. The issue re-emerged again at the 30 June 1953 meeting convened by the MoS during which the MCA restated that coordination of BEA and military requirements was essential for rapid and economic development of transport helicopters.[143] However, no agreement was reached to combine requirements and the Rotodyne remained a low-priority project. In part this was because there was

> a suspicion already existing in RAF circles that the real purpose of the meeting was to persuade the Services to support research and development on behalf of civil aviation as well as themselves, whereas Air Staff policy was to await the successful development of a civil aircraft and then buy it for the services.[144]

Equally important was BEA's unwillingness to risk a production commitment without military backing and support.

The net effect between 1951 and early 1953 had been to limit MoS R&D resource allocation to Rotodyne development. This lack of government investment had a detrimental effect on project innovation rates at Fairey that became evident in diminishing BEA confidence in the project. On 27 April 1953, BEA Chief Executive Peter Masefield expressed his deep anxiety to the MoS about Rotodyne technical progress to the extent of advocating that the MoS should support the development of a civil version of the Bristol Type 173 as an 'insurance policy' in case of further delays on the former.[145] The reaction of the MoS Assistant Secretary (Air) that 'Mr. Masefield does not appreciate the financial difficulties with which we are faced and I doubt very much whether we can make recommendations to the Treasury'[146] was indicative of what had become a chicken-and-egg problem. On the one hand, BEA were unwilling to risk firm orders for heavy-lift helicopter projects because of slow project-development rates while on the other, without BEA orders to increase development priority under 'Indigenous Procurement Process' arrangements, the MoS was powerless to release R&D resources to force the pace of heavy-lift project development.

BEA's frustrations were reiterated again by the firm's Chairman, Lord Douglas, directly with the Minister of Transport and Civil Aviation on 23 September 1953.[147] The BEA Chairman advocated that

> Greater priority should be accorded by the Government to the whole British helicopter programme . . . [currently] we are wasting our time and the taxpayers money unless we are seriously determined to get somewhere

> with helicopters. If that is our aim, we must clearly define our target, rationalise our manufacturing and operating programme and make up our minds to spend enough money to achieve worthwhile results.[148]

This line of criticism continued until late 1953, by which stage BEA Chief Executive Masefield complained to the MoS Deputy Secretary that development was lamentably slow

> ...towards the development of British transport helicopters other than the slowly moving and modest development programme for the Bristol 173 and the research project order for a prototype Fairey Rotodyne. The situation makes me despondent about the prospect of doing anything in scheduled transport for at least a decade with British-designed rotating-wing aircraft.[149]

By January 1954, the issue reached ministerial level when the Minister of Transport and Civil Aviation raised the subject of transport helicopters with the Minister of Supply.[150] Lobbying for additional MoS development resources to support BEA requirements, the Minister of Transport and Civil Aviation pointed to 'grave implications in the commercial field'[151] of the slow development of the Rotodyne and Bristol Type 173 projects because, on current predictions, neither would be in service within a decade. Criticism also focused on the limited prospects of the Bristol Type 173 as a 'stop-gap' programme. Citing Inter-Departmental Helicopter Committee findings, the Minister claimed that because of its small passenger capacity:

> even when developed to the maximum, it will still be a comparatively small helicopter with operating costs well in excess of those of current fixed wing aircraft. This will, in itself, limit the commercial future for the Bristol 173 to areas and routes where helicopter services can offer...advantages over other forms of transport...[152]

Finally, the Minister considered that, because of inadequate project funding, the Rotodyne was at too early a stage of technical development to 'pin hopes on'.[153]

Reacting to these observations, but unable to increase the development priority of the two transport projects without firm BEA orders, the MoS Deputy Secretary's response to the Minister of Transport and Civil Aviation during late 1954 was that

> if BEA could be more definite about the likelihood of their placing production orders, the firm prospect of civil orders as well as military would undoubtedly hearten...[industry]...even further with beneficial results. This, of course means that BEA must themselves determine their requirements – and it is only fair to mention that their various changes of mind have undoubtedly caused [project] uncertainty...which contributed to the lack of drive [in industry].[154]

Early 1954 was significant because it marked a new phase. Whereas factors in the 'Indigenous Procurement Process' had previously militated against large-scale MoS 'Development' funding and production orders for 'all-British' civil development, the growing divergence of UK and US production capabilities added a new dimension. In January 1954, the BEA Chief Executive informed the MoS Deputy Secretary that in contrast to the current estimated Rotodyne and Bristol Type 173 in-service dates of mid-1960, the 35-seat US Sikorsky S-56 transport helicopter was likely to enter commercial operation in the USA by 1958. More significant, the Belgian airline Sabena, which was a competitor to BEA for future European routes, had signed a 'letter of intent' with Sikorsky to acquire S-56s for short-haul operations. According to Masefield, BEA faced the prospect that S-56 helicopters would be operational with foreign airlines by the late 1950s while alternative British types would not be available until the mid-1960s. Masefield's conclusion was that

> As things now stand ... [the] prospects of receiving competitive British equipment have receded so far that there is no question that we shall be forced to purchase American equipment if our European competitors seem likely to acquire large American helicopters towards the end of this decade.[155]

Reiterating BEA concerns, the Minister of Transport and Civil Aviation informed the Minister of Supply that a real concern for 'all-British' projects was that British operators 'will be driven by the need to maintain their competitive position to the purchase of these American types'.[156] The thrust of his argument was that

> ... it does seem that we may already have been outstripped by the Americans in producing the first generation of genuinely economic helicopters for commercial operation. Unless we are content to allow them to gain initial advantages, which are always difficult subsequently to overtake, it seems that we should be clear that we have an adequate research and development programme with the emphasis, both in priority and type, on the right projects.[157]

Despite the deteriorating civil market prospects for the Rotodyne and the Bristol Type 173, and intensive lobbying by the Ministry of Transport and Civil Aviation, the MoS could do little under the 'Indigenous Procurement Process' to increase R&D funding levels for the projects without the priority that could only be generated by BEA orders.[158] At the same time, BEA were increasingly unwilling to commit themselves to such orders in the face of US Sikorsky alternatives which looked set to give rival civil airlines a competitive edge. By mid-1954, even the Ministry of Civil Aviation, with its remit of attempting to generate government funding and aircraft development in the interests of the domestic airlines, recognised the constraints affecting MoS attempts to foster 'all-British' projects. In a meeting of 10 March 1954 the Minister of Transport and Civil Aviation said that he appreciated both the difficulties facing MoS and the efforts made by MoS and he had no intention of blaming anybody for the present situation; this, however, showed alarming symptoms which the Government might well be called upon to account for.[159]

The 'Priority Problem' for the MoS Helicopter Programme, 1950–55

The factors affecting the MoS-sponsored helicopter programme between 1950 and 1955 – the period of the Korean War rearmament boom and the Churchill reversal – showed a remarkable continuity with the immediate post-war period. Bureaucratic factors in the 'Indigenous Procurement Process', the mismatch between design and development and user needs, and the availability in the UK of American-designed production technology continued to create constraints for MoS-sponsored 'all-British' projects in three crucial respects. First, rather than generating large-scale MoS funding to force the pace of development, MoS R&D investment was limited. Second, without this MoS development support and domestic manufacturing orders, the firms themselves were reluctant to risk their own private venture resources to stimulate more rapid project innovation. Third, Westland remained an indirect beneficiary because the factors retarding MoS-sponsored development enhanced the firm's relative position because of its access to the innovation incentives provided to Sikorsky in the USA.

These factors are illustrated by a number of key statistical indicators. The first was relative MoS expenditure on helicopter and non-helicopter R&D projects. Had helicopter and non-helicopter development been assigned equal priority, then *ceteris paribus* it can be assumed they would have attracted a *pro rata* share of MoS R&D expenditure. However, the relative under-funding of helicopter R&D projects provides important evidence that the lack of development priority and production demand limited the scale of MoS helicopter investment in industry.

Between 1945 and 1955, the MoS funded 26 aircraft R&D projects, comprising 10 helicopter (38 per cent by number) and 16 non-helicopter (62 per cent by number) developments. Expenditure trends show that helicopter programmes attracted a significantly lower proportion of MoS R&D funding than their numerical importance in the MoS aircraft programme implied (Table 9). Though accounting for nearly 40 per cent of the total *number* of projects, helicopter projects received no more than that 5.4 per cent of total *expenditure* in any one year. In addition, before 1954–55, aggregate helicopter expenditure remained even lower at between 1 per cent and 2.4 per cent of the total MoS extra-mural aircraft R&D budget. In the engine R&D category, the funding problem was more acute: between 1950–51 and 1952–53 helicopter powerplant funding was consistently under 1 per cent of all MoS aircraft engine funding. These statistics suggest that helicopter development was substantially underfunded by comparison with fixed-wing projects.

Table 9: MoS Extra-Mural Aircraft R&D Expenditure, 1950–55 (£000)

Description	*1950–51*	*1951–52*	*1952–53*	*1953–54*	*1954–55*
Airframes					
Service Prototypes	0	0	0	2	269
Civil Prototypes	0	0	0	0	200
Research Prototypes	192	246	423	440	820
Total of Helicopter Airframes	192	246	423	442	1,289
Total of All Airframes	12,351	12,898	17,700	20,527	22,550
Helicopter Airframes as a Proportion of All Airframes (%)	1.6	1.9	2.4	2.2	5.7
Engines					
Total Helicopter Engines	0	43	150	664	1,710
Total of All Engines	16,508	15,580	22,700	25,974	33,307
Helicopter Engines as a Proportion of All Engines (%)	0	0.3	0.7	2.6	5.1
All Helicopter Work					
Total of All Helicopter Work	192	289	573	1,106	2,999
Total of All Airframe and Engine Work	28,859	28,478	40,400	46,501	55,857
All Helicopter Work as a Proportion of All Work (%)	0.7	1.0	1.4	2.4	5.4

Notes: Actual expenditure at current prices.
Source: PRO AVIA 65/6, Extra-Mural Research and Development Expenditure on Rotating-Wing Aircraft, 1954.

A contrasting interpretation of the statistics is that helicopter projects were inherently less resource-intensive than fixed-wing development. However, this hypothesis is undermined by MoS assessments of helicopter project resource requirements during the period:

> ...basic knowledge on helicopters had been more limited in the United Kingdom than elsewhere at the end of the war, and much ground had to be made up. Furthermore, ...[helicopter projects initiated]... concerned radically different types of helicopters; some research was concerned with machines designed to carry light loads; some with medium and heavy loads and others with investigating new principles of helicopter flight.[160]

Instead, the figures imply that the lack of development priority was militating against large-scale MoS R&D support 'all-British' helicopter development in industry.

The second indicator related to MoS helicopter R&D funding on a project-by-project basis. The composition of the MoS helicopter programme after 1950 had reflected a number of factors. First, MoS policy was to support the development of the existing gear-driven Saunders-Roe Skeeter, Bristol Type 171 and Bristol Type 173 projects. Second, the MoS supported 'torqueless rotor' research on the assumption that the Fairey Rotodyne and the Percival P.74 with their associated power-plants would 'leap-frog' the US production lead in the longer-term. And third, the broader MoS policy approach was to encourage 'all-British' development by promoting a 'research programme designed to keep the helicopter industry in being'.[161] In practice, this had meant supporting projects against the criterion of maintaining existing helicopter design teams. The result was that between 1950 and 1955 the limited *aggregate* resources assigned to helicopter work were divided between some 20 major contracts (Table 10) placed with eight different UK firms.

MoS policy compounded the funding problem because it led to the dispersal of scarce R&D resources over 'too many' projects, causing underfunding and questionable project innovation rates. In its scrutiny of military aircraft development, the House of Commons Select Committee on Estimates in 1956 concluded that 'insufficient care had been shown [by the MoS] in limiting the number of helicopter projects'[162] and that 'the excessive number of projects, had an adverse effect on technical resources'[163] for individual projects.

A third indicator concerned basic helicopter research effort at the Government Research Establishments. Table 11 shows MoS intra-mural and extra-mural aircraft R&D expenditure between FY1950/51 and FY 1954/55. Analysis has already suggested that MoS extra-mural R&D support indicated a funding gap relative to fixed-wing efforts. Intra-mural expenditure figures highlight the problem in a more acute form. Throughout the period, helicopter-related work at government establishments did not exceed 0.6 per cent of total MoS intra-mural aircraft research expenditure. When set against the numerical importance of helicopters in the MoS extra-mural aircraft R&D programme, this provides an additional indicator that low development priority was also limiting government research investment to support project development in industry.

Table 10: MoS Extra-Mural Helicopter R&D Expenditure by Project, 1950–51 to 1954–55 (£000)

Type	*Spec./OR*	*Company*	*Contracts*	*50/51*	*51/52*	*52/53*	*53/54*	*54/55*
Service								
GP RAF	OR 280	Westland	8,724	–	–	–	2	–
B191 (RN)	HR 146	Bristol	10,843 10,462	–	–	–	–	250
GP RAF	OR 325	Bristol	–	–	–	–	–	50
Ultra-Light	OR 319	Fairey	9,912	–	–	–	–	50
Dev. of B171	–	Bristol	12,371	–	–	–	2	380
Research								
Small Ramjet	E.148	Bevan	2,079	–	–	3	–	–
Sycamore	E.20/45; E.34/46; A.9/49	Bristol	5,490 2,505	94	18	30 54	–	–
Type 173	E.4/47	Bristol	1,597	80	86	110	386	–
Air Horse	E.19/46	Saro	6,941 1,704	27	–	10	–	6
Crop Sprayer	E.10/48	Cierva	2,875	11	8	–	–	–
Jet Gyrodyne	E.16/47	Fairey	2,102 7,270	–	47	55	76	–
Rotodyne	E.H/42	Fairey	5,831	–	52	23	67	400
Skeeter	A.13/49	Saro	4,087	–	34	65	–	50
Gas Turbine (P.74)	E.H/25	Percival	7,054	–	–	52	105	175
Rotor Research			–		1	21	30	40
Sub-Total				212	246	423	668	1,401
Engines								
Eland (Rotodyne)		Napier		–	31	38	74	370
Oryx (P.74)		Napier		–	12	74	345	569
Leonides Major		Alvis		–	–	38	250	542
Free Turbine		Napier		–	–	–	–	200

Source: PRO AVIA 65/6, Air 2a, Statement of Expenditure on Rotary-Wing Aircraft, 10 May 1954.

Table 11: MoS Intra-Mural Aircraft Research Expenditure, 1950–55 (£000)

	1950–51	*1951–52*	*1952–53*	*1953–54*	*1954–55*
MoS Extramural Funding, Aircraft	28,859	28,478	40,400	46,501	55,857
MoS Extramural Funding, Helicopters	192	289	573	1,106	2,800
Helicopter Percentage	0.7	1.0	1.4	2.4	5.0
MoS Intra-Mural Funding, Aircraft	–	–	–	1,328	2,797
MoS Intra-Mural Funding, Helicopters	<100	<100	<100	100	120
Helicopter Percentage	<0.6	<0.6	<0.6	7.5	4.2

Note: Current prices.
Source: Extra-mural expenditure figures obtained from PRO AVIA 65/6, Extra-Mural Expenditure on Rotating-Wing Aircraft, figures for Parliamentary Question 10264, 1954; Intra-Mural Figures derived from estimates in PRO AVIA 65/6, MoS Air 2(a), 23 October 1953.

The adverse effects of limited intra-mural research effort for 'all-British' projects in firms became apparent in the 1953 Helicopter Committee of the Aeronautical Research Council (ARC) scrutiny of progress, in which:

> the Committee again reiterated the dire need for more rapid progress in this [helicopter-related] work to provide a rational backing for design work, both that now in progress and that which will be required for the new service and civil requirements. At no time since the birth of the ARC was the situation of fixed wing aircraft design in relation to fundamental work so lamentable as that of the helicopter . . . now.[164]

The ARC recommended an immediate increase in MoS expenditure on fundamental research,[165] and pointed to the detrimental effects on projects in industry of existing *ad hoc* full-scale and wind-tunnel aerodynamic research. They cited the urgent need for work on rotary-wing structures and propulsion at government establishments. The implications of underfunding in basic helicopter work was recognised by MoS officials:

> . . . it is felt that the expansion of effort by transferring half-a-dozen 'white paper' grades at RAE [Royal Aircraft Establishment] to full-time work in this field, and if possible the appointment of one officer at RAE as a co-ordinator of all fundamental work on rotating-wing aircraft

> would pay dividends quite out of all proportion to the additional expenditure (?£50,000 pa) involved. Some action of this kind is indeed essential.[166]

Without priority for basic research to enhance innovation on 'all-British' projects in industry, however, the MoS faced resource-allocation constraints: 'it is no doubt a question of priorities, and staff numbers and expenditure ceilings as well as the availability of facilities are bound to cause difficulties'.[167]

Thus far, the constraints affecting 'all-British' projects have been analysed in terms of policy developments, government R&D resource allocation and production orders. An equally important problem was that these constraints militated against private-sector helicopter investment. The MoS recognised that a lack of government R&D support and large-scale orders was undermining industrial effort. By December 1953 for example, in response to MCA concerns over progress on British MoS-sponsored projects, the MoS Deputy Secretary (Air) was forced to concede that

> we cannot but agree that there has been some lack of drive in the industry, but I think this has been understandable in the light of the lack of enthusiasm shown by users, both military and civil. After all, we cannot expect industry to be very keen on building up facilities and staff for work in a new field, even at our own expense, unless there are reasonable prospects of production to follow.[168]

Likewise, when reviewing the large helicopter field in 1954, the view of the MoS Deputy Secretary (Air) was that

> the slow progress to date had to a large degree been due to a lack of orders for helicopters. The Ministry had pursued a balanced programme of helicopter research and development, but the chief thing lacking was a substantial number of flying hours. The position was not, however, made easier by the fact that to date no service requirements for a large helicopter had been stated, and from time to time the services tended to disclaim interest in the development of such a machine.[169]

MoS officials were thus clearly concerned that the lack of production demand was undermining industrial effort and innovation on the projects under its sponsorship.

Illustrative of industry concerns was correspondence between the Bristol Aircraft Division and the MoS during 1953. During May 1953, Bristol conveyed its anxiety over 'all-British' helicopter development in general and the specific factors retarding development rates on the Type 173 project in particular.[170] Bristol's first point was that extensive flight testing on a number of prototypes was essential for the transition from development to production.[171] Instead, the MoS approach had been to limit funding to single prototype contracts, which was inadequate to support extensive flight testing. Second, Bristol were concerned about the lack of production orders on which to plan: on the Type 171 project, for example, the firm built 45 machines on a private venture basis yet only received orders 'at two or three at a time'; by 1953, only 21 had been purchased out of the total planned production of 45 units. Finally, Bristol indicated to the MoS that the firm were increasingly reluctant to risk further company resources on helicopter development because they had 'no reassurances even if that reasonable demand will exist for the B173'.[172] Bristol later reiterated its frustrations in a more direct manner by forwarding profit figures from the American helicopter firm Piasecki to the Ministry[173] which showed that with US government support and orders, the American firm had a backlog of helicopter orders amounting to $150 million, had tripled its net helicopter earnings between 1950 and 1951 and had annual sales approaching $64.5 million. Bristol's despondence was manifest: the figures 'indicate how far we have to go to approach helicopter development taking place in America, and Piasecki is only one of a number of such companies'.[174]

The final indicators of the constraints affecting MoS-sponsored helicopter projects were the *relative* levels of UK and US government support for helicopter development and the production output of British and American firms. Had the domestic UK helicopter market been protected against competition from US-sourced helicopter technology, these indicators would be of limited application. However, because Westland was a recipient of technology transfer with access to US innovation incentives, the comparison becomes relevant.

A 1954 MoS review of relative government helicopter R&D and production funding concluded that 'it is difficult to assess fairly the relative position of the UK and the USA'.[175] Statistics compiled in the same document, however, comparing predicted cumulative extra-mural R&D expenditure by the British MoS and the US Army between 1953 and 1956, indicated the considerable advantage enjoyed by US firms. Estimates were that between 1953 and 1956, the US Army would spend $61.5 million and that total UK government expenditure would be $21 million, indicating that US Army extramural helicopter investment would be approximately three times larger than total MoS funding in cumulative terms.[176] Moreover, while the UK figures represented overall government R&D expenditure, the US Army figures reflect only one portion of a wider programme supported by the US Navy, Air Force and civil users.

Analysis of the output performance of the British and US helicopter industries against selected indicators for the period between 1945 and 1953, again documented in the 1954 MoS review, also reveals key data. The first was the US industry's achievements in helicopter prototypes when compared with UK firms: American teams had developed 48 flying prototypes whereas British teams had developed just seven. Secondly, the proportion of American helicopter projects that proceeded to production was greater: one-in-four in the US as apposed to one-in-seven for indigenous UK designs.[177] Thirdly, in numerical terms, the 1954 MoS report showed that orders for Westland-built variants of US designs significantly exceeded the production figures for MoS-sponsored 'all-British' types. One implication, therefore, was that in addition to greater government inputs and user demand, fuelled in part by Korean War helicopter requirements, the US had retained a significant lead over the UK in terms of output. As a recipient of technology transfer, however, Westland was the direct recipient of this output lead. Another was that the US advantage in scale of output after the Korean War highlights the major problem that confronted MoS officials: how to plan and implement a programme of government-sponsored 'all-British' helicopter development in the face of US production dominance which Westland was accessing via licensed production.

WESTLAND IN-HOUSE INNOVATION AND THE 'TAILORING' EFFECT

Between 1950 and 1955 the strategy of exploiting Sikorsky's production lead and its ability to circumvent protectionism within the UK 'Licensed Production Procurement Process', enabled Westland to dominate British helicopter production. At the same time, Westland's manufacturing success and the bureaucratic factors in the 'Indigenous Procurement Process' undermined MoS R&D resources allocation, manufacturing orders and innovation rates on 'all-British' helicopter projects. As this section demonstrates, however, by 1955, these trends introduced new factors that both consolidated Westland's longer-term position in the British helicopter market and undermined MoS policies to foster 'indigenous' helicopter technology.

The first factor was Westland's technical strategy. By 1955, licensed production had become not only a means of winning short-term production orders but also a *modus operandi* through which the firm was accumulating a comprehensive and state of the art in-house design capability. The MoS-sponsored helicopter programme was now confronted with what MoS officials perceived to be undesirable competition from a new type of 'indigenous' helicopter technology in the form of Westland in-house designs. The second factor was that by 1955, the cycle of limited R&D investment, low development priority and small-scale production demand created a situation where 'the whole [MoS] programme was eventually to collapse like a pack of cards and leave a litter of prototypes and cancelled projects'.[178] The outcome was not only to undermine the MoS-sponsored helicopter programme further, but also to strengthen Westland's relative position in the UK helicopter market.

Westland, Licensed Production and Technology 'Anglicisation'

Between 1945 and 1955, Westland's primary commercial activity was to anglicise and manufacture proven Sikorsky helicopter production technology. After 1950, however, the firm implemented the second strand of its corporate strategy: the 'longer-term policy ... of training a design team in the rotary wing technique, able in due course to undertake its own designs'.[179] The decision to conduct in-house design and development meant that the MoS helicopter programme was to face a qualitatively different challenge. Westland's 'twin-track' approach meant that the MoS helicopter programme was confronted with both short-term manufacturing competition, and, in the longer term, rivalry from a new form of 'all-British' helicopter technology.

After 1950 and the receipt of orders for the S-55, Westland had succeeded in its immediate objective of making 'available both for service and civilian use, helicopters of proven design'.[180] In parallel, three factors encouraged the firm to concentrate on generating an in-house design and development capability. The first was the Westland Board's calculation that, while reliance on the Sikorsky lead could facilitate short-term orders, the lead would 'tend to diminish as time goes on'.[181] The assumption here was that MoS-sponsored designs could ultimately catch-up with Sikorsky developments and that Westland would therefore also require an in-house design capability to compete for future UK markets. The second was Westland's recognition that licensed production gave the firm 'unrivalled knowledge of the design and construction of helicopters', and practical flying experience 'to avoid almost all "blind alley" investigation to which the absence of that great practical experience might very well lead'.[182] Consequently, independent design was as attractive as it was essential because licensed production provided Westland with technological short cuts in relation to its UK rivals. The third was equally pragmatic: any MoS R&D funding that Westland received would be at the expense of investment on competing 'all-British' projects.

In implementing its design strategy, Westland embarked on a range of design studies and prototypes between 1950 and 1954: the 'Multi-Engined Design'[183] initiated in July 1950; 'Project W.80'[184] and 'Project W.81',[185] both initiated in April 1951; the 'BEA Design Study'[186] initiated in December 1952; the 'Widgeon'[187] initiated in June 1954; and, the 'Royal Canadian Navy Design Study'[188] initiated in October 1954. In each case, it was able to finance development and accumulate design expertise on a speculative private venture basis with revenues obtained through the sale of its licensed-produced Sikorsky variants.[189] The firm's overall strategy thus enabled Westland to remain external to the 'Indigenous Procurement Process' under which MoS-sponsored 'all-British' projects were largely reliant on government funding.

By late 1953, Westland's commercial strategy was to force a fundamental policy question for the MoS. In September 1953 Westland submitted a memorandum to the MoS outlining its design and development plans.[190]

The first issue raised was to ask for MoS endorsement to extend the firm's existing Sikorsky S-51 and S-55 licences to include manufacture in the UK of the larger Sikorsky S-52, S-56 and S-58 helicopters. The second was a request for MoS R&D funding support for a programme of in-house helicopter development. Westland's justification for the funding request was that

> The design and engineering efforts associated with the Westland enterprise appears to have been seriously underrated [by the MoS], and notwithstanding design studies undertaken, a design team which can be fairly described as the most experienced helicopter design team in Great Britain has so far not been considered suitable to carry out a[n in-house] helicopter project [with MoS R&D funding].[191]

To support this position, the memorandum pointed out that, although Westland after 1945 had risked private venture capital on licensed production, generated £7 million of UK service production contracts, and received 200 manufacturing orders, throughout the period it had received from 'the Ministry [of Supply] Research and Development vote only £53,000 – less than 1% of our total business'.[192] Finally, the Westland Board claimed that it viewed

> with great concern the situation whereby the experience accumulated by its design staff is not being given its proper place in prototype development. At the same time it knows that other firms with little or no practical helicopter experience are receiving government support, which means that Westland, unless it can develop its own designs, must inevitably be at a serious disadvantage with regard to its competitors.[193]

The initial MoS response was to reject both requests in defence of its own helicopter programme. Aware of the commercial dangers posed by the new Westland licensed-manufacturing proposals, the position by 7 October 1953 of the MoS Assistant Secretary (Air) was that

> ... the introduction of the S-51 and the S-55 are considered to have held back the full potentialities of their nearest British rivals the Bristol 171 and the Bristol 173 ... Any extension of a Westland/Sikorsky licence agreement to include a wider range of helicopters raises again a real problem ... any further extension of US design in this country would make a nonsense of our efforts to stimulate a positive policy into British helicopter efforts. Our policy in the latter direction is crystallising out and, I think, in such manner as to make it abundantly clear that we should still take this line with US licence agreements.[194]

At a meeting of 18 October 1953, senior MoS officials decided that Westland had 'set back' British development and should thus be given no further encouragement to extend their Sikorsky licensing arrangements.[195] Of most concern to the MoS were Westland's S-56 licensed-production proposals which would 'reach fruition in time to deal a death blow to our [MoS] efforts to provide a Bristol 30/40 seater'[196] with the Type 173 project. On the issue of government R&D support for Westland, the MoS assessment was that 'while Westland had gained considerable experience in anglicising American designs . . . they certainly did not possess the best helicopter design team in the United Kingdom'.[197] In part, the MoS view was that the Bristol helicopter design team was superior to the Westland design team and that the latter had 'no particular claim' upon MoS resources.[198] More important, however, was MoS reluctance to provide Westland with R&D support because of its industrial policy of keeping the design teams covered by its own R&D programme in being. As the MoS Assistant Secretary (Air) pointed out

> We cannot settle the problem raised by Westlands without considering the position of other firms: Bristol's, Saro's, Percival's and Faireys . . . It is quite clear we shall require to implement some form of size and shape policy when we have taken stock of the present situation [namely, Westland's proposals]. Saro could, I think, raise a more pathetic case than Westland's on this kind of issue.[199]

While the 18 October 1953 meeting did not endorse Westland's proposals, its significance was that it prompted the MoS to question for the first time the fundamental tenets of its post-war helicopter industrial policy. Against the growing constraints of the divergence of UK and US helicopter production achievements, Westland's commercial success as a licensed producer, the potential threat posed to 'all-British' projects posed by Westland in-house designs and the lack of development priority and production demand for MoS-sponsored projects, the MoS Director General of Technical Development was forced to concede that

> an important stage had been reached at which it must be decided whether to pursue vigorously, abandon, or compromise our research and development programme. It was important to decide how much reliance should be placed on American helicopters, to consider the financial aspects, and formulate a policy accordingly.[200]

Under increasing pressure, the MoS was eventually forced to consider the fundamental policy choice between 'getting on and getting out'[201] of the helicopter development field.

On 5 March 1954, an evaluation of MoS policy alternatives had been produced in a secret report entitled 'Rotary Wing Aircraft'[202] by the MoS Assistant Secretary (Air) 2(a). The analysis considered four alternative policy approaches:

A) To abandon helicopter development at government expense entirely, and meet service and civil needs by the use of either American-built machines or British-built machines of US design.
B) To limit British development to the Bristol 173 in its present (piston-engined) and 'stretched' (turbine-engined) forms, so as to meet the smaller Service requirements and get a share of the market for small civil machines, but to resign the field of larger and more advanced designs to the USA.
C) To continue with the present programme but on a firmer financial footing with the approval of a separate 'Rotating Wing Aircraft Budget' not liable to be 'raided' in the interests of the Defence Budget, or of Treasury attempts to prune non-defence expenditure. If this programme is to proceed on a sound basis and not be held up unnecessarily, additional effort will have to be put into rotating wing aircraft research at MoS Establishments.
D) To increase the effort on rotating-wing aircraft (both intra- and extra-mural) immediately and to make an all-out effort to establish a lead over the USA over the whole field.[203]

The implications of each option was assessed as follows:-

A) A continuing dollar drain on licence agreements or on purchasing US machines and spares would follow UK abandonment of helicopter development, and very promising export markets would be largely abandoned. Some £2m of expenditure on developing British types might be saved in 1954–55 and nearly £3m in 1955–56 and 1956–57, but this would be offset by the cost of the modification needed to adapt US types to British service requirements.
B) To limit development to the Bristol 173 would mean a smaller dollar drain than A, and larger export earnings could be expected. But as the demand for larger machines grew, the dollar drain would increase, and in all probability many markets would prefer to have all sizes of machines from the one source from which their larger machine would have to come, so that British sales would dry up. This course might save rather less than £1m in 1954–55 of expenditure on developing British types, and between £1m and £1.5m in each of 1955–56 and 1956–57, again offset by the cost of modification to meet British service requirements.
C) ...[MoS] expenditure could be expected to rise, but simultaneously, sales of the Bristol 173's should start to build up, to be followed by sales of other more advanced types. The additional intramural expenditure involved would probably not exceed £50,000 p.a. at the most, unless additional capital facilities, such as rotor spinning towers, had to be provided.
D) No substantial acceleration of the rate of progress forecast for the main

> projects . . . is feasible, even if additional money were made available. The present programme however does represent the bare minimum number of projects for which requirements, largely service were foreseen . . . if sufficient money were available, additional projects could be started at once for research and civil purposes. It should be noted that such an expansion of the programme would not result in very much increase of expenditure in 1954–55, but it would build up considerably in 1955–56 and later years; such an expansion would not be worth starting if financial stringency and expenditure ceilings were to strangle it as it got under way.[204]

The primary conclusion was that on economic and national prestige grounds, option D should be adopted; if additional funding was affordable, option C was recommended as 'second best'.[205] This recommendation was made with two important caveats, however, that got to the heart of the constraints and impediments that had affected the MoS helicopter programme after 1945. The first, in either case, was that ministerial approval for the programme in 'unequivocal terms' was essential before the programme could proceed on a 'stable and assured basis instead of being subject to perpetual challenge by Treasury, DRPC and others' and that a statement should be made by the government 'of the importance attached to rotating wing development'.[206] The second was that Westland should be precluded from licence agreements to build helicopters comparable with 'machines in the UK programme'.[207]

By 10 March 1954, the primary recommendations in 'Rotary-Wing Aircraft' had been accepted within the MoS at Ministerial level. The Minister of Supply prepared a paper for Cabinet discussion, making a case for allocating a greater proportion of the defence budget for R&D and, within this, a 'provision for increased expenditure on helicopters'.[208] However, despite the high-level MoS policy reassessment during 1954, the fact remained that in the 'Indigenous Procurement Process' decisions over R&D funding provision and production orders for MoS-sponsored projects remained outside MoS control. By 1955, events would deal a more serious blow to the MoS-sponsored helicopter programme.

The 'Tailoring' Effect and MoS-Sponsored Helicopter Programme Cancellations, 1955

The MoS optimism of March 1954 was to be short-lived. By late 1955, the Ministry had been forced to cancel key projects in its helicopter R&D programme, the primary reasons for which were the lack of firm production demand and the downstream effects of low development priority.

Helicopter projects were only one subset of the overall MoS aircraft R&D and production programme. The lack of service and civil production demand had limited MoS helicopter R&D investment not only in absolute terms but also relative to other aviation branches. In *de facto* terms, therefore, it had rendered helicopter projects of 'peripheral' importance when compared to other 'core' aircraft programmes. After 1950, the significance of this 'peripheral' characteristic was that when the MoS was required to make *marginal* R&D expenditure economies, the low priority of helicopter projects made them prime candidates for R&D funding reductions under what was termed by the MoS the 'tailoring' effect.

The 'tailoring' effect was a recurring feature after 1950 when the MoS were required to make a succession of aircraft R&D budget cuts as a result of financial crises affecting the UK economy, or forced to focus industrial assets on aircraft production as part of the Korean War rearmament programme.[209] During April 1953, for example, in the face of Air Ministry/War Office inter-service rivalry, the concern of the MoS Under Secretary (Air) was that

> I cannot help feeling that one of the main troubles is that the Air Ministry are so nervous about letting the army develop their own ideas for aircraft including helicopters. The Air Force in nearly every case put Army requirements at the bottom of their list and the result accordingly is that when money is short army requirements suffer.[210]

In the same month, the 'tailoring' effect, which stemmed directly from the reluctance of potential military purchasers to specify their likely production demand, had also undermined MoS estimates of future helicopter resource allocation:

> Current economy exercises under the auspices of DRPC aimed at 'tailoring' the programme to the amount of Defence Budget money likely to be available in 1955–56 have resulted in the deletion of the military heavy-lift helicopter, and have placed the Rotodyne in jeopardy, since for neither aircraft (unlike the Bristol 173) at this stage has any firm military requirement been stated ... Lack of firm military interest may well place the Percival project in the same position.[211]

Evidence of growing MoS frustrations were also manifest in the 1954 'Rotary-Wing Aircraft'[212] report and its recommendations that helicopter programmes could only proceed on a 'stable and assured' basis with a separate budget not liable to be 'raided' in defence R&D reductions or Treasury cuts.

Despite the Minister of Supply's endorsement of the 'Rotary-Wing Aircraft' report, however, the most serious manifestation of the 'tailoring' effect occurred in late 1955. During November 1955, the Cabinet introduced public expenditure cuts that reduced total MoS Defence R&D Estimates for financial year 1956–57 of £73.9 million by £10 million and incorporated a cumulative savings target of £18 million on MoS Estimates for financial year

1958–59.[213] The DRPC was required to implement the expenditure reduction and, after evaluating aircraft R&D projects on a priority basis, decided that the MoS helicopter R&D helicopter estimates on the defence Budget Account for financial year 1958–59[214] should be reduced by £2 million, a 58 per cent cut in the original estimate of £4.88 million. In addition, helicopter expenditure for for financial years 1956–57 and 1957–58 were to be reduced by 17.5 per cent and 22 per cent, respectively, on original estimates.[215]

Against these constraints, a working party was assembled under the MoS Deputy Secretary[216] operating

> on the assumption that . . . the UK could not afford to abandon all idea of developing British helicopters to meet home and export needs and leave the entire market to helicopters of American origin . . . [and] with a view to cutting [the MoS helicopter programme] down on an 'austerity' basis . . . , which will yet make the most profitable use of the money already spent on helicopter development in the UK, the experience gained and the skill of the existing British helicopter design teams.[217]

The policy outcome, reluctantly endorsed by the Minister of Supply on 20 December 1955,[218] was the withdrawal of government R&D support for key helicopter programmes. First, as the Percival design team was 'weakest in the helicopter field' and 'furthest from yielding a useful operational machine', the MoS concluded 'with considerable reluctance that since one major project must be sacrificed' it should be the P.74 and associated Oryx engine.[219] The P.74 cancellation achieved savings of £1.13 million for the financial year 1958–59 estimates.[220] Second, the decision was taken to cancel the Fairey Ultra-Light project, with associated savings of £0.138 million, and leave the Army reliant on the Saunders-Roe Skeeter development. Third, to achieve further economies on the Defence Vote, the Fairey Rotodyne was reclassified as a civil project, and the Bristol Type 173 and its associated variants for the Admiralty (designated B191) and the Air Ministry (designated B192) were to be charged in part on the civil budget. Finally, some £0.4 million, provisionally earmarked for Westland's S-56 'Westminster' for financial year 1958–59, was cancelled.[221]

The industrial picture emerging from these cuts was that while 'Bristols will continue as our [the UK's] major domestic design team and we shall also have a substantial domestic design team in Faireys,'[222] the result would also be that 'Hunting Percival Aircraft would drop out of the helicopter field, and Saunders-Roe would fade out gradually after the Skeeter'.[223] Confronted with the 'tailoring' effect, however, the MoS Deputy Secretary had no alternative but to accept that,

> although the loss of the Saunders Roe team would be regrettable, I do not think that in present circumstances we can justify any larger number of firms working on helicopters at public expense in this country.[224]

Whereas licensed production had provided by 1955 the mechanism for Westland to consolidate its design and production capability, the legacy of constraints affecting MoS-sponsored development had undermined key elements of the MoS industrial strategy.

SUMMARY

Between 1950 and 1955 the variables affecting UK helicopter R&D and production were characterised by a remarkable degree of similarity with the immediate post-war period. On the one hand, by exploiting the US technological lead and accessing the innovation incentives provided by Sikorsky, Westland was able to consolidate its dominance of UK helicopter production. Equally important, the objectives of the organisations making up the 'Licensed Production Procurement Process' facilitated Westland's access to UK manufacturing orders despite the protection policies pursued by the MoS. On the other hand, the lack of production demand caused by Westland's production success, coupled with the bureaucratic arrangements in the 'Indigenous Procurement Process', further militated against R&D resources, production orders and innovation rates on those projects making up the MoS helicopter programme.

The major difference with the immediate post-war period, however, was one of degree. Through its commercial success, Westland had begun after 1950 the process of assimilating know-how derived from Sikorsky to generate an in-house design and development capability. In effect, Westland began to challenge MoS-sponsored 'all-British' designs with a new form of indigenous helicopter technology. Over the same period, Westland orders and the lack of demand from potential UK civil and military users further undermined MoS-sponsored helicopter development. The playing-out of these factors would create the conditions by 1960 for Westland to emerge as Britain's sole helicopter design and manufacturing firm.

NOTES

1. See R. Sturtivant, *British Research and Development Aircraft: Seventy Years at the Leading Edge* (Yeovil: Haynes, 1990), p. 187.
2. For more details see 'Hunting Percival P.74', *Flight*, 23 December 1955, p. 938.
3. Ibid.
4. For a more extensive discussion see P. London, *Saunders and Saro Aircraft since 1917* (London: Putnam, 1988), p. 239.
5. See K. Watson, 'Activities of Weir, Cierva and Saunders-Roe, 1933–1962' in R.A.C. Brie (ed.), *A History of British Rotorcraft, 1866–1965* (Yeovil: Westland Helicopters, 1968), p. 60.
6. London, *Saunders and Saro Aircraft*, p. 239.
7. Extensive descriptions of both the design features and the technical development of the projects already exist in published form. Throughout this section the reader is referred to relevant texts dealing with these issues. See Appendix 1 for a summary of projects.

8. For a detailed technical description of the Jet Gyrodyne design and project development, see E.J Everett-Heath, *British Military Helicopters* (London: Arms & Armour Press, 1986), pp. 61–4; G.S. Hislop, 'Helicopter Activities of Fairey, Westland and British European Airways 1947–1965', in R.A.C. Brie (ed.), *A History of British Rotorcraft, 1866-1965* (Yeovil: Westland Helicopters, 1968), p. 125; and Sturtivant, *British Research and Development Aircraft*, pp. 185–7. The relevant MoS technical file covering Jet Gyrodyne development is PRO AVIA 53/485, Fairey Design.
9. Texts covering technical and development information on the Fairey Rotodyne project are numerous. For a key contemporaneous account see 'Rotodyne Report: Development Aspects and Commercial Applications of Fairey's VTOL Transport', *Flight*, 20 December 1957, pp. 953–60. Comprehensive recent analyses include: Everett-Heath, *British Military Helicopters*, pp. 64–8; and D. Wood, *Project Cancelled: The Disaster of Britain's Abandoned Aircraft Projects* (London: Tri-Service Press, 1990), pp. 102–7. Relevant MoS files covering Rotodyne development between 1950 and 1955 are: PRO AVIA 54/742, Large Helicopter for BEA (1951–53); PRO AVIA 65/262, Proposals for Fairey Rotodyne (1949–51); and, PRO AVIA 65/263, Proposals for Fairey Rotodyne (1951–56).
10. For a description of the project see: H.A. Taylor, *Fairey Aircraft since 1915* (London: Putnam, 1974), p. 401; and Everett-Heath, *British Military Helicopters*, pp. 68–71. Relevant MoS files covering the Ultra-Light project are: PRO AVIA 46/483, Supply of Ultra-Light HR 144D; and, PRO AVIA 53/551, Contract for Design of Jet for Ultra-Light.
11. For more details see: C.H Barnes, *Bristol Aircraft since 1910* (London: Putnam, 1988). Relevant Ministry of Supply files covering project developments include: PRO AVIA 54/741, Conversion of B171 (1951–52); PRO AVIA 54/731, Sycamore (1951-1953); PRO AVIA 54/792, Sycamore Mk.1 (1952–53); PRO AVIA 54/873, B171 Mk.10 (1952–53); PRO AVIA 54/903, Sycamore Service Trials in Malaya (1952–55); PRO AVIA 54/832, B173 (1952–55); PRO AVIA 54/865, ASW Helicopter (NSR NA43) Considerations (1952-1954); and, PRO AVIA 65/4, Bristol B191: Finance and Policy (1952–55).
12. See T.L. Ciastula, 'Saunders-Roe Helicopter Activities, 1951–59', in R.A.C. Brie (ed.), *A History of British Rotorcraft 1866–1965* (Yeovil: Westland Helicopters, 1968), pp. 129–33.
13. See 'Hunting Percival P.74', *Flight*, p. 938.
14. See 'Rotary-Wing Power', *Flight*, 12 March 1954, pp. 318–22.
15. See J.W.R. Taylor and M.F. Allward, *Westland 50* (London: Ian Allan, 1965), p. 113. Relevant Ministry of Supply files covering project developments include: PRO AVIA 54/786, Westland Sikorsky S-51 (1952); PRO AVIA 54/889, S-55 Leonides (1953); and, PRO AVIA 54/860, Armament for S-55 (1952–55).
16. Ibid.
17. PRO AVIA 65/6, Memorandum on Westland Helicopter Design and Development, September 1953.
18. For more detail on the Westland S-51 variants, see Everett-Heath, *British Military Helicopters*, pp. 80–91; Jane's, *All the World's Aircraft, 1964–1965* (London: Jane's, 1960); Taylor and Allward, *Westland 50*, p. 112; and, PRO AVIA 54/565–54/567, S-51 and Variants.
19. See, for example, Taylor and Allward, *Westland 50*, p. 110; and D. Wettern, *The Decline of British Seapower* (London: Jane's, 1982), p. 69.
20. See, for example, P.A. Towle, 'The RAF and the Malayan Insurgency', *Air Clues*, Vol. 43, No. 8, August 1989, pp. 284–90.
21. Everett-Heath, *British Military Helicopters*, p. 91.
22. Ibid., p. 57. See also: PRO AVIA 54/828–54/831, B171 for the Australian Navy (1952–1954).

23. See Barnes, *Bristol Aircraft*, p. 365.
24. Ibid., p. 48.
25. Figures calculated from Report of the Committee of Inquiry into the Aircraft Industry, *Cmnd. 2853* (London: HMSO, 1965), pp. 121–2; and, R. Hafner, 'British Rotorcraft', *Journal of the Royal Aeronautical Society*, Vol. 70, Part I, January 1966, p. 241. Westland S-55 Whirlwind production was 308 units out of a total production output by the UK industry of 1022 units.
26. L.B. Bryson, F.E. Heenan and C.A. Johnson, 'Helicopters in the Royal Navy', *Royal Aeronautical Society Journal*, Vol. 76, August 1972, p. 472.
27. Ibid.
28. PRO T 225/1103, Letter from the Air Branch, Admiralty, to Mr. Humphreys-Davies, HM Treasury, 24 November 1951.
29. For more details see, for example, Wettern, *Decline of British Seapower*, p. 34.
30. PRO T 225/1103, Letter from Air Branch, Admiralty, to Mr. Humphreys-Davies, HM Treasury, 24 November 1951.
31. Ibid.
32. Ibid.
33. PRO ADM 1/20933, Helicopters in Anti-Submarine Warfare, 1946-47, Tactical Employment of ASW Helicopters, 28 November 1946, cited in G. Hartcup, *The Silent Revolution: Development of Conventional Weapons, 1945–85* (London: Brassey's, 1993), p. 264.
34. Bryson *et al.*, 'Helicopters in the Royal Navy', p. 472.
35. Ibid.
36. For more detail, see G. Swanborough and P.M. Bowers, *United States Navy Aircraft since 1911* (London: Putnam, 1968), p. 345.
37. J. Chartres, *Westland Sea King* (London: Ian Allen, 1984), p. 9.
38. Hartcup, *Silent Revolution*, p. 264.
39. PRO ADM 1/24148, 9th Report by British Helicopter Crews Participating in USN Evaluation of Helicopter Dipping Sonar, 1 December 1951, cited in Hartcup, *Silent Revolution*, p. 264.
40. PRO T 225/1103, Letter from the Air Branch, Admiralty to HM Treasury, 28 December 1951.
41. O. Fitzwilliams, 'Westland Helicopter Activities 1946–1960', in R.A.C. Brie (ed.), *A History of British Rotorcraft, 1866–1965* (Yeovil: Westland Helicopters, 1968), p. 116.
42. See: E. Rees, *World Military Helicopters* (London: Jane's, 1986), pp. 130–2.
43. Chartres, *Westland Sea King*, p. 9.
44. Swanborough and Bowers, *United States Navy Aircraft*, p. 345.
45. Ibid.
46. Chartres, *Westland Sea King*, p. 11.
47. PRO T 225/1103, Letter from the Air Branch, Admiralty, to HM Treasury, 28 December 1951.
48. AHB ID9/94/10/Pt. 1 (Air Historical Branch Records), Report of the Air Attaché in Washington, cited in J. Dowling, *RAF Helicopters: The First Twenty Years* (London: HMSO, 1992), p. 55.
49. PRO T 225/1103, Letter from the Air Branch, Admiralty, to HM Treasury, 28 December 1951.
50. Ibid.
51. Ibid.
52. Ibid.
53. Ibid., Letter to F.C. Herd, Admiralty, from D.F. Hubback, Treasury, 28 November 1951.
54. Ibid., Letter from the Air Branch, Admiralty, to HM Treasury, 28 December 1954.
55. Ibid.
56. Ibid.

57. Ibid.
58. Ibid., Letter from the Ministry of Defence to HM Treasury, 4 January 1952.
59. Ibid.
60. Ibid., Minute from D.F. Hubback to Mr. Humphreys-Davies, S-55 Helicopters for the Navy, 7 January 1952.
61. Ibid.
62. Ibid., Letter from HM Treasury to the Admiralty Air Branch, 8 January 1952.
63. PRO AVIA 65/6, The Helicopter and its Potential, by A. McClements, Assistant Director of Research and Development (Helicopters), 6 February 1953.
64. Everett-Heath, *British Military Helicopters*, p. 91.
65. Ibid.
66. PRO AVIA 65/6, The Helicopter and its Potential, by A. McClements, Assistant Director of Research and Development (Helicopters), 6 February 1953.
67. Ibid.
68. Ibid.
69. PRO AVIA 65/264, Minute from the Ministry of Supply Assistant Director, Aircraft Research and Development (Research), 25 May 1951.
70. See Sturtivant, *British Research and Development Aircraft*, p. 78.
71. Ibid., p. 187.
72. PRO AVIA 65/6, Memorandum by the Ministry of Supply to the Ministry of Defence Defence Research Policy Committee, Large Helicopters and Vertical Lift, 27 November 1952.
73. For a discussion on this point see Wood, *Project Cancelled*, p. 97.
74. PRO AVIA 65/6, Memorandum by the Ministry of Defence Defence Research Policy Committee, Large Helicopters and Vertical Lift, 27 November 1952.
75. Ibid.
76. PRO AVIA 65/6, Minutes of a Meeting held on 30 June 1953 in the House of Commons to discuss Development and Production of Helicopters in the UK, 30 June 1953.
77. Ibid.
78. Ibid.
79. The MoS helicopter programme between 1949 and 1955 comprised the Bristol Type 171, Bristol Type 173, Percival P.74, Fairey Rotodyne, and the Fairey Jet Gyrodyne. During 1954, Fairey commenced development of the 'Ultra-Light' type with MoS funding. Despite the cancellation of 'Air Horse' development at Cierva, MoS 'Experimental' funding continued until FY 1951/52.
80. PRO AVIA 65/6, Note on the MoS Helicopter R&D Programme with Special Emphasis on the Civil Transport Role, MoS Air 2(a), 17 October 1953.
81. Ibid., Ministry of Defence Defence Research Policy Committee Helicopter Requirements for the Three Services, Memorandum by the Vice Chief of the Air Staff, 10 September 1952.
82. PRO AVIA 65/6, Minutes of the DRP Committee on Helicopters Meeting of 7 October 1952.
83. PRO AVIA 65/6, The Helicopter and Its Potential, by A. McClements, Assistant Director of Research and Development (Helicopters), 6 February 1952.
84. Ibid., Minutes of a Meeting held on 30 June 1953 in the House of Commons to Discuss Development and Production of Helicopters in the UK, 30 June 1953.
85. Ibid.
86. Ibid.
87. Ibid.
88. Ibid.
89. Ibid., Minute by DCA for US (Air), 9 July 1954.
90. Figures calculated from Dowling, *RAF Helicopters*.
91. E.W. Rawlins and W.J. Sambito, *Marines and Helicopters, 1946–1962* (Washington,

DC: US Marine Corps, History and Museums Division, 1976), p. 108.

92. M. Allen, *Military Helicopter Doctrines of the Major Powers, 1945–1992* (London: Greenwood Press, 1993), p. 4.
93. Figures from S.C. Williams, *Report on the Helicopter: The Helicopter and Its Role As a Transport Vehicle* (New York: Brundage Story & Rose, 1955), p. 23.
94. The most comprehensive account of internal perceptions within the Air Ministry during this period is contained in Dowling, *RAF Helicopters*, pp. 103–112.
95. For the most detailed accounts of War Office developments, see: A. Farrar-Hockley, *The Army in the Air: The History of the Army Air Corps* (Stroud: Allan Sutton, 1994), pp. 165–179; R.A. Norman-Walker, 'The Formation of the AAC – 1955–1957', *Army Air Corps Journal*, 1982, pp. 9–16; A.W. McTaggart,'Helicopter Air Power', *Air Clues*, Vol. 43, No. 3, March 1989, pp. 83–8; N. Crookenden, 'Aviation in the British Army Today', *RUSI Journal*, August 1956; P.W. Mead, 'Army Aviation', *RAF Quarterly*, Summer 1962, pp. 189–93; B.H. Reid, 'Civil War Between Services', *Military History*, January 1984, pp. 1–7; and, J. Waddy and S. Moss, 'The Saga of the Soldier and His Helicopter', *The Army Quarterly and Defence Journal*, Vol. 116, No. 4, October 1986, pp. 391–6.
96. For policy developments, see PRO AVIA 65/268, Army Helicopter Working Party: Reports (1953–54); and, PRO WO 32/12214, Recognition Air to Ground, (1946–1955).
97. Ibid., p. 101.
98. Air Historical Branch File ID/53/1/60/Pt.3: 13 January 1947, cited in Dowling, *RAF Helicopters*, p. 128.
99. PRO WO 32/15177, Minute to CIGS, 2 February 1953, cited in P.A. Towle, *Pilots and Rebels: The Use of Aircraft in Unconventional Warfare, 1918–88* (London: Brassey's, 1989), p. 127.
100. PRO WO 32/13525, Executive Committee of the Army Council: Cargo Helicopters, Paper by the Deputy Chief of the Imperial General Staff for Consideration by the Executive Committee of the Army Council at a Future Meeting, 25 February 1953.
101. Ibid.
102. Ibid. For a day-to-day account of the activities of the Working Party see PRO WO 32/15177, Cargo Helicopters (1953).
103. Towle, *Pilots and Rebels: Use of Aircraft*, 1989, p. 127. Analysis of PRO WO 32/13525, Executive Committee of the Army Council: Cargo Helicopters, Paper by DCIGS for Consideration by the Executive of the Army Council at a future meeting, 25 February 1953, reveals that the planned composition of the Committee was an officer of brigadier rank to act as chairman, a lieutenant-colonel with staff experience, a major and 'a technical officer or civil servant with knowledge of the maintenance problems involved' from the Ministry of Supply.
104. PRO AIR 2/15149, RAF Helicopter Policy, by the Deputy Chief of the Air Staff, undated.
105. Ibid., Letter from the War Office to the Under-Secretary of State, Air Ministry, 23 December 1952.
106. Ibid.
107. Ibid.
108. Ibid., Minute by the Air Ministry Director of Policy (A.S.), 12 January 1953.
109. Ibid., Minute by the Assistant Chief of the Air Staff, 24 March 1953.
110. Ibid., Minute by Air Vice-Marshal G. Tuttle, Assistant Chief of the Air Staff (O.R.), 20 January 1953.
111. Ibid.
112. Ibid., Draft Letter to the Under Secretary of State, War Office, from the Air Ministry, 4 July 1953.
113. Ibid.
114. Ibid.

115. PRO WO 32/13525, The Army Council: Light Aircraft Support for the Army, Paper by the Deputy Chief of the Imperial General Staff for Consideration at a Future Meeting, 26 August, 1953.
116. Ibid.
117. Ibid.
118. Ibid.
119. Ibid.
120. Ibid.
121. Ibid.
122. PRO DEFE 11/79, Letter from the Secretary of State for War to the Minister of Defence, 24 May 1954.
123. Ibid.
124. Ibid.
125. Ibid.
126. Ibid.
127. Ibid., Service Ministers' Committee: Extract from S.M./M (54) 7th Meeting Held on 31 May 1954.
128. Ibid., Letter from the Secretary of State for Air to the Minister of Defence, 25 May 1954.
129. Ibid.
130. Farrar-Hockley, *Army in the Air*, p. 175.
131. Ibid.
132. G.S. Hislop, 'Activities of Fairey, Westland and BEA', p. 127.
133. Wood, *Project Cancelled*, p. 110.
134. Taylor and Allward, *Westland 50*, p. 112.
135. Ibid.
136. *Keesing's Contemporary Archives*, 1959–1960 (London: Keesing's, 1960) 125420.
137. Taylor, *Fairey Aircraft*, p. 410.
138. 'Rotodyne Report', p. 935.
139. PRO AIR 2/10797, Minute from Air Commodore A.J. Kirkpatrick (DOR(A)) on the Development of the Fairey Rotodyne, 3 October 1955. BEA was unaware of War Office heavy-lift proposals then under discussion with Air Ministry Officials.
140. Ibid.
141. Ibid.
142. Wood, *Project Cancelled*, p. 103.
143. PRO AVIA 65/6, Minutes of a Meeting held on 30 June 1953 in the House of Commons to discuss Development and Production of Helicopters in the UK, 30 June 1953.
144. Dowling, *RAF Helicopters*, p. 106.
145. Ibid, Letter from P. Masefield, Chief Executive, BEA, to Mr L.J. Dunnett, Ministry of Supply, 27 April 1953.
146. Ibid., Minute to the Ministry of Supply Under-Secretary (Air) from the Assistant Secretary (Air), 29 April 1953.
147. Ibid., Letter from Lord Douglas of Kirtleside, Chairman, BEA, to the Minister of Civil Aviation, 23 September 1953.
148. Ibid.
149. Ibid., Letter from P.G. Masefield, Chief Executive, BEA, to L.J. Dunnett, Deputy Secretary, MoS, undated.
150. Ibid., Letter from Minister of Transport and Civil Aviation to the Minister of Supply, 11 January 1954.
151. Ibid.
152. Ibid.
153. Ibid.
154. Ibid.

155. Ibid.
156. Ibid.
157. Ibid.
158. Ibid.
159. Ibid., Comments by the Minister of Transport and Civil Aviation contained in Notes of a Meeting Held on 10 March 1954.
160. Second Report with Evidence taken before Subcommittee E of the Committee of Session 1956–57, The Supply of Military Aircraft, *HCP 34* (London: HMSO, 1956), p. vii.
161. PRO AVIA 65/6, Minutes from a Meeting Held on 30 June 1953 in the House of Commons to Discuss Development and Production of Helicopters in the UK, 30 June 1953.
162. Ibid., p. viii.
163. Ibid.
164. Ibid., cited in Rotating-Wing Aircraft, by Ministry of Supply Air 2(a), 5 March 1954.
165. Ibid.
166. Ibid.
167. Ibid.
168. Ibid., Letter from L.J. Dunnet, Deputy Secretary (C), Ministry of Supply, to Sir George Cribbett, Ministry of Transport and Civil Aviation, 31 December 1953.
169. Ibid., Comments by the Deputy Secretary (C) of the Ministry of Supply, contained in Notes of a Meeting held on 10 March 1954.
170. Ibid., Letter to L.J. Dunnett, Under Secretary (Air), Ministry of Supply, from the Aircraft Division, The Bristol Aeroplane Company Ltd., 13 April 1953.
171. Ibid.
172. Ibid.
173. Ibid., Letter to L.S. Dunnett, Under Secretary (Air), Ministry of Supply from the Aircraft Division, the Bristol Aircraft Company Ltd., 5 May 1953.
174. Ibid.
175. Ibid., Rotating-Wing Aircraft, by Air 2(a), 5 March 1954.
176. Ibid.
177. Ibid. Of the 48 US flying helicopter prototypes, 12 programmes proceeded to quantity production. In the case of the UK, just one of the seven projects that had reached the prototype stage was in quantity production.
178. Wood, *Project Cancelled*, p. 98.
179. PRO AVIA 65/6, Memorandum on Westland Helicopter Design and Development, September 1953.
180. Ibid.
181. Ibid.
182. Ibid.
183. For more details, see O. Fitzwilliams, 'Westland Helicopter Activities', pp. 117–20; and, PRO AVIA 54/803, Westland Proposals for High-Speed Helicopters (1952). The 'Multi-Engined Design' was outlined in Westland Brochure B.128. The design was based on two Alvis Leonides engines mounted on the nose of an S-55 fuselage.
184. PRO AVIA 65/6, Memorandum on Westland Helicopter Design and Development, September 1953. Outlined in Westland Brochure B.131, the design was based initially on four, but later two Leonides engines.
185. Ibid. 'Project W.81' was outlined in Westland Brochure B.132. The design was based on cabin-roof-mounted Armstrong Siddeley Mamba engines, and a model was exhibited at the 1951 Society of British Aircraft Constructors Show.
186. Ibid. Outlined in Westland Brochure B.141, this was a three-engine design with an estimated payload of 45 passengers at speeds in excess of 200 knots.
187. Ibid. Outlined in Westland Brochure B.148, the 'Widgeon' was a refined and updated version of the Sikorsky-designed S-51. The 'Widgeon' included a redesigned cabin

and enhancements to S-55 rotor technology that increased payload and range.

188. Ibid. This project was outlined in Westland Brochure B.152.
189. Ibid.
190. Ibid.
191. Ibid.
192. Ibid.
193. Ibid.
194. Ibid., Memorandum from AS/Air (2) to US (Air), 'Extension of Manufacturing Licence Agreement by Westland Aircraft Ltd: Financial and Policy Considerations', 7 October 1953.
195. Ibid., The Helicopter Development Position: Minutes of a Meeting held on 18 October 1953.
196. Ibid., Memorandum from AS/Air (2) to US (Air), Extension of Manufacturing Licence Agreement by Westland Aircraft Ltd: Financial and Policy Considerations, 7 October 1953.
197. Ibid.
198. Ibid.
199. Ibid.
200. Ibid., The Helicopter Development Position: Minutes of a Meeting held on 18 October 1953.
201. Ibid., Rotary-Wing Aircraft, by Air 2(A), 5 March 1954.
202. Ibid.
203. Ibid.
204. Ibid.
205. Ibid.
206. Ibid.
207. Ibid.
208. Ibid. Comments by the Minister of Supply in Notes of a Meeting Held on 10 March 1954.
209. M. Edmonds, 'The Higher Organisation of Defence in Britain, 1945-85: The Federal-Unification Debate', in M. Edmonds (ed.), *The Defence Equation: British Military Systems Policy, Planning and Performance* (Brassey's: London, 1986), p. 13.
210. PRO AVIA 65/6, Letter to PDSR (A) from US (Air), 24 April 1953.
211. Ibid., Rotary-Wing Aircraft by Air 2(A), 5 March 1954.
212. Ibid.
213. Ibid., Minute from US/(Air) B to AS/Air B2, 2 November 1955.
214. PRO AVIA 65/723, Minute from the Deputy Secretary of the Ministry of Supply to the Minister of Supply, 30 November 1955.
215. Ibid., MoS Helicopter Programme, undated.
216. Ibid., Minute from the Deputy Secretary of the Ministry of Supply to the Minister of Supply, 30 November 1955.
217. Ibid.
218. Ibid., Minute from the Minister of Supply to the Deputy Secretary of the Ministry of Supply, 20 December 1955.
219. Ibid., Ministry of Defence – Defence Research Policy Committee, Note by the Ministry of Supply on the Helicopter Programme, 24 November 1955.
220. Ibid.
221. Ibid.
222. Ibid., Minute by the MoS Deputy Secretary (C), 30 November 1955.
223. Ibid., Ministry of Defence – Defence Research Policy Committee, Note by the Ministry of Supply on the Helicopter Programme, 24 November 1955.
224. Ibid., Minute by the MoS Deputy Secretary (C), 30 November 1955.

6

Helicopter Developments, 1955–60

Ministerial endorsement of the March 1954 'Rotary-Wing Aircraft' report had reaffirmed MoS policies of 'getting on' rather than 'getting out' of government-sponsored 'all-British' development, and attempting to preclude further Westland licensed production. By 23 March 1960, however, the industrial and policy scenarios had undergone a quantum shift: with UK government endorsement, Westland had acquired or taken over the helicopter interests of Saro, Bristol and Fairey, and emerged as Britain's sole helicopter designer and manufacturer.

The factors leading to Westland's emergence as the single united helicopter manufacturer resulted from an intensification of the underlying post-1945 trends. In 1956, Westland acquired a further licence for the Sikorsky S-58 helicopter. This agreement led to decisive orders that consolidated Westland's manufacturing supremacy. Moreover, increasing MoS recognition that Westland's corporate strategy was not merely to replicate Sikorsky equipment, but also to 'anglicise' and qualitatively improve US-sourced designs, led to official acceptance and backing for this new form of 'indigenous' helicopter technology. Crucially, therefore, a turning point after 1955 was Westland's absorption into MoS helicopter industrial policy. Conversely, Westland's success in satisfying UK production demand, the shift in MoS industrial policy to include Westland, and recurring bureaucratic impediments in the 'Indigenous Procurement Process', all compounded the demand and resource problems afflicting rival 'all-British' development.

FIRMS AND PROJECTS

Between December 1955 and Westland's absorption of Saro, Bristol, and Fairey in February 1960, only one major structural change occurred in the British helicopter industry. After the MoS decision to cancel its long-term commitment to the Percival P.74,[1] contract development continued until July 1956. Following an unsuccessful attempt to flight test the P.74 prototype in late 1956,[2] and with no prospects for further MoS funding, Percival withdrew from the helicopter field. After 1956, therefore, the restructured British helicopter industry comprised the four teams at Bristol, Fairey, Saro and Westland.

In the immediate aftermath of the December 1955 MoS helicopter programme cuts, eight projects remained. The Bristol Helicopter Division had two commitments: manufacture and refinement of the single-rotor Type 171 Sycamore;[3] and development of the tandem-rotor Type 173 and associated RN (B191) and RAF (B192) variants.[4] Fairey's major project was the Rotodyne,[5] though small-scale private venture development of the tip-jet Ultra-Light[6] was continued after the 1955 cancellation of MoS R&D contracts. The Saro Helicopter Division focused on refinement and manufacture of Skeeter[7] variants. Finally, in addition to scale manufacture of the S-55 Whirlwind,[8] Westland's work was extended in 1954 to include two new initiatives: production of the Westland-designed Widgeon derivative of the S-51 Dragonfly;[9] and incorporating main and tail-rotors, the transmission and flying controls of the Sikorsky S-56 to Westland's own heavy-lift 'Westminster' design.[10]

After 1955, in addition to numerous design studies by the industry,[11] two new helicopter projects were initiated. The first was the Saro P.531.[12] During 1956, Saro's Helicopter Division commenced design of a general-purpose turbine-powered light helicopter, intended primarily as a Skeeter replacement. Saro's initial approach was to use existing Skeeter components and the first prototype with a Blackburn Turmo 325 shp (shaft horse power) engine flew on 18 July 1958.[13] The second 1956 venture was Westland's extension of its S-55 license to include manufacture in the UK of the Sikorsky S-58 helicopter.[14] The result was that, by late 1956, some ten projects were in train at British helicopter firms.

This spectrum of projects formed discrete market segments. In the 'light' helicopter sector, with the Skeeter and P.531 projects, Saro occupied a niche sector immune from UK rivals. Likewise, the 'medium' weight Westland S-55 Whirlwind (3,402 kg auw) had no domestic competitor. Following Westland's 1953 completion of its production run of 139 S-51 Dragonflies, Bristol's Type 171 Sycamore (2,449 kg auw) was the sole project in the 'light-medium' sector. However, in the remaining two categories there were competing projects. In the 'heavy-lift' sector, the Fairey Rotodyne (14,969 kg auw) and the Westland Westminster (14,969 kg auw) were contending types. In the 'medium-heavy' field, Westland's decision to produce the Sikorsky S-58 (estimated auw of 5,715–6,124 kg) under licence introduced a rival for the Bristol Type 173/B191/B192 series (estimated auw of 6,124–8,616 kg).

Finally, Bristol, Fairey and Saro continued with their core post-war expectations that in-house 'all-British' development would bring government R&D support and protected domestic markets. In contrast, the Westland Board calculated that the strategy of accessing the US manufacturing lead through licensed production, 'anglicising' American designs, and 'indigenising' the know-how obtained through technology transfer in Westland's own in-house designs would continue to provide the crucial commercial edge. Westland was again correct in its core assessment.

BRITISH HELICOPTER PRODUCTION, 1955–60

Between 1955 and 1960, two MoS-sponsored 'all-British' helicopter projects were in scale production. The Bristol Helicopter Division consolidated earlier service orders[15] with new contracts for the Type 171 Sycamore Mk14. Cumulative sales reached 175 units when production ceased in 1959. Following the 1955 cancellation of the Fairey Ultra-Light, Saro finally secured Skeeter orders to meet the War Office Air Observation Post (AOP) requirements. When Saro's Skeeter contracts were completed in July 1960, production had totalled 88 units in a range of variants.[16]

Despite the moderate commercial success of its competitors, Westland remained the dominant UK helicopter manufacturer. Westland's combined orders for the S-51 Dragonfly and the S-55 Whirlwind accounted for 59.3 per cent of the UK helicopter industry's unit production,[17] and approximately 74.3 per cent of total sales revenue.[18] By 1960, in addition to its sales performance, Westland had made important qualitative technical improvements to the Sikorsky S-55 parent version. Westland's Series 1 variants of the S-55 (Mks 1 to 4) had differed little from the Sikorsky-built versions, and included imported American 600hp Pratt & Whitney Wasp engines. However, in the Series 2 variants (Mks 5, 7 and 8),[19] Westland's value-added contribution was to re-engine the S-55 with the British-built Alvis Leonides Mk 155 powerplant. Finally, in the Series 3 (Mks 9, 10 and 12)[20] the firm's technical achievement was the development of a turboshaft-engined S-55 version through the incorporation of the Bristol Siddeley Gnome H.1000 engine.

A more important development was Westland's 1956 licence for the Sikorsky S-58 helicopter. Despite competition from the MoS-sponsored Bristol Type 173/B191/B192 series, technology transfer again provided Westland with a mechanism with which to win UK service contracts for the S-58 Wessex.

Westland S-58 Orders

The Admiralty's overriding objective in 1955 was rapid and cost-effective procurement of an anti-submarine helicopter to meet Requirement NA 43.[21] Previously, during June 1953, the Admiralty had agreed to order 65 Bristol B191s as part of the inter-departmental Air Ministry/Admiralty purchase to meet NA 43, but with some reservations about the cost of the project.[22] In early 1956, however, the Admiralty cancelled its B191 contracts and placed a new order with Westland for a development batch of 12 S-58 Wessex helicopters with Napier Gazelle turboshaft engines.[23] By March 1958, Royal Navy production orders for 40 S-58s followed;[24] orders which paved the way for further sales to the Royal Navy, RAF, civil operators and export markets,[25] and an eventual S-58 production run of 369 units.

Westland's ability to win S-58 contracts reflected the now-established three-stage process. First, through the S-58 licence, Westland would obtain a competitive edge by accessing the US design and manufacturing lead over its British rival. Secondly, factors in the 'Licensed Production Procurement Process' undermined the 'buy-British' tenets of declaratory MoS helicopter industrial policy, and facilitated Westland's crucial Admiralty S-58 contracts. Thirdly, Westland consolidated these initial contracts because of its success in 'anglicising' and 'indigenising' the know-how obtained through technology transfer.

By obtaining the Sikorsky S-58 licence, Westland again acquired the US helicopter industry's lead, measured by innovation incentives, production expertise and scale of output. In contrast to the limited production success of Westland's UK competitors, by the end of 1954 the US helicopter industry had achieved total sales of $155 million, a sales backlog of $550 million, a work force of 14,460 with 11 helicopter types in scale production and a further 23 types at the prototype or design stage.[26] The S-58 licence provided Westland with access to know-how from an American industry whose exports alone exceeded the cumulative production output of Westland's domestic UK rivals.[27]

In extending its links with Sikorsky, Westland consolidated and strengthened its relationship with the major US helicopter firm. Between 1946 and 1954, Sikorsky's cumulative production amounted to approximately 1,200 helicopters, or 35 per cent of the US helicopter industry total.[28] By 1954, Sikorsky's design and manufacturing workforce of 6,815 personnel accounted for 47 per cent of the US industry total.[29] In the same year Sikorsky achieved annual sales of $52,300,000 (33 per cent of the US industry total) and by 31 December 1954 the firm had a sales backlog of $260,000,000 (47 per cent of the US industry total).[30] By obtaining the S-58 licence, therefore, Westland had again acquired a mechanism to exploit the experience, investment and technological gains made by the premier American helicopter manufacturer.

Sikorsky's development of the S-58 helicopter was based on US military R&D support, large-scale production orders, and low-risk incremental refinements to the proven S-55 configuration. In early 1952 the US Navy (USN) had formulated a requirement for a larger and more up-to-date ASW helicopter to replace its Sikorsky S-55s.[31] The pressures for the requirement included USN concerns about S-55 performance limitations, primarily its limited range, while the 'small useful load which could be carried severely restricted its usefulness in operations'.[32] The requirement specified a larger helicopter capable of carrying a pilot, co-pilot, sonar equipment plus ordnance with a three-hour flight duration, and dimensions compatible with storage in and operation from battleships and cruisers.[33] By 27 February 1952, the US Chief of Naval Operations had directed the Bureau of Aeronautics (BuAer) 'to proceed without delay with a programme for the development of the Sikorsky HRS aircraft with the large engine – ASW configured,'[34] specifying service release to the USN in January 1955. On 5 December 1952, the Chief of Naval Operations also informed BuAer of a high-priority US Marine Corps requirement for a utility helicopter of similar dimensions, for which a further order for 33 S-58s (designated HUS-1) was placed.[35] Consequently, by the end of 1952, Sikorsky had received both government development resources from the US Armed Services and had the prospects of large-scale domestic military orders.

Sikorsky's design strategy after 1952 was to build on its established technical approach. The S-58 retained the basic S-55 layout, but included the more powerful 1,525 hp Wright R-1820-84 piston engine, an upgraded transmission system,[36] and modifications to the tailboom configuration.[37] With this limited development risk, on 8 March 1954 the first flight of a Sikorsky S-58 prototype was achieved. After US Navy evaluation, the HSS-1 variant entered production on 20 September 1954[38] and began operational service with the USN in August 1955. Consequently, with the S-58 licence, Westland acquired blueprints for a proven ASW production helicopter that had been developed with extensive US government resources and large-scale production orders. By contrast, at the same time, the 'all-British' MoS-sponsored Bristol B191 was at the early prototype testing stage, and severe engine and transmission problems were hampering development.[39] The S-58 licence, therefore, meant that Westland had again obtained a mechanism to exploit the American technological lead over a competing British design.

However, Westland's ability to win UK service orders against the rival Bristol project lay not only in its access to this lead but also on account of the bureaucratic objectives of the organisations in the 'Licensed Production Procurement Process'. Until late 1955, the MoS had 'made it perfectly clear that the [Royal Navy] anti-submarine task had been allocated to the Bristol Company and that there was no interest in any Westland proposal'.[40] By December 1955, however, the Admiralty had informed the MoS of its wish to cancel the B191 contract in favour of a purchase of Westland-built S-58s because it considered the latter 'an apparently cheaper solution of much lower risk'.[41] On technical grounds, Admiralty officials were concerned about development difficulties on the B191 project. After 1953, technical problems had affected the Leonides Major powerplant, and successive airframe modifications had increased the overall weight to the extent that by 1955, the Admiralty had concluded the B191 was 'too large' for carrier-borne operations.[42] Moreover, they had also identified additional 'difficulties anticipated in handling large twin-rotor helicopters on carriers, particularly in conjunction with fixed-wing aircraft'.[43] On financial grounds, their estimates were that the

> ...anti-submarine helicopter requirement could be met with substantially (perhaps £10M) less cost to public funds using...[the S-58]...than with the 191 – even allowing for the cost of development of the [S-58] which might be from £1.5M to £5M depending on the choice of engine.[44]

Consequently, despite the earlier MoS policy on Westland's proposals, Admiralty assessments of operational requirements and cost meant that the RN posed no protectionist barrier to Westland S-58 orders.

The second bureaucratic factor facilitating Westland orders was the position of HM Treasury. Throughout late 1955 and early 1956, the Treasury's preoccupation was to limit aircraft R&D and production expenditure. Consequently, the predicted cost savings anticipated by replacing the Admiralty B191 contracts with an S-58 order were entirely acceptable to the Treasury. Moreover, enthusiasm about potential economies provided by the Westland alternative led Treasury officials to suggest that the Air Ministry should cancel its outstanding Bristol B192 contracts and follow the Admiralty's approach on 27 February 1956.[45] On the basis of comparative S-58 and B191 costs, Westland had thereby circumvented the second potential organisational impediment to orders.

Paradoxically, the final bureaucratic facilitator was the MoS. Despite its declaratory 'buy-British' policy, the MoS could do little to oppose the Admiralty's cancellation of its B191 order because of the overwhelming operational and financial arguments in favour of the Westland-built S-58. The MoS were aware that the Admiralty were

> ...showing reluctance to maintain their order for [Bristol] 191's, not because its performance falls below the requirement, but because of difficulties anticipated in handling large twin-rotor helicopters on carriers, particularly in conjunction with fixed-wing aircraft.[46]

Moreover, faced with the December 1955 financial stringency that precipitated the Percival P.74 and Fairey Ultra-Light cancellations,[47] MoS advice on the Defence Research Policy Committee's submission on the S-58 was that

> the Navy wish to have this aircraft instead of the Bristol 191 as their anti-submarine helicopter for operation from carriers, and since the use of the [S-58] Wessex in place of the 191 should result in a saving on naval votes of some £10-£12M, it is considered that the development cost of this additional project should be accepted...[48]

Consequently, with MoS endorsement, Westland had satisfied the final bureaucratic hurdle in the 'Licensed Production Procurement Process', and secured vital first orders.

Subsequent S-58 contracts, however, were attributable to Westland's success in 'indigenising' the technology that the Sikorsky licence had provided. On receipt of the 1956 licence, Westland began the process of 'anglicising' the S-58 design rather than merely replicating the Sikorsky blueprints. Westland elected to adopt a low-risk technical approach, limiting 'anglicisation' to the incorporation of British-built turboshaft engines into the proven Sikorsky airframe. A measure of the limited technical uncertainty in Westland's strategy was that in the space of four years, the firm had succeeded in 'indigenising' the S-58 design when the Napier Gazelle HAS Mk1 Wessex variant entered service with the Royal Navy.[49] The significance of Westland's low-risk approach, was that the firm was able to produce the S-58 HAS Mk 1 within original 1956 MoS lead-time predictions for the first quarter of 1960[50] and with no cost escalation on original 1956 estimates.[51]

This 'anglicisation' strategy was crucial for subsequent UK production orders because it enabled Westland to tailor its designs to specific Service requirements. After the first HAS Mk 1 entered RN service, Admiralty orders for a further 129 were placed with Westland.[52] In addition, by 1960 Westland began development of a twin-engined Wessex variant (Mk 2), employing two coupled 1,350 shp Bristol Siddeley H.1200 Gnome turboshaft engines to meet specific RAF tactical transport, casualty evacuation and general duties requirements.[53] A measure of the firm's success in incremental 'anglicisation' and 'indigenisation' was contained in the 1965 Plowden Report

> Westlands have the most successful and consistent profit record of all the major groups in the aircraft industry . . . They have . . . avoided research and development risks which unduly strained their finance; and they have rarely had to incorporate in any new venture more than one major development. New types they have taken on have had either new engine installation, a new airframe, or a new major system, but not normally a combination of these.[54]

With its S-58 licence, therefore, Westland repeated the pattern established with its earlier S-51 and S-55 ventures: accessing state of the art know-how from Sikorsky, successfully winning UK service orders on the basis of this technical edge, and 'anglicising' Sikorsky technology to compete for subsequent UK requirements. It was this approach with the S-58 Wessex, coupled with Westland's existing S-55 orders, that enabled the firm to dominate UK helicopter manufacturing output between 1955 and 1960.

CONSTRAINTS AFFECTING THE 'ALL-BRITISH' MOS-SPONSORED HELICOPTER PROGRAMME, 1955–60

Westland's manufacturing success was only one factor accounting for overall patterns of UK helicopter R&D and production after 1955. The second was the recurring problems that had plagued MoS-sponsored 'all-British' projects throughout the post-war period. After 1955, however, events entered a new and decisive phase. Shifts in MoS helicopter industrial policy, the availability of Westland-manufactured American technology, and bureaucratic factors in the 'Indigenous Procurement Process', together undermined concerted MoS R&D funding and domestic UK production orders for 'all-British' projects. When confronted with these constraints, Bristol, Fairey and Saro were increasingly reluctant to invest scarce private venture capital and resources to force the pace of 'all-British' development. The result was that these barriers to 'all-British' innovation again enhanced Westland's relative position in the UK helicopter market.

MoS Helicopter Industrial Policy, 1955–60

Until late 1955, the two tenets of MoS helicopter industrial policy were to support 'all-British' development, and to oppose Westland's licensed-production strategy on the grounds that the latter would make 'nonsense' of Ministry attempts to stimulate 'indigenous' designs.[55] By December 1955, however, though the MoS did not alter its declaratory policy, the significant shifts declared Ministry recognition that Westland was acquiring in-house design expertise through technology transfer and acceptance that the firm had become the *de facto* leader in British helicopter production.

The December 1955 DRPC-imposed budgetary reductions leading to the Percival P.74 and Fairey Ultra-Light cancellations had been crucial in prompting an MoS review of the status of UK helicopter firms. What emerged was an MoS re-evaluation of Westland's activities, and MoS acknowledgement that licensed production was a mechanism for technology indigenisation. The revised MoS assessment was that

> Westland have successfully produced in quantity the S-51 and S-55 under licence from Sikorsky in America; although they have entered for various design competitions, they have not so far built a helicopter to completely original design; their latest proposals for versions of the Sikorsky S-58 and S-56 with British gas turbine engines are however less slavish copies of the original than the S-51 and S-55, and their private venture Widgeon though based on the S-51, has some original features.[56]

While the MoS view was still that Bristol had 'much the strongest design team,'[57] the importance of the review was official recognition that Westland was acquiring an in-house development capability through its relationship with Sikorsky.

The outcome was an MoS decision to incorporate Westland in its helicopter industrial policy. Critically, this decision was not only premised on the short-term financial expediency that led the Ministry to support the Admiralty's decision to procure Westland S-58s, but also on wider MoS acceptance that

Westland had become an important constituent of the UK helicopter industry which warranted government R&D support. The Ministry's revised assessment was that Westland had 'shown willingness to put their own money' into helicopter development, though it was 'doubtful whether they could manage the [S-58] wholly as a private venture'.[58] The resulting analysis was that

> MoS support for the development of the [S-58] would . . . prevent a problem arising at Westland's . . . While the disappearance of Westland's helicopter team in the absence of any project beyond the S-55 might strengthen the surviving teams unless the staff were lost to the industry altogether, the disappearance of an organisation which has produced and sold more helicopters and earned more foreign exchange by doing so than any other British helicopter maker would rightly be a matter for considerable regret and public criticism . . . it seems reasonable that provided the Admiralty's interest is sustained, MoS should support to some extent the development of the [S-58].[59]

The significance of the November 1955 scrutiny was that in addition to the cancellation of key MoS projects, Westland had effectively been absorbed into the MoS helicopter programme. The extent of new MoS thinking was the Ministry's evaluation of the industrial picture after the review

> On the assumption that the UK could not afford to abdicate entirely from the helicopter field, a reasonable programme which would make the best use of expenditure on helicopters to date and experience already gained, and which would be tailored to our resources, could be achieved consisting of three major projects, the Bristol 173-191-192 and the Rotodyne, including civil versions of both, and the Westland [S-58] Wessex.[60]

What was crucial was the MoS perception that the resulting programme would consist 'of one project at each of the three *major* firms,'[61] namely Bristol, Fairey and Westland. In December 1955, therefore, Westland's achievement was its inclusion in MoS helicopter industrial policy and unhindered access to government R&D resources and domestic markets. Conversely, the MoS policy shift had zero-sum implications for Westland's rivals relying on MoS sponsorship to develop 'all-British' designs, as Bristol, Fairey and Saro were confronted with new competition for scarce MoS R&D resources and domestic production orders.

The second major factor that led to a reshaping of MoS helicopter policy and which had adverse implications for 'all-British' projects occurred in 1956. During February 1956, the House of Commons Select Committee on Estimates was tasked to investigate whether value for money had been obtained 'for the large sums of money voted for the supply of military aircraft'[62] after 1945. *The Supply of Military Aircraft* report[63] that emerged was the first substantive public scrutiny of the performance of post-war aircraft procurement policy. As a whole, the report was critical, pointing to serious deficiencies in key areas including aircraft supply administrative arrangements, policies towards aircraft research, as well as identifying evidence of excessive duplication in aircraft development and questionable contracting and project management procedures.

More important was the specific indictment of MoS post-war helicopter industrial policy. The Select Committee was 'surprised' that 10 out of a total of 26 aircraft research programmes initiated after 1945 related to helicopters.[64] The Committee's assessment was that 'insufficient care had been shown in limiting the number of helicopter research projects'[65] and there was 'evidence also of an excessive number of helicopters being put into production'.[66] The MoS was also criticised for initiating 'too many' helicopter projects because of its reliance on the fact that '"the services had indicated . . . that they had an interest" in a [helicopter] type as a criteria for starting a project'.[67] Finally, the Committee expressed major concerns about MoS management of helicopter projects:

> The Ministry [of Supply] it seems have no criteria for deciding when a research project has gone on for long enough. Your Committee feel that there is insufficient control in this field. Once a project has been continuing for some time there are obviously powerful vested interests in keeping it going and in a few years millions of pounds may be spent.[68]

The report's overall conclusions were particularly scathing:

> Some research projects are bound to fail, that being the nature of research, and rapidly changing strategic decisions must affect service requirements, but to begin projects without ascertaining that there is likely to be a real and continuing need for them would indicate a complete failure of the Ministry to carry out what is supposed to be one of its chief functions and advantages as an ordering agent: namely, supplying technical knowledge and advice to the services.[69]

The significance of this public criticism was that it had a profound impact on MoS R&D policy towards 'all-British' helicopter projects after 1956. The principal effects were that it forced the MoS to challenge for the first time its support for 'all-British' helicopter development proposals from industry and rendered new proposals increasingly reliant on firms' private-venture resources. An example of the downstream effects of the report occurred in 1958, following recommendations from the MoS Assistant Director, Royal Navy (1), that the services should urgently produce firm statements of requirements to cover the Fairey Ultra-Light, the Whirlwind/Sycamore replacement and the Army's heavy-lift helicopter requirements.[70] A less than enthusiastic response of the MoS Under-Secretary (Air B) typified the increasing Ministry reluctance to endorse funding for development suggestions from industry:

> The Ministry [of Supply] . . . has already been criticised once for allowing too many different helicopter developments to proceed at public expense. We must ensure that this does not happen again.[71]

The consequences of the shifts in MoS helicopter policy during late 1955 and early 1956 were severe for those firms that had adopted the in-house 'all-British' helicopter development route. Bristol, Fairey and Saro had assumed that they would receive large-scale MoS R&D resources and domestic market protection from Westland. The reality was that they were now confronted with MoS-sanctioned Westland competition for government R&D funding and manufacturing orders. Moreover, increasing Westland rivalry was compounded by tighter controls over MoS development resources in the light of *The Supply of Military Aircraft* report. Bristol, Fairey and Saro, therefore, lost a traditional post-war bureaucratic ally and the *carte blanche* MoS commitment to 'all-British' technology. The corollary was that Westland was the net beneficiary of this MoS policy shift.

Admiralty Helicopter Demand, 1955–60

A further factor compounding the lack of production demand for the MoS-sponsored 'all-British' helicopter programme was the Admiralty's procurement preferences. Between 1955 and 1960, the Royal Navy remained the major UK purchaser of production helicopters and Admiralty helicopter purchasing had a remarkable continuity with the earlier post-war period: orders were almost exclusively for Westland licensed-produced types to the extent that by 1958, 97.3 per cent of their helicopters had been sourced from Westland while only 2.7 per cent were purchased from other UK suppliers.[72] The effect was that after 1955, Admiralty helicopter requirements again undermined the release of large-scale MoS R&D resources and development priority for MoS-sponsored 'all-British' projects, further enhancing Westland's relative position in UK helicopter markets by default.

Typical here was the 1955 decision to cancel its Bristol B191 orders in favour of the Westland S-58 Wessex. The first implication was that Westland had succeeded in gaining orders that enabled it to consolidate its market position at the expense of a rival 'all-British' project. Equally significant, the Admiralty's B191 cancellation was to place the residual Air Ministry order for 25 B192 variants under constant Treasury financial pressure. Shortly after the Admiralty's withdrawal of support, on 27 February 1956, the Treasury 'tried to get the Air Ministry to drop their requirement for the B.192, taking the Wessex [instead]'.[73] Again, during 1957, major Treasury concerns

> ...existed on the desirability of proceeding with the development of the B.192 in respect of a production order of only 25 aircraft and the Ministry of Supply were asked... [by HM Treasury]... to explore the possibility of buying some foreign helicopter to meet the RAF requirement and also to evaluate its production cost on assumptions relating to the size of the B.192 order and the cost of foreign helicopters.[74]

The core problem that the Admiralty cancellation generated was the diseconomies of scale that the reduced order had for unit-cost estimates on the Bristol project. During February 1954, when the initial Admiralty and Air Ministry orders had been placed, total production cost estimates for the combined order of 90 helicopters was £6.8m, or £75,555 per unit.[75] By April 1958, total production cost estimates for the Air Ministry's residual order for 25 B192s had risen to £6.4m, or £257,000 per unit.[76] After 1955, in addition to ongoing pressure on the Air Ministry for B192 cancellation in favour of the Westland S-58 Wessex, the impact of this cost escalation made the Treasury increasingly reluctant to authorise MoS development expenditure on the Bristol project.[77] The result, therefore, was that the Admiralty's preference for the Westland alternative had exacerbated the problems for a major 'all-British' project by undermining both MoS R&D resources and manufacturing orders.

By 1958, longer-term Admiralty helicopter requirements had crystallised and again, the clear RN preference was for Westland-built helicopters. Admiralty requirements fell into four categories: Anti-Submarine Warfare, General Purpose, Commando and 'Future Developments'. For Royal Navy medium-weight anti-submarine requirements, in-service Westland S-55 Mk 7s provided sufficient capability. For its foreseeable needs, the Admiralty's 1958 assessment was that 'there are at present no future anti-submarine requirements beyond [S-58] Wessex development possibilities'.[78] The 1958 Navy Estimates[79] had announced the establishment of a Royal Marine Commando Carrier equipped with troop-carrying helicopters. Here, the Admiralty preference was for further Westland S-58s, as the 'role will be more clearly defined in the near future, and a special Commando version of the Wessex may be the outcome'.[80] For longer-term requirements, the Admiralty view was that

> other roles such as troop carrying and communications are likely to emphasise increased range and safety. Development to meet this requirement in the medium-weight bracket should aim at a twin-turbine version of such aircraft as the Wessex in the Commando role where a considerable increase in range could be achieved by single-engine cruise.[81]

By contrast, in 1958 the Admiralty's interest in the array of MoS-sponsored 'all-British' projects remained only marginal. Though the Royal Navy briefly investigated the Fairey Ultra-Light as a potential light anti-submarine helicopter, the requirement was only for evaluation purposes and the project remained a private venture at Fairey.[82] Likewise, during 1958 the RN was involved in formulating a joint service requirement for a general purpose helicopter which was written around the Saro P.531 design, but at this stage the specification was in a preliminary phase, and P.531 development at Saro remained on a private-venture basis.[83] In essence, therefore, the MoS were supporting an array of 'all-British' designs for which the Admiralty had no firm production demand nor development priority.

Air Ministry and War Office Relations, 1955–60

Between 1945 and 1955, there were major differences in helicopter procurement arrangements for land forces in the USA and the UK. On the one hand, the relative autonomy of the US Army to purchase helicopters on its own behalf had resulted in a major expansion of army rotary-wing aviation after the Korean War. In doctrinal terms, by the mid-1950s senior US army officers including Generals Gavin, Ridgeway and Maxwell Taylor began developing a general theory of air mobility which stressed 'the importance of cavalry actions such as reconnaissance, screening, exploitation and pursuit' which they 'believed would best be performed by units equipped with armed, troop-carrying and supply helicopters'.[84] On the other hand, over the same period purchasing arrangements in the UK meant that British Army helicopter requirements and orders had suffered because of the hierarchy of spending priorities within the Air Ministry.

After 1955, two substantive changes did occur in the policies and processes affecting British Air Ministry and War Office helicopter procurement. The first was Air Ministry acceptance that the helicopter offered considerable operational potential. Following a gradual shift in Air Ministry thinking, by 1955

> official attitudes had changed considerably: it was now recognised that there was an immediate need to put an adequate number of helicopters into service not only to gain wide operating experience but also to stimulate industry . . .[85]

This policy revision reflected RAF assessments that helicopter reliability had improved considerably and recognition of the utility of helicopter operations in the campaign in Malaya.[86] The second major innovation was the Air Ministry's decision to cede operational control and procurement responsibility for army helicopters up to 4,000 lb all-up-weight to the War Office, a move that paved the way for the formation of the Army Air Corps (AAC) in 1957.[87]

Prima facie, two of the major bureaucratic impediments that had contributed to the post-war lack of production demand and development resources for the MoS-sponsored 'all-British' helicopter programme had been removed. However, the reality was very different. On the one hand, the new Air Ministry enthusiasm was for readily available Westland licensed-produced variants of Sikorsky designs, rather than for 'all-British' alternatives. On the other, though RAF and Army helicopter production demand increased after 1955, a further organisation in the 'Indigenous Procurement Process', HM Treasury, imposed purchasing limitations that adversely affected investment and production contracts for 'all-British' types.

Before 1955, Air Ministry helicopter orders were predominantly for 'all-British' designs. Though the Air Ministry had procured 16 Westland-built

S-51s, the major RAF contracts had been for 93 Bristol Type 171 Sycamores, 27 Saro Skeeters and 25 Bristol B192 helicopters. After 1955, a significant shift occurred in Air Ministry purchasing patterns: all of the 205 helicopters subsequently ordered were sourced from Westland. Like the Admiralty, in the absence of an 'all-British' replacement for the S-51 and Type 171 to meet RAF search and rescue requirements, the Air Ministry placed contracts for 133 Westland S-55 Whirlwinds. In addition, by 1960, the Air Ministry had followed the Admiralty's approach and placed orders for 72 Westland S-58 Wessex helicopters.

The most significant example of the impact of Treasury-imposed constraints after 1955 affected the Air Ministry's procurement of the Bristol B192 Belvedere helicopter.[88] Following the Admiralty's 1956 decision to withdraw from the combined Royal Navy/Royal Air Force Type 173/B191/B192 contract in favour of the S-58 Wessex, the residual Air Ministry order for 25 B192 helicopters to meet OR 325[89] came under considerable Treasury pressure for cancellation. By 1960, a combination of Treasury-imposed financial stringency, development difficulties on the Bristol project, and the availability of the proven Westland S-58 Wessex led the Air Ministry to select the Westland alternative for its subsequent requirements.

Until the 1956 Admiralty B191 cancellation, the Bristol programme 'meandered without much control by the Ministry of Supply or the Treasury'.[90] The immediate impact of the Admiralty's decision to purchase the S-58 Wessex was a Treasury suggestion on 27 February 1956 that the Air Ministry should cancel its B192 orders in favour of the Westland project. The Air Ministry refused to abandon its B192 order, but the Treasury strategy was to limit expenditure on the B192 project and to press repeatedly for RAF procurement of the S-58 Wessex.

Between February 1956 and January 1957, the issue of whether to continue with the B192 order or adopt the Westland S-58 was debated extensively in the Air Council. The approach recommended by the Air Ministry Deputy Chief of the Air Staff was that the B192 order should be cancelled in favour of an S-58 Wessex buy.[91] However, this suggestion met strong opposition from the Assistant Chief of the Air Staff (OR) and the Ministry of Supply.[92] In the event, the Air Council decision was that the B192 order should stand and Treasury approval should be sought to re-engine the B192 with Napier Gazelle engines.[93] The Treasury reaction was to refuse authority for B192 re-engining[94] and to repeat the suggestion that the S-58 Wessex should be adopted to meet part of the Air Ministry requirement.[95] Though the Treasury did reluctantly acquiesce to the Air Ministry re-engining request, vital financial authority was delayed until 22 April 1958.[96]

Again during April 1958, Treasury officials put pressure on the Air Ministry to cancel the B192 order in favour of the Westland S-58 Wessex.[97] The Air Ministry's defence of the Bristol project was that contracts should be continued because 'the greater part of the expenditure on its development and production [had] already been committed'.[98] Redundancy costs on the B192 would be £3.5m, whereas introduction of the Wessex at that stage would incur at least an additional £2m expenditure.[99] However, by 1960 the combination of Treasury-imposed financial constraints affecting the B192 project and the opportunities provided by the Westland S-58 alternative forced two decisive shifts in Air Ministry policy: first, on the basis of a comparison between the projects 'after assessing relative costs and taking into account the unproven features of the [B192] Belvedere, [the Air Ministry] decided not to increase the present order'[100] for 25, and second, plans were set in train for procurement of the Westland S-58 Wessex Series 2 to meet future RAF transport requirements.[101] Consequently, between 1955 and 1960 the interaction of Treasury-driven financial stringency and Westland's production success with the S-55 Whirlwind and the S-58 Wessex undermined production demand and R&D resources for the Bristol project.

A major organisational innovation after 1955 was the Air Ministry's delegation of control and responsibility for aspects of helicopter procurement and operations to the War Office. By late 1954, two Air Ministry rationales for allowing the War Office to assume a role in helicopter procurement, subject to overriding control by the Chiefs of Staff Committee,[102] had emerged: the first was that the Air Ministry would be in a 'stronger position to keep them [the War Office] on the rails through its influence in the Chiefs of Staff Committee,[103] while the second was that the Air Ministry would benefit because 'under the existing system, when we [the Air Ministry] fail to meet their [War Office] requests we give the impression that we are influenced by selfishness or inertia rather than by the merits of the case...'.[104] By 6 May 1954, the Chief of the Air Staff (CAS) had accepted these arguments in principle, particularly the implication that the War Office Vote should bear the cost of army aircraft.[105]

Despite this 1954 shift in Air Ministry thinking, no substantive changes to the structure and procedures for procurement were to occur until late 1956, when the issues were debated at the ministerial level.[106] On 27 June 1956, however, ministerial decision was precipitated by the Vice Chief of the Air Staff's suggestion that a transfer of responsibility to the army should occur within all-up-weight limits for aircraft that 'would oblige the War Office to come to terms with the financial implications of this responsibility, at the same time relieving the Air Ministry from negotiations on their behalf with the Treasury'.[107] What resulted was War Office/Air Ministry agreement that:

i) The army should assume full responsibility for purchasing, manning, maintaining and operating unarmed aircraft used solely for its own purposes in the AOP and light liaison roles. The maximum all-up-weight – the weight of the aircraft plus whatever load was to be carried in flight – would not exceed 4,000 pounds.
ii) The Air Ministry in conjunction with the War Office would remain responsible for formulating specifications.

iii) In the field, army aircraft would be subject to the overall direction of the air force commander.[108]

By early 1957, formal approval for the transfer of light aviation procurement and operations to the War Office was sanctioned, and the Army Air Corps (AAC) was formed during early 1957.

The 1957 reorganisation illustrates two important factors. First, the scale of subsequent War Office helicopter bids indicated the extent to which pre-1957 Air Ministry purchasing controls had suppressed army production requirements. Second, the War Office's post-1957 dealings with the Treasury demonstrated new constraints that were concurrently afflicting Air Ministry attempts to procure the Bristol B192 helicopter.

Evidence of the degree to which the pre-1957 War Office/Air Ministry procurement arrangements undermined production orders for the only light UK helicopter then under development, the 'all-British' Saro Skeeter, was reflected in War Office proposals after the formation of the AAC. Before the transfer, total Air Ministry Skeeter purchases to meet Army AOP roles were 27 units.[109] After assuming purchasing responsibility, the War Office bid to the Treasury on 29 May 1957 was for an additional 31 Skeeters to equip the newly formed AOP flights. The bid was indicative of the scale of latent Army helicopter demand and, therefore, the extent to which pre-1957 procurement arrangements had stifled War Office production requirements.

Internal Treasury debates about how to respond to the War Office Skeeter bid was indicative of Treasury-imposed barriers to production orders. The Treasury were sceptical about endorsing the War Office request because of the former's assessment:

> that the Air Ministry having a much wider experience of aircraft were able to sort out the sensible and economic proposals from the over-enthusiastic pipe dreams of the military [under the pre-1957 regime]...Against this background one can only look with some caution at the proposals to expand the Army 'force' so soon after the change-over. Considering the speed with which the War Office machine usually works it is clear that they must have had this proposal in mind when the changeover was under discussion last Christmas. This may well be the sort of requirement which, for one reason or another, might never have 'got through' the Air Ministry, but which is now confidently advanced to the Treasury.[110]

The Treasury tactic was that the Air Ministry should be 'sounded out' discreetly for RAF views on the War Office proposal and the significance of the Army's timing.[111] At a meeting on 18 September 1957,[112] Treasury officials began the process of capping War Office Skeeter orders. The conclusion of the meeting was that

> ...we [the Treasury] can hardly withhold complete authority for further purchases of Skeeters, but that we should endeavour to keep purchases at as low a level as possible. This would mean restricting our authority to the minimum number of 20....[113]

Consequently, after 1955 new factors undermined R&D resources and production orders for 'all-British' MoS-sponsored helicopter projects. In the case of Air Ministry helicopter requirements, this arose because of the availability of Westland production technology and Treasury-imposed financial constraints. For War Office operational requirements, where the only UK project under 4,000 lb was the 'all-British' Saro Skeeter, earlier barriers to procurement stemming from Air Ministry control were replaced after 1957 by Treasury attempts to restrict expenditure. These trends compounded the lack of orders and investment on MoS-sponsored 'all-British' projects at precisely the stage at which Westland was consolidating its production dominance.

Civil Helicopter Requirements, 1955–60

In the civil helicopter field the situation confronting the sole 'all-British' heavy-lift design intended for commercial airline operations, the Fairey Rotodyne, was a familiar one.[114] Without military backing, BEA remained unwilling to commit themselves to firm production orders. At the same time, the MoS remained unable to release large-scale R&D for the Fairey project without a definite BEA purchasing commitment.

Under the December 1955 DRPC-imposed helicopter-programme cuts and without firm Service or civil orders, the Fairey Rotodyne was rendered wholly dependent on the MoS civil budget as a research prototype.[115] The primary reason for continued MoS support for the project was that 'the Minister [of Supply] said he regarded this as a project which it was important to keep going'.[116] However, between early 1956 and December 1957, the Rotodyne project continued to be denied development priority and orders because of what was a vicious circle. On the one hand, without extensive R&D backing, major technical problems were encountered in project development leading to an increased all-up-weight and excessive noise output from the tip-jet propulsion system;[117] on the other hand, concerned about these development difficulties and the lack of military backing for the Rotodyne, BEA was still unwilling to commit itself to issue production orders. The result was that on 31 December 1957, Treasury authorisation for the Rotodyne was discontinued and all 'Government financial support for the project was terminated'.[118] At the same time, the MoS received further confirmation from the Naval[119] and Air Staffs[120] that they had no requirement for the Rotodyne.

Between December 1957 and September 1959, the Rotodyne project became the subject of protracted negotiations between the MoS, BEA and

Fairey.[121] MoS proposals were that it would fund 50 per cent of project development costs to an upper limit of £4m from the MoS Civil Vote, on the condition that BEA order at least six Rotodynes.[122] Conversely, BEA's position was that it would only place contracts if the MoS agreed to bear all the costs of introducing the Rotodyne into service.[123] Despite correspondence from Prime Minister Macmillan to the Minister of Supply, Aubrey Jones, on 6 July 1958 saying that the 'project must not be allowed to die,'[124] no agreement on development-funding arrangements or orders was reached between the MoS, BEA and Fairey. Throughout, BEA 'refused to buy [the Rotodyne] until it could be satisfied that performance, economic and noise guarantees could be achieved'.[125]

The major implication was that until September 1959, the Fairey project remained deprived of government R&D support and without production contracts; to continue, it remained reliant on the firm's private-venture capital. The wider effect of these problems afflicting the Rotodyne was that, between 1955 and 1960, Westland's relative position in the UK helicopter market was enhanced by the constraints affecting one of its major domestic rivals.

The 'Priority Problem' for MoS-Sponsored 'All-British' Projects, 1955–60

The predicament of MoS-sponsored 'all-British' projects between 1955 and 1960 reflected remarkable continuity with the earlier post-war period: bureaucratic factors in the 'Indigenous Procurement Process' and the availability in the UK of American-designed production technology militated against production orders, R&D funding and development priority. After 1955, however, what was different was that Westland's *de facto* inclusion in the MoS helicopter programme improved the firm's already dominant position.

The effects of these trends are shown by a number of statistical indicators. The first was relative MoS R&D expenditure on Westland and non-Westland helicopter projects between 1955 and 1960 (Table 12). After Westland's receipt of Admiralty orders for the Wessex in 1955, the data indicate that the firm attracted an increasing proportion of MoS R&D resources. In financial year 1957/58, Westland received approximately 44 per cent of total MoS helicopter airframe R&D investment. By financial year 1960/61, MoS estimates were that this proportion would increase to approximately 65 per cent.

A second indicator concerns MoS investment in basic helicopter research. Whereas Westland's licensed-production approach enabled it to exploit basic research conducted by Sikorsky in the USA, Bristol, Fairey and Saro were reliant on experimentation conducted in UK Government Research Establishments. Before 1955, intramural helicopter research had been marginalized.[126] Aware of the innovation constraints this posed for 'all-British' designs, the MoS Rotating-Wing Committee formulated during July 1958 its 'Research and Development Programme'[127] with three objectives: to review the general progress of rotary-wing research and development in the

Table 12: MoS Estimates of R&D Expenditure on Helicopter Airframes, 1957–58 to 1960–61

Company	*Project*	*1957–58*	*1958–59*	*1959–60*	*1960–61*
Saro	Skeeter	65	56	55	35
Bristol	B192	908	773	634	320
Westland	Whirlwind	230	223	110	50
Westland	Wessex	540	855	800	630
Fairey	Ultra-Light	–	5	5	5
Total Airframe Expenditure		1,743	1,912	1,604	1,040
Percentage of MoS Expenditure at Westland		44.2%	56.4%	56.7%	65.4%
Percentage of MoS Expenditure other than at Westland		55.8%	43.6%	43.3%	34.6%

Note: Current prices
Source: PRO AVIA 65/723, Helicopter Research and Development, 14 March 1958

preceding eight years, to recommend relative priorities (A or B) for necessary areas of helicopter research, and to revise and recast intramural helicopter research in light of 'general progress and the facilities currently available'.[128] The Programme was compiled

> ... on the assumption that although the helicopter is now at an operational stage, it is still far from being a satisfactory aircraft from the point of view of the operator, be he service of civil. It requires as much development in the engineering and operational fields as it does in that of basic research.[129]

Three research areas were considered vital to support 'all-British' projects. The first was 'Engineering and Structural', or the need for extensive research into structural design criteria, fatigue aspects, methods of propulsion, operational sub-systems and mechanical reliability.[130] The second was essential work on 'Flight Operations' to meet 'various operational role requirements,'[131] including all-weather and blind flying, and deck-landing techniques. The third, and most significant, request was for urgent research into 'Aerodynamic Stability and Performance', or issues concerned with helicopter aerodynamic control and stability.

During April 1959, an internal MoS review was conducted into the extent to which the 1958 Research and Development Programme was being implemented. The 1959 Review had a familiar tone: 'In general, partly because of the low priority accorded to helicopter work, progress was slow and effort available very short'.[132] The primary conclusion was that

> the official research and experimental effort on rotorcraft in the past two to three years has contracted very considerably. In fact, with the exception of work on all-weather operation . . . few of the items on the Programme are receiving any worthwhile attention on the R&D side.[133]

In key research areas identified by helicopter firms conducting 'all-British' development, intramural effort was still either limited or non-existent in the Government Research Establishments. In the 'Aerodynamic Performance and Stability' sector, negligible work was being done. In the 'Rotor Performance' category, 'little basic research [was] underway' despite that fact that it was 'frequently stated . . . by ['all-British'] designers that there [was] a pressing need to augment our present knowledge'.[134] In the 'High Speed Flight' field, no research was being conducted and in the 'Airframe Aerodynamics' sector there was no Establishment effort despite its 'increasing importance as higher cruising speeds are demanded'.[135] Finally, due to a lack of priority for 'all-British' projects, wind-tunnel experimentation was in complete abeyance despite pressing requirements from designers in industry for investigation into rotor/tunnel size and tunnel interference.

The limited priority assigned to basic helicopter research was also evident in the allocation of government-employed qualified scientists and engineers (QSEs) between 1955 and 1960. Helicopter work at the Royal Aircraft Establishment (RAE), Farnborough, was centred primarily in four departments: the Naval Aircraft Department (NAD), the Instruments and Photographic Department, the Mechanical and Engineering Department (MED) and the Structures Department. Total intramural manpower on helicopter research 'was about 15/20 staff, of which 10/15 were at NAD, with a number of others employed for part of their time'.[136] Consequently, of the total 1,515 QSEs[137] employed at the RAE, only 1.3 per cent were employed on helicopter research. More importantly, in the specific departments where helicopter research was concentrated, a measure of low priority was that out of some 417 QSEs[138] only 4.7 per cent were working on helicopter-related activities.

A further indicator of the constraints affecting 'all-British' projects was the distribution of QSEs in the helicopter industry. Table 13 shows employment statistics for Bristol, Fairey, Saro and Westland segregated into production and R&D categories during 1958. Westland's dominance of UK helicopter manufacturing output was reflected in its production labour, which accounted for approximately 59 per cent of the industry total. More significant, however, was that Westland had by 1958 accumulated the industry's largest concentration of R&D manpower. Consequently, therefore, Westland's success in winning production orders and attracting MoS R&D

funding through its 'anglicisation' strategy, was reflected in the firm's QSE employment levels.

Table 13: Labour Employed in UK Helicopter Firms, 1958

	Bristol	*Saro*	*Fairey*[c]	*Westland*	*Total*
Production					
Direct Labour	500	160	50	1,130	1,840
Indirect Labour[b]	1,100	200	100	1,900	3,300
Total	1,600	360	150	3,030	5,140
Research and Development[a]					
Drawing Office	87	22	62	99	270
Technical Staff	127	30	56	145	358
Total	214	52	118	244	628

Notes: [a] R&D figures include only technical and drawing office staff directly engaged in R&D design work and exclude staff employed to provide services for them.
[b] Indirect labour under the Production heading includes the R&D staff.
[c] Note that Fairey's R&D establishment is large compared to the firm's production labour because it had no helicopters in scale manufacture.
Source: PRO AVIA 65/723, Helicopter Research and Development, 14 March 1958.

The lack of production demand and development priority not only undermined MoS R&D resource allocation and production orders for 'all-British' helicopter projects; it also undermined private sector investment by Westland's competitors. An example of this trend was Fairey's approach on the Ultra-Light project. By March 1958, the Admiralty had expressed some interest in a developed version of the Ultra-Light as a frigate-borne anti-submarine helicopter.[139] However, in the absence of firm RN orders and MoS development support, the project was 'proceeding slowly [at Fairey] on a private-venture basis'.[140] Without explicit orders and MoS development funding, the Fairey Board's position was that it would 'not proceed with development without a Contract'.[141] Consequently, against growing Westland production dominance, Fairey were unwilling to risk private-venture resources to force Ultra-Light development.

A second example was the Bristol Helicopter Division's increasing reluctance to fund new development in the face of market trends. By 1958, Bristol were aware that no further orders would be sanctioned for its only major project, the B192, when the firm had completed its one outstanding Air Ministry order. To meet this shortfall in orders, Bristol initiated the design of the Type 203, a development of the Type 171 Sycamore. This was intended as a contender for a probable future Air Ministry requirement for an S-55/Type 171 replacement, and financed on a private-venture basis.[142] In the absence of further B192 orders, the Type 203 was Bristol's only helicopter under development and the firm were 'aware that the continuation of the [Bristol] Helicopter Division may depend on the success or otherwise of the Type 203'.[143] However, the extent of the Bristol Board's scepticism about potential Type 203 market opportunities in the face of Westland competition and the pressures on the MoS R&D budget was reflected in the firm's decision to invest only limited private-venture resources, to the extent of 'authorising the development on a "month by month" basis'.[144]

By 1958, the anxieties of firms conducting 'all-British' ventures were of concern to MoS officials. Summarising the problem, the MoS Assistant Director (RN1) advocated that

> ...the three Services should be encouraged to hasten firm statements of their future requirements for Helicopters as time is being lost, and considerable money, (albeit P.V.) is being spent on airframe, rotor system and engine developments which may not be wholly relevant to these requirements. This applies particularly to the Fairey Ultra Light (RN), the General Purpose Helicopter (Joint Services), and the Whirlwind/Sycamore utility and communications replacement (RAF), and to a lesser extent to the possible heavy lift, crane requirement (RAF/Army).[145]

A final constraint affecting the firms that had adopted the 'all-British' strategy concerned the high levels of technological risk associated with their projects in comparison to Westland's licensed-production and 'anglicisation' strategy. Evidence here is provided by the comparative performance of two competing projects: the Bristol Type 173/B191/B192 series and the 'anglicised' Westland S-58 Wessex. In adopting the licensed-production/ 'anglicisation' approach, Westland were able to minimise development uncertainty in two crucial respects. First, technical risk was limited to re-engining the operationally proven Sikorsky airframe, rather than design and development of new transmission and fuselage, and second, by relying on R&D already conducted in the USA by Sikorsky, Westland's development approach involved only minor modification to the original Sikorsky blue-prints rather than a major re-design. This reduced technical uncertainty was central to Westland's ability to place the S-58 Mk 1 in production within the original lead-time and cost estimates at project initiation.[146]

By contrast, the 'all-British' Type 173/B191/B192 project was characterised by considerably higher levels of technical uncertainty because it involved simultaneous airframe development, engine installation and systems integration. The manifestation of this uncertainty was reflected in the performance of the Bristol project against indicators of lead-time and cost. When initial Admiralty and Air Ministry orders were placed in 1954, MoS and Bristol estimates were that production would commence in April 1957.[147] The reality was that, as a result of development difficulties,[148] the B192 finally entered RAF service some three-and-a-half years late during September 1961.

Table 14: Type 173/B191/B192 Project Cost Escalation

Year	*Estimated Production Unit Cost (£)*	*Estimated Total Production Cost (£m)*	*MoS – Airframe Development Expenditure (Annual)*	*MoS – Engine Development Expenditure (Annual)*
1947	–	–	£0	£0
1948	–	–	£0	£0
1949	–	–	£60,000[c]	£0
1950	–	–	£80,000[c]	£0
1951	–	–	£86,000[c]	£0
1952	–	–	£110,000[c]	£38,000[c] (Leonides Major)
1953	–	–	£386,000[c]	£250,000[c]
1954	£77,000[a]	£6.8 for a total order of 90 aircraft[a]	£250,000[c]	£542,000 (Leonides Major)[c]
1955				
1956				£800,000[b]
1957			£250,000[b]	
1958	£257,000 (Gazelle)[a]; £185,000 (Leonides)[e]	£6.4 for a total order of 25[a] aircraft	Total Expenditure (airframe plus engine) to £4.25m authorised by HM Treasury[b]	
1959				
1960	£370,000 (Gazelle)[a]	£9.25 for an order of 25[a]	Cumulative engine and airframe development costs of £6.25m[a]	

Note: Current prices.
Sources:
[a] PRO T 225/1611, Bristol 192, 11 March 1960.
[b] PRO T 225/1611, Bristol 192, 2 March 1960.
[c] PRO AVIA 65/6, Air 2(a), 10 May 1954.
[d] PRO AIR 2/14888, Belvedere, October 1960.
[e] PRO T 225/1611, Letter from Air Ministry to HM Treasury, 16 April 1958.

Likewise, the project encountered major cost overruns on original 1954 predictions (Table 14). During June 1952, MoS estimates of the all-up-price of the Type 173 in production form were put at £116,000, based on anticipated potential orders for three aircraft.[149] The large-scale Admiralty/Air Ministry production orders placed in 1954 led to revised MoS unit cost estimates of £77,000 for the RN production version, and £72,000 for the RAF production variant.[150] However, when the first production B192 was released in 1961, the all-up unit cost had risen to £390,000.[151] Moreover, between 1958 and 1960 alone, technical modifications[152] required in the system integration process precipitated an overall programme cost escalation of 44 per cent.[153]

The relative development experiences of the Westland S-58 and the Bristol Type 173/B191/B192 series highlight the two-fold problems for 'all-British' projects more generally. First, following Westland's post-1955 absorption into MoS helicopter industrial policy and the removal of residual market-entry barriers, firms conducting 'all-British' designs were subjected to inherently greater technological risk than Westland. Second, relative levels of risk were reflected subsequently in Westland's improved commercial performance. On the basis of its success in 'anglicising' the S-58, Westland obtained further UK service contracts; by contrast, the development difficulties, lead-time slippage and cost escalation on the B192 project were instrumental in the Air Ministry's decision to place no further orders after its initial batch. Consequently, evidence suggests that Westland's technological strategy itself was a major variable that both contributed to and exacerbated the lack of production demand and resources for 'all-British' helicopter programmes.

THE MERGER PROCESS AND WESTLAND MARKET DOMINANCE

On 14 July 1959 Westland acquired Saro, and on 23 March 1960, the Bristol Helicopter Division became the Bristol Helicopter Department of Westland Aircraft Limited. By 2 May 1960, when it acquired Fairey Aviation Limited's aviation interests, Westland became Britain's sole helicopter manufacturer. Westland's emergence as the sole unified British helicopter company was the result of two factors. The first was wider UK government policy initiatives to rationalise the structure of the aircraft industry as a whole. The second was the playing-out of the variables that had both facilitated Westland's manufacturing success and retarded the market potential of 'all-British' projects.

Between 1955 and 1960, pressure was generated for government to use selective contracting to induce industrial coalescence and reduce the total number of firms in the UK aircraft industry. The primary drivers were technological progress and the long-run decline in the number of aircraft demanded.[154] 'The changing nature of the military aircraft market during this period made it inevitable that contraction and reorganisation would soon be necessary',[155] while the increasing cost and complexity of aircraft meant that production numbers at fixed rates of expenditure were declining.

As Hartley points out, during 1954 a total of 155 combat aircraft represented a value of £6.164 million but, by 1958, the production of 178 combat aircraft was valued at £29 million.[156] These cost increases were due entirely to greater aircraft technical complexity. In addition, by 1958 the cost profile of a civil aircraft had increased to the extent that it was difficult for any single firm to undertake its development as a private venture. These trends created economic pressures for industrial rationalisation and increased market concentration as a means to amortise R&D costs and achieve economics of scale in production.

In policy terms, these pressures precipitated government policy initiatives to encourage industrial mergers and acquisitions. The first manifestation of the government's commitment to market concentration was the 1956 Report by the Select Committee on Estimates, *The Supply of Military Aircraft*,[157] which highlighted the inadequate technical capacity of the large number of small companies making up the aircraft industry. The Report endorsed 'the view expressed by the Ministry of Supply that they would like to see a certain measure of coalescence', and that 'preferably with the agreement of the industry, steps should be taken to limit the number of firms receiving government contracts for the manufacture of air-frames and aero-engines'.[158] Moreover, the Report recommended that the MoS 'should use the method of selective allocation of contracts to bring about the measure of coalescence in the aircraft industry which they agreed was desirable'.[159]

Though *The Supply of Military Aircraft* report raised the industrial re-organisation issue, the primary policy impetus was the Duncan Sandys May 1957 Defence Statement which signalled an intent to cut back on defence spending to help the British economy.[160] In proposing a policy to replace manned combat aircraft with missiles, the implication of the Sandys Review was that contraction was essential if the UK aircraft industry were to survive. The process of reorganisation emerged gradually throughout 1958. On the one hand, whilst anticipating a reduction in aircraft expenditure of 9 per cent between 1958 and 1960/61 and a decline in industrial employment from 250,000 in 1958 to 150,000 by 1963, a government commitment was made to the continuing need for domestic aircraft production on strategic, industrial and export grounds.[161] On the other hand, the government's position was that further public research and development funding would be fruitless without industrial reorganisation. As the primary customer, the government intended to use selective contracting to reduce the number of airframe and aero-engine firms.[162] By 1960, the fourteen major airframe firms and the five major aero-engine companies had merged to form five major groups.[163]

Against these government-induced pressures for industrial coalescence, Westland's emergence as Britain's sole helicopter firm during 1960 marked the culmination of two trends. The first was the downstream effect of Westland's *de facto* absorption into MoS helicopter industrial policy during 1955. Hartley makes the point in his analysis of the overall merger process that, with the exception of the partnership between Vickers-Armstrong (Aircraft) and English Electric Aviation,

> in all other consortia and later mergers, there is no evidence to indicate that the Government directed firm A to merge with firm B. In other words, within the framework of the Government's competing groups policy, the actual mergers were a function of market forces.[164]

Because the 1955 MoS policy shift signalled acceptance that Westland were a legitimate 'all-British' company, with laissez-faire government policies towards market concentration, Westland was not confronted with bureaucratic barriers to the acquisition of its rivals. The second key trend was the downstream effect of the lack of production demand and development priority that had afflicted Westland's UK rivals. After 1958, confronted with the loss of key helicopter contracts to Westland, and attracting a diminishing proportion of government R&D resources, Saro, Fairey and Bristol finally succumbed to acquisition by Westland through the direct effect of market forces.

After 1958, the laissez-faire MoS approach towards industrial restructuring was indicated by a succession of internal Ministry reviews of the future prospects for UK helicopter firms. In its first major review of March 1958, the MoS assessment of the helicopter industry illustrated the impact of the problems for firms conducting 'all-British' development, and Westland's relative commercial strength. The primary conclusions were that

> Westlands have a fair load of work on the Wessex and the private-venture Westminster for some time ahead, but the future of the other three firms' helicopter work is uncertain. Bristols and Saunders Roe are dependent very largely on getting the order for the new Joint Services' small helicopter. Fairey's helicopter future depends on the Rotodyne, although if the Fairey Ultra-Light helicopter proved an outstanding success, they could probably keep together a small team.[165]

Between March 1958 and June 1959, two decisive procurement decisions further eroded the remaining prospects for Westland's two main competitors, Fairey and Bristol. The first was the Admiralty's decision not to purchase the Ultra-Light during mid-1959,[166] which rendered the prospects for the Fairey Helicopter Division entirely dependent on the Rotodyne project. The second was Bristol's failure to win orders for its new Joint Services small helicopter proposals after the Services elected to procure the Saro P.531. The implication for Bristol was that by mid-1959, with the exception of design studies for a possible Whirlwind replacement, the firm's Helicopter Division had no definite orders beyond its Air Ministry B192 production contracts.

In its second major review[167] during June 1959, the MoS industrial survey concluded that

> the present programme and possible future requirements suggest that our work will concentrate on Westlands and Saunders Roe ... Westlands and Saunders Roe appear to be the most viable firms at present in the military helicopter field.[168]

By August 1959, two significant developments had further consolidated Westland's market position and undermined the longer-term commercial threat posed by its rivals. The first was that Westland acquired Saro on 14 July 1959.[169] Westland's rationale for the take-over was in part defensive: following Saro's receipt of P.531 contracts, Westland was eager to prevent the acquisition of Saro by either Bristol or Fairey.[170] In addition, the Westland Board were aware that Saro was negotiating a reciprocal licensed-production relationship with the American helicopter manufacturer, Hillier,[171] so acquisition provided a mechanism for Westland to prevent any potential competition from a Saro/Hillier partnership. Finally, following the withdrawal of government support for the Saro SR. 177 rocket aircraft programme in 1957,[172] 'company resources [at Saro] were at a low ebb and this helped to encourage [the Westland] take-over'.[173]

The second development was that, by August 1959, the prospects for the Bristol Helicopter Division had further deteriorated. After the failure of its Joint Services small helicopter proposals, the Division's most promising remaining design project was the B203,[174] intended primarily for the Air Ministry's planned procurement of a Whirlwind/Sycamore replacement. By July 1959, however, the familiar effects caused by Westland licensed-produced variants had again militated against Bristol. On 27 July 1959 the Air Ministry decided to meet the requirement with Westland Whirlwinds re-engined with De Havilland Gnome 6 gas-turbine engines,[175] and by August 1959 Bristol was forced to abandon its B203 design after the firm had 'been told [by the MoS] there [was] no military requirement for it'.[176]

After the B203 cancellation, the Bristol Helicopter Division's residual chances of remaining a viable development and production unit rested effectively on two paper designs: the B214, a proposed utility class helicopter intended as a competitor to the Westland Wessex,[177] and the B194, a proposal to augment the B192 design for civil helicopter applications.[178] However, by 16 September 1959 the attraction of the Westland S-58 Wessex to the MoS and the UK services on cost and lead-time criteria forced Bristol to abandon its B214 proposals. After service assessment[179] of the B214, the MoS informed Bristol that it foresaw 'no military requirement' for the project because

> provisional estimates of the production price of the B214 suggested it would be slightly cheaper than the Wessex but at least an extra £2.25m would be needed to develop it and it would be considerably later in Service.[180]

In the aftermath of Westland's acquisition of Saro, and the failure of the Bristol B203 and B214 to secure support or orders, the MoS assessment of the industry's prospects during October 1959 was that

> the absorption of Saunders-Roe's strong helicopter team by Westland has created a very strong helicopter group and Westland with their subsidiary seems to have an assured future in the helicopter business until at least 1965 ... On the aircraft side, therefore, Westlands with Saunders-Roe is a strong helicopter design and production unit with an assured future. Fairey's future depends on the Rotodyne, but Bristol unless the B.194 proves a worthwhile development seems to have little chance of survival.[181]

The relative strength of Westland after the Saro take-over was evident to Ministry officials. On the manufacturing side, Westland had production contracts for 167 military helicopters and outstanding military requirements accounted for a further 229 potential orders.[182] By contrast, the Bristol Helicopter Division's order book was limited to its outstanding contract for 26 B192s for the Air Ministry. On the basis of these figures, the October 1959 conclusion by Ministry officials was that

> ... the production capacity of Westland and their subsidiary Saunders Roe will be fully occupied [until at least 1965]. Employment will be maintained at about the present level, and it might even be possible for Westland/Saunders-Roe to absorb possible redundancies from the Bristol Helicopter Division.[183]

In terms of estimates of future government helicopter R&D funding, officials also recognised that Westland would be the major recipient of subsequent expenditure. Discounting funds already committed to B192 development and Sycamore modification at Bristol, provisional estimates were that during FY1960–61 and FY1961–62 Westland would receive approximately 60 per cent of 'Approved Project' expenditure.[184] More significant, however, was that with the new orders won by Westland and Saro in late 1959, Ministry funding for the 'Projects Not Yet Approved' at Westland accounted for all estimated future helicopter expenditure.[185]

In the three months after October 1959, the commercial position for Westland's two remaining UK helicopter rivals became increasingly unsustainable in the face of Westland's *de facto* monopoly over future UK Service orders and government R&D resources. In the Bristol Helicopter Division's case, with its failure to obtain government support for the remaining B194 proposal, Bristol Aircraft Ltd. signed an agreement on 11 January 1960 allowing for a Westland take-over 'in principle'.[186] Denied government development support for the Rotodyne, and spending £70,000 per month[187] of the firm's private capital to keep the project going, Fairey's acquisition by Westland soon followed on 2 February 1960.[188]

February 1960, therefore, marked the closing chapter in the process by which Westland emerged as the single united British helicopter manufacturer. The factors that had facilitated Westland's helicopter manufacturing success through licensed-production and technology indigenisation, coupled with the variables that had undermined the commercial performance of UK government-sponsored 'all-British' alternatives after 1945, culminated in a final and decisive shift in UK government helicopter industrial policy. By 23 January 1960, the UK government position had come full circle from the original 1945 starting point, with formal acceptance by Minister of Aviation Duncan Sandys that

> ...the formation of a British single specialist helicopter Group would be in accordance with Government policy and...Westland would be acceptable, and welcome, as the basis and leaders of this; the government would not view this as a monopoly contrary to the public interest, but in fact in that interest, whilst naturally giving no guarantees as to continuing orders it would not expect to sponsor the development of any competing group and, given satisfactory service, would expect to obtain whatever were its relevant requirements from the Westland group. It was recognised that the curb to the monopoly would be foreign competition and that the Government would, if necessary owing to technical or other circumstances, be free to purchase from abroad.[189]

SUMMARY

The five years between 1955 and 1960 witnessed the playing-out of the underlying factors that had affected patterns of UK helicopter R&D and production throughout the earlier post-war period. On the one hand, a combination of Westland's access to the US technological lead, its ability to 'indigenise' the know-how obtained through technology transfer and, ultimately, UK-government recognition after 1955 that Westland were generating an in-house design and development capability, all contributed to the firm's domination of British helicopter manufacturing. On the other hand, the impact of Westland's ability to attract MoS R&D funding and domestic production orders, coupled with bureaucratic impediments in the 'Indigenous Procurement Process', both militated against government investment, production orders and innovation rates for rival 'all-British' projects. The intensification of these processes after 1955 resulted in a legacy of cancelled indigenous R&D projects and the situation whereby Britain had finally become dependent for its future domestic helicopter sourcing on a firm that had specialised in the licensed production and 'anglicisation' of foreign technology.

NOTES

1. See Chapter 5.
2. For a detailed description of the abortive attempts to flight test the P.74, and other technical constraints affecting development during 1956, see D. Wood, *Project Cancelled: The Disaster of Britain's Abandoned Aircraft Projects* (London: Tri-Service Press, 1990), pp. 97-100. The relevant MoS file for the project is PRO AVIA 65/265, Percival Gas Turbine Helicopter (1951–8).
3. For detailed technical descriptions of post-1955 Bristol Type 171 Sycamore development, see E.J. Everett-Heath, *British Military Helicopters* (London: Arms & Armour Press, 1986), pp. 41–8; C.H. Barnes, *Bristol Aircraft since 1910* (London: Putnam, 1988); and, K. Munson, *Helicopters and other Rotorcraft since 1907* (London: Blandford Press, 1968), pp. 123–4. The main MoS files covering technical development after 1955 are: PRO AVIA 54/687, B171 HC.Mk11; PRO AVIA 54/680–54/683, B171 Helicopter; PRO AVIA 54/662, Sycamore Helicopter; and, PRO AVIA 54/626–54/627, B171 Helicopter. Details of Air Ministry operational requirements are contained in: PRO AIR 2/15308, Sycamore Mks 11, 13, 14 General Purpose Helicopter: Operational Requirements (1959–60).
4. The most detailed published account of Type 173/191/192 technical development are contained in Everett-Heath, *British Military Helicopters*, pp. 48–57; and, A. McClements, 'The Westland Belvedere Mk1', *Journal of the Royal Aeronautical Society*, Vol. 66, August 1962, p. 521. MoS technical files covering project development are extensive after 1955, including, *inter alia*, PRO AVIA 54/880, Design and Development of B191 to Spec. HR146 (1953–62); PRO AVIA 54/916, Proposed use of B173 against NA 43 (1952–56); PRO AVIA 65/8, Bristol B173 Development Programme; PRO AVIA 65/784, Development of the Napier Gazelle for B191, B192 and Westland (1954–62); and, PRO AVIA 54/787, Fitment of Stub Wings to B171, (1952–56). For Air Ministry requirements and technical evaluations of project development, see PRO AIR 2/14890, General Purpose Helicopter ASR 325: Bristol 192 Belvedere (1958–59); PRO AIR 2/15353, Bristol 192 Belvedere: General Purpose Helicopter (1959); PRO AIR 2/15354, Bristol 192 Belvedere: General Purpose Helicopter (1959–60); PRO AIR 2/15693, Belvedere Helicopter: Air Staff Requirements (1960); and, PRO AIR 2/16085, Bristol Belvedere: Operational Requirements (1961).
5. For detailed accounts of project development after 1955, see Wood, *Project Cancelled*, pp. 102–7; and, H.A. Taylor, *Fairey Aircraft since 1915* (London: Putnam, 1974). MoS files covering the technical aspects of Rotodyne development after 1955 are PRO AVIA 65/39, BEA Helicopter Policy (1951–58); PRO AVIA 65/85, Reduction of Helicopter Noise (including Rotodyne) (1954–61); PRO AVIA 65/211–65/212, Engine Requirements for the Rotodyne; PRO AVIA 65/263, Proposals for Fairey Rotodyne (1951–56); and, PRO AVIA 65/614, Rotodyne: Policy Proposals (1956–59). Relevant Treasury files include: PRO T 225/1607, Rotodyne Helicopter (1955–1958); PRO T 225/1608, Rotodyne Helicopter (1955–58); and, PRO T 225/1609, Rotodyne Helicopter (1958–60).
6. For a description of project development, see Everett-Heath, *British Military Helicopters*, pp. 68–71. For the MoS file covering Ultra-Light technical development after 1955, see PRO AVIA 65/1309, Ultra-Light: Naval Staff Requirement and Specification (1957–58).
7. The most detailed accounts of project development after 1955 are contained in P. London, *Saunders and Saro Aircraft since 1917* (London: Putnam, 1988), pp. 236–63; and, Everett-Heath, *British Military Helicopters*, pp. 33–40. Relevant MoS technical files covering Skeeter development are PRO AVIA 54/541–54/544, A13/49

Skeeter; and, PRO AVIA 65/638, Specification H163P2 Saro Skeeter (1956–62).

8. For an overview of project development, see J.W.R. Taylor and M.F. Allward, *Westland 50* (London: Ian Allan, 1965). The major MoS files covering S-55 Whirlwind technical development after 1955 are PRO AVIA 54/585, Sikorsky S-55 Helicopter; and, PRO AVIA 65/1305, Specification: Whirlwind (1957–63). Relevant Admiralty files include PRO ADM 264/90, Whirlwind HAS Mk 7 Aircraft: Flight Test Schedule (1959); and, PRO ADM 264/48, Whirlwind HAR Mk 1 Aircraft (1953–68).
9. See Everett-Heath, *British Military Helicopters*, pp. 79–80.
10. For detailed technical accounts of the project, see O. Fitzwilliams, 'Westland Helicopter Activities, 1946–60', in R.A.C. Brie (ed.), *A History of British Rotorcraft, 1866–1965*, (Yeovil: Westland Helicopters, 1968), pp. 120–1; Taylor and Allward, *Westland 50*; and, Wood, *Project Cancelled*, pp. 110–112. The relevant MoS policy and technical file covering the project is PRO AVIA 65/24, Westland Proposals for S-56: Finance and Policy (1954–56).
11. Between 1955 and 1960 the major helicopter firms undertook a range of design studies that did not proceed to prototype development. For an overview of these studies see R. Hafner, 'British Rotorcraft', *Journal of the Royal Aeronautical Society*, Vol. 70, Part 1, January 1966, p. 238. For more detail on Westland's project studies, see Fitzwilliams, 'Westland Helicopter Activities', pp. 117–23.
12. The most detailed technical and development account of the Saro P.531 project is provided by the former Chief Designer, Light Helicopters, Westland Aircraft Limited, Fairey Aviation Division, in T.L. Ciastula, 'The Development of the P.531', *Journal of the Royal Aeronautical Society*, Vol. 68, June 1964, pp. 399–417. See also London, *Saunders and Saro Aircraft*, pp. 263–76; and, Everett-Heath, *British Military Helicopters*, pp. 113–27. The relevant MoS file covering P.531 development between 1956 and 1960 is: PRO AVIA 65/1418, Alouette as Stop-Gap for P.531, 1958–67. Treasury papers covering the project are contained in PRO T 225/1606, Ordering of P.531 Helicopter (1959–60).
13. Ciastula, 'Development of the P.531', p. 400.
14. Ministry of Supply files covering project development include: PRO AVIA 53/525–53/526, 1956–60: S-58 and Spec. HAS 170D; PRO AVIA 53/527, S-58 Supply; and, PRO AVIA 65/1302, Specification: Wessex (1956–60). For Air Ministry documents covering project development, see PRO AIR 2/15709, Wessex Helicopter: Standards of Preparation (1960–61); PRO AIR 2/16438, Wessex Helicopter: Standards of Preparation (1962); and, PRO AIR 20/10927, Wessex Helicopter: Standards of Preparation (1960–62).
15. See Chapter 5.
16. For a detailed description of the Skeeter variants, see Everett-Heath, *British Military Helicopters*, pp. 33–40; and, London, *Saunders and Saro Aircraft*, pp. 236–63.
17. Between 1945 and 1960, Westland produced 139 S-51 Dragonflys and 245 S-55 Whirlwinds, a total of 384 units. Over the same period, Bristol produced 175 Type 171 Sycamores and Saro's output was 88 Skeeters.
18. Between 1945 and 1960, Westland sold 139 S-51s at £22,180 per unit and 245 S-55s at £66,000 per unit, leading to total cumulative sales of approximately £19.25 million. At £25,000 per unit, Bristol's orders for 175 Type 171s generated revenue of approximately £4.37 million. At £26,100 per copy, Saro's orders for 88 Skeeters generated revenue of approximately £2.29 million. Financial data in current prices compiled from PRO AIR 2/11428, Minute by D.Pol (AS), 15 June 1952; and, PRO AVIA 65/723, Note on the Ministry of Supply Helicopter Programme and Policy, 16 September 1959.

19. For more details, see Taylor and Allward, *Westland 50*, p. 113.
20. For more details about the Series 3 models, see Jane's, *All The World's Aircraft*, 1964–65 (London: Jane's, 1965), p. 164.
21. See Chapter 5.
22. See Chapter 5.
23. PRO AVIA 65/723, Helicopter Research and Development, 14 March 1958.
24. Ibid.
25. For a breakdown of S-58 sales, see Everett-Heath, *British Military Helicopters*, p. 112.
26. Figures in current prices derived from S.C. Williams, *Report on the Helicopter: The Helicopter and Its Role As a Transport Vehicle* (New York: Brundage Story & Rose, 1955), p. 28.
27. Cumulative US helicopter exports between 1948 and 1954 were 353 units that had a total reported value of $15.3 million. Total US helicopter industry exports for 1954 alone were 74 units that had a reported total value of $4.04 million. Figures in current prices derived from R. Modley and T.J. Cawlay, *Aviation Facts and Figures 1955* (Washington, DC: Lincoln Press, 1955), p. 81, cited in S.C. Williams, *Report on the Helicopter*, p. 25.
28. Figures derived from S.C. Williams, *Report on the Helicopter*. US industry is defined as the main firms: Bell, Hillier, Kaman, Piasecki and Sikorsky.
29. Ibid. US industry defined as the main firms plus Cessna and Doman.
30. Ibid. Figures in current prices. US industry is defined as the main firms: Bell, Hillier, Kaman, Piasecki and Sikorsky.
31. Munson, *Helicopters*, pp. 137–8.
32. G. Swanborough and P.M. Bowers, *United States Naval Aircraft since 1911* (London: Putnam, 1968), p. 349.
33. E.W. Rawlins and W.J. Sambito, *Marines and Helicopters, 1946–1962* (Washington, DC: US Marine Corps, History and Museums Division, 1976), p. 55.
34. Ibid.
35. Ibid.
36. For more details, see E. Rees, *World Military Helicopters* (London: Jane's, 1986), p. 132.
37. See N. Polmar and F.D. Kennedy, *Military Helicopters of the World: Military Rotary-Wing Aircraft since 1917* (London: Arms and Armour Press, 1981), p. 296.
38. Munson, *Helicopters*, p. 138.
39. PRO AIR 2/14888, Loose Minute, Review of Helicopters on Order for the Royal Air Force and the Army Air Corps by Group Captain D.F. Rickson, DDOR (7), 7 October 1960.
40. Fitzwilliams, 'Westland Helicopter Activities', p. 116.
41. Everett-Heath, *British Military Helicopters*, p. 95.
42. PRO AVIA 65/723, Ministry of Defence – Defence Research Policy Committee, MoS Helicopter Programme, Note by the Ministry of Supply, 24 November 1955.
43. Ibid., Air B.2(a), MoS Helicopter Programme, 24 November 1955.
44. Ibid.
45. PRO T 225/1611, B.192, 2 March 1960.
46. PRO AVIA 65/723, Air B.2(a), MoS Helicopter Programme, 24 November 1955.
47. See Chapter 5.
48. PRO AVIA 65/723, Ministry of Defence – Defence Research Policy Committee: MoS Helicopter Programme, Note by the Ministry of Supply, Undated.
49. There were a number of key development landmarks in the Westland S-58 'Anglicisation' process. On 17 May 1957, Westland achieved first flight of an S-58 prototype equipped with the 1,100 shp Napier Gazelle Nga.11 turboshaft engine.

The first flight of two pre-production Westland S-58s equipped with 1,450 shp Gazelle Mk161 turboshaft engines took place on 20 June 1958. During 1959, the Wessex HAS Mk1 entered production and by April 1960, Westland commenced delivery to the Royal Navy. For more information on this process, see Everett-Heath, *British Military Helicopters*, pp. 95–6.

50. See PRO AVIA 65/723, Helicopter Research and Development, 14 March 1958.
51. Ibid.
52. Everett-Heath, *British Military Helicopters*, p. 96.
53. Ibid., p. 98.
54. Report of the Committee of Inquiry into the Aircraft Industry, *Cmnd. 2853* (London: HMSO, 1965) p. 67.
55. See Chapter 5.
56. PRO AVIA 65/723, Air B.2(a), MoS Helicopter Programme, 24 November 1955.
57. Ibid.
58. Ibid.
59. Ibid.
60. Ibid.
61. Ibid., Ministry of Defence – Defence Research Policy Committee: MoS Helicopter Programme, Note by the Ministry of Supply, Undated.
62. Second Report with Evidence taken before Subcommittee E of the Select Committee on Estimates of Session 1956–57, The Supply of Military Aircraft, *HCP 34* (London: HMSO, 1956), p. iv.
63. Ibid.
64. Ibid., p. vii.
65. Ibid., p. xxxiv.
66. Ibid., p. xv.
67. Ibid.
68. Ibid.
69. Ibid., p. viii.
70. PRO AVIA 65/723, A Review of Probable Future Military Requirements in Relation to Present Developments of Aircraft and Power Plants in Industry, by AD/RN1, MoS.
71. Ibid., Minute from MoS Under-Secretary (Air B) to MoS Assistant-Secretary (Air B.2), 24 June 1958.
72. Statistics calculated from PRO AVIA 65/723, Helicopter Research and Development, 14 March 1958. According to MoS figures, cumulative Admiralty helicopter orders by 1958 totalled 336 units, of which 327 were contracts with Westland. The remaining nine purchases were contracts with Bristol for the Mk 50 and Mk 51 variants of the Type 171. See also the papers contained in PRO T 225/1612, Helicopters: RN Production Requirements (1957–60); PRO T 225/1319, Admiralty: Fleet Air Arm: Provision of Aircraft (1954–56); PRO T 225/1104, Fleet Air Arm: Provision of Aircraft (1954–60); PRO T 225/1261, Admiralty Fleet Air Arm: Provision of Aircraft and Associated Equipment (1958–60); PRO T 225/1263, Provision of Aircraft (1955–60); and, PRO T 225/1264, Provision of Aircraft (1958–60).
73. PRO T 225/1611, Minute by Mr. Judd, HM Treasury, B.192, 2 March 1960.
74. Ibid.
75. Ibid.
76. Ibid.
77. For more details, see, for example, PRO T 225/1611, Minute, Bristol 192, 22 April 1958.
78. PRO AVIA 65/723, A Review of Probable Future Military Requirements in Relation to Present Developments of Aircraft and Power Plants in Industry, by

AD/RN1, MoS.
79. Explanatory Statement on the Navy Estimates 1957–58 by the First Lord of the Admiralty, *Cmnd. 151* (London: HMSO, 1958).
80. PRO AVIA 65/723, A Review of Probable Future Military Requirements in Relation to Present Developments of Aircraft and Power Plants in Industry by AD/RN1, MoS.
81. Ibid.
82. Ibid.
83. Ibid.
84. M. Allen, *Military Helicopter Doctrines of the Major Powers, 1945–1992* (London: Greenwood Press, 1993), p. 6.
85. J. Dowling, *RAF Helicopters: The First Twenty Years* (London: HMSO, 1992), p. 103.
86. Ibid., Chs 2 and 3. See also AIR 2/14309, Helicopters for Use in Malaya (1954–55); PRO AIR 2/14887, British Helicopter Development (1958–60); and, PRO AIR 2/15120, Helicopter Requirements (1952–64).
87. For background information, see J.F. Scott, 'Joint Experimental Helicopter Unit', *Air Power*, Spring 1959.
88. For an overview of Air Ministry policy towards the Bristol 192 Belvedere helicopter, see PRO AIR 2/14744, General Purpose Helicopter OR 325: Policy, (1956–57); and PRO AIR 2/14745, General Purpose Helicopter OR 325: Policy, (1957–1964).
89. Ibid.
90. PRO T 225/1611, B.192, 2 March 1960.
91. PRO AIR 2/14888, Loose Minute, Review of Helicopters on Order for the Royal Air Force and the Army Air Corps by Group Captain D.F. Rickson, DDOR (7), 7 October 1960.
92. Ibid., Belvedere, October 1960. See also PRO AIR 20/10294, Helicopters: ACAS Papers (1957–58).
93. Ibid.
94. PRO T 225/1611, Note by HM Treasury concerning Bristol 192 – Air Ministry Letter of 30 April 1957.
95. Ibid., Letter from HM Treasury to the Air Ministry, 17 May 1957.
96. Ibid., Bristol 192, 22 April 1958.
97. Ibid., Letter from the Air Ministry to HM Treasury, 16 April 1958.
98. Ibid.
99. Ibid.
100. PRO AIR 2/14888, Belvedere, 11 October 1960.
101. Ibid.
102. Cited in A. Farrar-Hockley, *The Army in the Air: The History of the Army Air Corps* (Stroud: Alan Sutton, 1994), p. 174.
103. Ibid.
104. Ibid., p. 175.
105. Ibid.
106. See Chapter 5.
107. Farrar-Hockley, *Army in the Air*, p. 178.
108. Ibid.
109. See the papers contained in PRO AIR 2/13518, Financial Aspects and Purchase of Skeeter Aircraft (1954–59).
110. PRO T 225/696, War Office Letter of the 29 May, 1957, 5 June 1957.
111. Ibid.
112. Ibid., Army Air Corps, October 1957.
113. Ibid.

114. See Chapter 5.
115. See Chapter 5.
116. PRO AVIA 65/723, Notes of a Meeting Held on 30 December 1955.
117. See 'Rotodyne Report: Development Aspects and Commercial Applications of Fairey's VTOL Transport', *Flight*, 20 December 1957, pp. 953–58.
118. PRO AVIA 65/723, Helicopter Research and Development, 14 March 1958.
119. Ibid.
120. See PRO AIR 2/10797, Minute by A.J. Kirkpatrick, DOR (A), The Development of the Fairey Rotodyne, 3 October 1955. The Air Council's refusal to place orders was based on the assessment that the Rotodyne could not meet the Air Ministry's heavy-lift Operational Requirement, was 'too complicated' for use in forward areas, had a 'Catherine Wheel' effect at the blade tips, and made too much noise when hovering or coming to the hover. Additional information is provided in PRO AIR 2/14410, Fairey Rotodyne: Policy (1954–59); PRO AIR 2/15377, Fairey Rotodyne: Policy (1959–61); and PRO AIR 2/15376, Fairey Rotodyne: Standards of Preparation (1959–66).
121. For a summary see PRO T 225/696, Rotodyne, 20 February 1959.
122. PRO AVIA 65/723, Note on the Ministry of Aviation Helicopter Programme and Policy, October 1959.
123. Ibid.
124. Cited in Wood, *Project Cancelled*, p. 105.
125. Ibid.
126. For more details see Chapter 5.
127. PRO AVIA 65/723, A Note on the Rotary-Wing Research and Development Programme Prepared by the Ministry of Supply Rotating-Wing Committee, April 1959. This document outlines Ministry of Supply Rotating-Wing Committee Paper No. RWC 130, Rotating-Wing Research and Development Programme, Issue No. 1, July 1958. See also PRO AVIA 65/107, MoS Rotating-Wing Committee (1951–58) for an overview of the Committee's overall activities.
128. Ibid.
129. Ibid.
130. Ibid.
131. Ibid.
132. Ibid., Note of Meeting on Wednesday, 22nd April, 1959 to Consider Future Helicopter Work and the Best Organisation to Cope with it, 24 April 1959.
133. Ibid.
134. Ibid.
135. Ibid.
136. Ibid.
137. Figures derived from M.J. Lighthill, 'The Royal Aircraft Establishment' in J. Cockcroft (ed.), *The Organization of Research Establishments* (Cambridge: Cambridge University Press, 1965), p. 30.
138. Ibid.
139. PRO AVIA 65/723, A Review of Probable Future Military Requirements in Relation to Present Developments of Aircraft and Power Plants in Industry by AD/RN1, MoS, May 1958.
140. Ibid.
141. Ibid.
142. Ibid.
143. Ibid.
144. Ibid.
145. Ibid.

146. Ibid., Helicopter Research and Development, 14 March 1958.
147. Ibid.
148. PRO AIR 2/14888, Belvedere, October 1960.
149. PRO AIR 2/11428, Minute by D.Pol (AS): Summary of Activities, 15 June 1952.
150. PRO T 225/1611, Bristol 192, 11 March 1960.
151. PRO AIR 2/14888, Loose Minute: Review of Helicopters on Order for the Royal Air Force and the Army Air Corps, 7 October 1960.
152. PRO T 225/1611, Bristol 192, 11 March 1960.
153. A detailed breakdown of the unit cost escalation is as follows. During 1958, total unit cost estimates for the B192 were £257,000. By 1960, the estimated total unit cost had risen to £370,000, an increase of 44 per cent. The major source of this increase was the predicted cost of the airframe (including tooling), which rose from £152,000 per unit in 1958 to £260,000 per unit in 1960, a 76 per cent increase. By 1960, unit cost estimates for the Gazelle engine had fallen from £95,000 to £92,000, or three per cent less than 1958 estimates. Estimates for 'Installed Items' remained constant at £10,000 per unit. Figures compiled from PRO T 225/1611, Letter from the Air Ministry to HM Treasury, 25 February 1960.
154. K. Hartley, 'The Mergers in the UK Aircraft Industry, 1957–60', *Journal of the Royal Aeronautical Society*, Vol. 69, December 1965, p. 864. For Treasury deliberations on this issue, see PRO T 225/1296, Future of UK Aircraft Industry: Aircraft Industry Working Party (1957); and, PRO T 225/1297, Future of UK Aircraft Industry: Aircraft Industry Working Party (1958).
155. Ibid.
156. Ibid.
157. Second Report from the Select Committee on Estimates, *HCP 34*, p. iv.
158. Ibid., p. xxix.
159. Ibid., pp. xxix–xxx.
160. Ministry of Defence, Defence – Outline of Future Policy, *Cmnd. 124* (London: HMSO, 1957).
161. For a discussion see Hartley, 'Mergers in the UK Aircraft Industry', p. 847.
162. Ibid., p. 848.
163. For more details, see P. Gummett, 'Civil and Military Aircraft in the UK' in J. Krige (ed.), *Choosing Big Technologies* (Reading: Harwood, 1993), pp. 206–13; D. Edgerton, *England and the Aeroplane: An Essay on a Militant and Technological Nation* (London: Macmillan, 1991), pp. 95–100; and, Hartley, 'Mergers in the UK Aircraft Industry', pp. 846–52.
164. Hartley, 'Mergers in the UK Aircraft Industry', p. 849.
165. PRO AVIA 65/723, Helicopter Research and Development, 14 March 1958.
166. See previous sections in this chapter.
167. PRO AVIA 65/723, Military Helicopter Programme and Policy, 9 June 1959.
168. Ibid., Note by AS/Air B.2, 9 June 1959.
169. Westland acquired the whole of Saro's capital in exchange for the issue of 3,200,000 new Westland 5-shilling shares and a cash payment of £100,000. With a Stock Exchange quotation of 10 shillings for Westland shares, the total consideration was equivalent to approximately £1,700,000. See *Keesing's Contemporary Archives, 1959–1960* (London: Keesing's, 1960), p. 17227.
170. See Hartley, 'Mergers in the UK Aircraft Industry', p. 850.
171. PRO AVIA 65/723, Military Helicopter Programme and Policy, June 1959.
172. This decision was contained in Defence – Outline of Future Policy, *Cmnd. 124*, p. 9.
173. London, *Saunders and Saro Aircraft*, p. 48. For a detailed account of the P.177 project and the factors leading to its cancellation, see pages 44–8.

174. For technical details of the B203 design proposal, see PRO AVIA 65/723, A Review of Probable Future Military Requirements in Relation to Present Developments of Aircraft and Power Plants in Industry, by AD/RN1, MoS, May 1958.
175. For more details, see PRO T 225/1611, Letter from the Air Ministry to HM Treasury, 27 July 1959; and, PRO AIR 2/14886, Sycamore/Whirlwind: Replacement Helicopter OR 348, 1958–60.
176. PRO AVIA 65/723, Note on the Ministry of Supply Helicopter Programme and Policy, 9 August 1959.
177. Ibid., Note on the Ministry of Aviation Helicopter Programme and Policy, October 1959.
178. Ibid.
179. Ibid. The conclusion of the Official Working Party, which considered War Office helicopter requirements during September 1959, was that the Westland Wessex with Gnome engines should be selected to meet future Army requirements.
180. Ibid., Note on the Ministry of Supply Helicopter Programme Policy, 16 September 1959.
181. Ibid., Note on the Ministry of Aviation Helicopter Programme and Policy, October 1959.
182. Ibid. The breakdown of Westland orders was as follows: Whirlwind H.C.C.8 – two units on order; Whirlwind (turbine) – 12 units on order from a total Air Ministry requirement of 16; Whirlwind HAS Mk 7 – 28 units remaining on order from a total purchase of 129 units; Wessex HAS Mk 1 – 92 units on order from a total Admiralty requirement of 170 units. There were also additional orders acquired by Westland as a result of the Saro take-over: P.531 – three units on order for evaluation and a total estimated requirement of 140 to 150 units; Skeeter – 30 units on order.
183. Ibid.
184. Ibid., Second Draft Estimate 1960/61, Vote Letter Supplement No. 5, Research and Development Work in Industry, DFB Air B.2, Military Helicopters. For financial years 1960–61, 'Approved Project' expenditure at Westland was £820,000, as compared with £610,000 at Bristol. For financial years 1961–62, 'Approved Project' expenditure at Westland was £720,000, as compared with £490,000 at Bristol.
185. Ibid. In the 'Projects Not Yet Approved' category for financial years 1960–61, some £460,000 was earmarked for Westland projects, and for financial years 1961–62 Westland was expected to receive £1,030,000. No provisional funding was allocated to Bristol under this expenditure category.
186. Westland secured agreement 'in principle' for the acquisition on 11 January 1960. On 23 March 1960 Westland bought the helicopter interests of Bristol Aircraft Ltd. in return for a 10 per cent interest in Westland Aircraft Limited. This was achieved by Westland's issue to Bristol of 2,000,000 new 5-shilling shares and payments by instalments of £1,000,000 cash. For more details see *Keesing's Contemporary Archives*, p. 17227; and, Taylor and Allward, *Westland 50*, p. 131.
187. See Wood, *Project Cancelled*, p. 106.
188. On 2 February 1960 Westland acquired the entire share capital of Fairey Aviation Ltd for £1,400,000 in cash and 2,000,000 Westland shares of 5 shillings nominal value. The purchase price was equivalent to approximately £3,000,000. See *Keesing's Contemporary Archives*, p. 17227.
189. PRO AVIA 65/723, Westland Aircraft Limited, Notes for Meeting with The Rt Hon. Duncan Sandys, Minister of Aviation, 10 February 1960.

Conclusion

After 1945, Ministry of Supply (MoS) policy was to foster a self-sufficient helicopter industry founded on an indigenous R&D and manufacturing capability. As the guardians of aircraft industrial policy, MoS officials assumed that a combination of government R&D contracts and 'buy-national' procurement policies would generate an 'all-British' helicopter design and production capacity to meet domestic and export requirements. By the late 1950s, the failure of this policy became manifest in a serious inability in Britain to produce commercially viable indigenous helicopter technology leading to a reliance on American design manufactured in the UK under licence by Westland. This section summarises why these trends occurred, outlines the lessons of the helicopter experience for the broader historiography of early post-war British aircraft industrial policy, and considers the scope and limitations of licensed production as a procurement strategy for national governments.

DETERMINANTS OF BRITISH HELICOPTER R&D AND PRODUCTION, 1945–60

This study shows that trends in British helicopter R&D and production stemmed from two interrelated factors. Westland's decision to circumvent in-house R&D and focus instead on manufacturing proven US designs provided the firm with a competitive edge and a route to British helicopter market dominance. Correspondingly, a series of constraints affecting MoS helicopter industrial policy undermined the emergence of competitive 'all-British' alternatives to Westland, but also led to a range of commercially questionable prototypes intended to fulfil civil and military requirements for which Westland did not compete.

A critical factor underpinning Westland's post-war commercial success was the comprehensive technological lead that the US helicopter industry maintained over its British counterpart throughout the 1940s and 1950s. Though Britain had entered the Second World War at the state of the art in helicopter experimentation, resource constraints and the higher priority of other aviation programmes led to an official policy of opting out of the helicopter field in 1940 for the duration of hostilities. In the US between 1940 and 1945, urgent wartime military requirements and government financial and technical investment enabled firms to transform the helicopter from an experimental to a production technology during Britain's absence from the field. After 1945, US industry maintained this lead because of important government innovation incentives. Large-scale public development funding was channelled to helicopter firms in the form of major helicopter procurement programmes initiated by the US armed services, which translated into large-scale production orders. Measured in financial and technical terms, post-war US R&D investment dwarfed British government-sponsored efforts. Similarly, measured by production lead-times, cumulative manufacturing orders and helicopter sales, the American technological lead over British efforts during the 1940s and 1950s remained considerable.

A second determinant of post-war market trends was Westland's access to this American technological edge through its long-term relationship with the US Sikorsky firm. By obtaining a series of Sikorsky licences, Westland acquired the means to exploit the experience, investment and technological gains made by America's premier helicopter manufacturer. The pattern after 1947 was that successive licences allowed Westland to access Sikorsky know-how which had been derived, in turn, from substantial US government R&D backing, accumulated manufacturing process expertise, and incrementally refined and operationally proven production technology. Moreover, the licences meant that Westland's development challenge was qualitatively different from its UK competitors. By relying on Sikorsky's manufacturing edge, Westland's task was to adapt and re-engine proven production technology. Conversely, Bristol, Fairey and other UK firms bound by the MoS-sponsored 'all-British' programme were conducting development of unproven and experimental rotor technology, airframe layouts and components. These fundamental differences in activities, each involving radically different levels of technological risk, enabled Westland to enter scale manufacture ahead of its UK competitors.

Sikorsky licences provided Westland with a production edge. However, the third factor underpinning Westland long-term commercial success was the firm's ability to circumvent the implied protectionism of MoS helicopter industrial policy. Westland's core assumptions in adopting the licensed-production route were two-fold: by harnessing the US technological lead, it could manufacture helicopters before its UK rivals, and by employing private venture capital the Westland Board judged that licensed designs were unlikely to encounter protectionism in competition for UK public sectors orders. In the event, Westland's calculations were to prove correct because of the objectives of the British government ministries with a role in the helicopter procurement process. For the armed service ministries a preoccupation with equipment lead-time and performance overrode considerations of helicopter design origin. This was reflected in a preference for proven Westland technology rather than unproven 'all-British' designs and prototypes. The fact that Westland employed its own capital to cover licence costs undermined potential Treasury opposition to service and civil orders on balance of payments grounds. The most serious potential bureaucratic barrier to Westland orders was the MoS, and its policy of fostering 'all-British' helicopter technology. However, initial post-war MoS complacency that Westland licensed production posed no long-term threat to the emergence of 'all-British' designs, coupled with the autonomy that the service ministries enjoyed in selecting and paying for helicopters, undermined the final bureaucratic hurdle to UK civil and military contracts.

The factor that enabled Westland to emerge as the UK's sole helicopter manufacturer was its ability to assimilate and indigenise the know-how obtained from successive Sikorsky licences. Between 1945 and 1955, MoS policy was to support 'all-British' development and oppose Westland licensed production on the grounds that the latter undermined the emergence of an indigenous helicopter design and development capability. By 1955, however, a crucial turning point was MoS recognition that Westland had acquired an in-house design expertise through technology transfer from Sikorsky. This had two important effects. First, Westland now had unhindered access to MoS R&D resources and domestic markets, whereas its rivals developing 'all-British' designs now confronted increased competition for scarce development funding and production contracts. Second, against a backdrop of more general pressures for industrial coalescence in the aircraft sector during the late 1950s, it was these in-house design credentials that removed potential government opposition to Westland's acquisition of its domestic rivals.

Correspondingly, the study shows that the questionable performance of the MoS-sponsored helicopter programme reflected a vicious circle. After 1945, the firms adopting the in-house 'all-British' route to market entry shared the MoS expectations that large-scale government development funding would be forthcoming and that 'buy-British' procurement policies would ensure protected domestic markets. However, the extent to which these expectations were fulfilled was not the sole domain of the MoS. Instead, under the 'Indigenous Procurement Process', the armed service ministries, the Ministry of Civil Aviation, the Ministry of Defence and HM Treasury dictated the scale of R&D funding and production demand.

Throughout the 1940s and 1950s, the very different priorities of these user ministries undermined MoS and industry expectations about government funding and domestic markets. The ready availability of US-designed production helicopters from Westland left little residual development priority or demand for 'all-British' projects. In the Royal Navy's case, the pattern during the 1940s and 1950s was that Westland-licensed production met immediate maritime helicopter requirements. This gave the Admiralty little incentive to endorse MoS R&D funding on 'all-British' helicopter projects that would compete with expenditure on other fields of naval aviation. Despite War Office interest in acquiring helicopters, RAF scepticism about the operational value of helicopters and the Air Ministry's *de facto* control over aircraft purchasing for the army deprived the MoS programme of production orders and development priority. In the absence of military backing for the 'all-British' programme, the MCA and nationalised airlines were reluctant to place firm production orders. The net effect, therefore, was that the MoS was sponsoring an indigenous helicopter programme that bore little relation to the needs of the potential purchasing ministries.

This situation created a 'priority problem' for the 'all-British' helicopter programme. The pattern between 1945 and 1960 was that the lack of development priority and production demand militated against MoS R&D support for 'all-British' development in industry and the Ministry's own research establishments. Without large-scale MoS development support and definite production orders Bristol, Fairey, Saro and other firms adopting the in-house design route were reluctant to risk their own capital and technical resources to stimulate project innovation. Conversely, Westland both contributed to and benefited from this 'priority problem' as it continued to access the significant innovation incentives provided in the USA to Sikorsky. By 1960, Westland's accumulated design expertise and commercial success, coupled with the repeated 'tailoring' of the MoS-sponsored 'all-British' programme as a result of its limited priority, created the conditions for Westland's emergence as the UK's single united helicopter manufacturer.

HELICOPTERS AND HISTORIOGRAPHY

The story of British helicopter R&D and production between 1945 and 1960 is significant in its own right because it bridges a gap in the historical record of a major branch of post-war aviation. However, it is also relevant to broader interpretations of early post-war British aircraft industrial and procurement policy. Historians agree that Britain's performance in converting promising designs into production aircraft between 1945 and 1960 was questionable – a consensus reflecting the high proportion of government-funded aircraft R&D projects that were either abandoned or failed to enter scale manufacture. Illustrative is Fedden, who observes that

> when history comes to be written, it will be found that the years 1946–1956 have played an enormously important part in aeronautical advance, but in spite of this the period has not been a vintage one for Britain.[1]

This study shows that government-sponsored 'all-British' helicopter efforts conform to a wider pattern of project cancellations. At issue is the extent to which events and developments in the helicopter field correspond with the competing assumptions that purport to explain what went wrong with Britain's advanced aviation projects.

The literature on British aircraft procurement is dominated by a popular mythology that holds, in essence, that industry-generated, potentially world-beating aircraft designs and prototypes were wrongly abandoned because of flawed or shortsighted government policies. This view is generally predicated on three assumptions. The first is that the 'genius of British designers and the skills of British engineers and craftsmen'[2] placed the UK in the vanguard of post-war aircraft innovation, in part because the Second World War 'left [only] Britain, the United States and the Soviet Union as the three nations capable of building aircraft on a large scale and with the resources to provide all component parts'.[3] Second, it assumes that it was post-war governments – as the main sponsor, regulator and customer of the aircraft industry – that impeded the conversion of this 'design excellence' into production aircraft. Finally, it presents an alternative counter-factual history: a sanguine conjecture about 'what the aerospace situation in Britain would be now if even a small number of the first-class designs… had been carried through to production and service'.[4] As Edgerton observes, this mythology reflects

> a vast literature which takes these cancellations as indicative of the traditional English lack of commitment to technology. If only we had continued with the TSR-2, especially, we would not be in the mess we are in now. In part, this is part of a larger literature which argues that England should have had the Miles supersonic plane in the 1940s, and the Fairey Delta and V1000 in the 1950s.[5]

It may be the case that this thesis captures the root cause of Britain's questionable performance in a range of aviation sectors. However, it is clearly at variance with trends and developments in the helicopter field. Throughout the 1940s and 1950s, Britain did import some American fixed-wing aircraft, largely as a stopgap until domestic designs became available. However, it was only in the helicopter market that clear technological battle lines were drawn between indigenous design in the form of the MoS 'all-British' helicopter programme and Westland licensed production as a proxy for the US state of the art, competing on what was a *de facto* level playing field. Rather than finding evidence of indigenous British design and manufacturing leadership, this study shows that it was the comprehensive US helicopter development and production lead exploited by Westland that explained UK market trends. Equally, the fundamental disconnection between the 'all-British' programme and actual production demand arose precisely because UK civil and military helicopter requirements were defined by reference to US state of the art that Westland licensed production offered. Importantly, therefore, this study reveals a flaw in the myth that early post-war British aircraft designs were necessarily at the cutting edge.

Britain's helicopter experience also challenges the premise that government failed to support aircraft design efforts in industry. A perennial problem afflicting the 'all-British' helicopter programme throughout the 1940s and 1950s was not a lack of commitment by MoS officials, but rather an acute scarcity of development funding and production orders for 'all-British' projects. In part, this reflected Westland's success in winning major military and civil contracts that served to deprive the MoS-sponsored programme of development priority and markets. Equally, the MoS supported a range of R&D projects for which there was little production demand. In these cases, the lack of demand reflected budgetary constraints affecting the armed service ministries and civil aviation. Throughout the 1940s and 1950s, the relatively low cost and simplicity of airframe design allowed the MoS to fund competing research aircraft and military prototypes within available resources because development to the prototype stage involved 'very low financial demands'.[6] By contrast, because production to the point of operational release 'involved continuously high levels of funding',[7] the potential user ministries were precluded by budgetary constraints from placing orders for all these development projects. In effect, therefore, though available government funds could sustain parallel R&D projects it was inevitable that numerous 'promising' designs and prototypes would fall by the wayside as the armed service ministries and civil aviation were forced to select between competing designs. Consequently, events in the helicopter sector cast doubts over the popular myth that Britain developed potentially world-beating designs that were wrongly cancelled by government. Instead, they raise the issue of why Britain persisted for so long with an ambitious programme of aviation development that it could ill-afford to convert into operational aircraft.

It is precisely this point that underpins the second major critique of Britain's legacy of cancelled aircraft programmes. This view argues that government contracting policies between 1945 and 1960 were deficient precisely because they supported 'too many' aircraft development projects and competing firms.[8] It holds that the failure of successive governments to induce industrial mergers and focus the country's design and industrial efforts on fewer projects starved promising projects of funds and technical manpower, and militated against economies of scale for aircraft types which did enter production.[9] It also assumes that innovation on British aircraft projects was undermined because government industrial policies wrongly emphasised preserving the existing industrial structure instead of fostering genuine competition between individual aircraft-design teams.[10] Correspondingly, this critique presents the alternative counter-factual history that if Britain had encouraged competition and focused 'design teams and production capabilities on fewer development projects more contracts might have been completed'.[11]

In part, the history of 'all-British' helicopter development between 1945 and 1960 lends credence to this 'too many' firms/projects thesis. Over the period, scarce MoS R&D resources were dissipated across 16 helicopter projects of radically different all-up-weights and design configurations at the UK's six helicopter firms. This pattern was replicated in the fragmentation of basic and enabling research at government research establishments. Equally, the MoS criteria for awarding helicopter development contracts were consistently driven as much by the goal of preserving separate design teams as with investing in prototypes with definite production potential. Helicopter firms working on MoS helicopter R&D contracts were given little incentive to reduce development costs or invest private venture capital to force the pace of innovation and they faced limited financial risk in the event of project cancellation. Consequently, with the benefit of hindsight there is ample evidence that successive British governments did support 'too many' helicopter firms and projects.

However, the value of an in-depth study of the policy decisions and events affecting the 'all-British' helicopter programme lies in identifying why UK governments supported the 'all-British' helicopter programme that they did. At one level, the helicopter case points to serious deficiencies in the aircraft procurement process that militated against the focus of funding and resources on fewer projects. These deficiencies stemmed from the very different remits and perspectives of the various government ministries and the degree of autonomy each ministry enjoyed in the aircraft supply process. Throughout the 1940s and 1950s, a combination of policies to diversify industry away from large-scale fixed-wing manufacture, to 'catch up' in fields neglected during the Second World War, official predictions about market potential and a mindset firmly wedded to faith in the superiority of British design created the imperative for the MoS to support the helicopter industrial policy that it did. The MoS was able to implement this policy because it had the autonomy to sponsor R&D in industry. Correspondingly, the various user ministries had the autonomy to exploit American technological advances in the form of Westland licensed production. It was this institutional autonomy that created a fundamental disconnection between helicopter industrial policy and the demands of potential users. This disconnection – mirrored in other aircraft sectors – contributed directly to the 'all-British' helicopter programme that emerged and the subsequent sequence of cancellations.

At another level, however, the helicopter case also reveals limitations in the 'too many' firms/projects critique. Throughout the 1940s and 1950s, the MoS confronted an ongoing problem of positioning an 'all-British' helicopter programme in the face of US-backed Westland competition. Westland was able to draw on the US technological edge, considerable production experience and levels of government investment that were of an order of magnitude greater than funding available in the UK. On this basis, it is difficult to visualise how MoS sponsorship of fewer 'all-British' helicopter projects would have made a difference to longer-term market trends. The dispersal of government R&D funds across an ambitious spectrum of 'all-British' projects, therefore, was only one of a far more complex set of variables that accounted for the legacy of cancelled helicopter projects.

Consequently, though it lends weight to the general assertion that Britain funded 'too many' advanced aviation projects in the 1940s and 1950s, the helicopter case questions the extent to which this provides a sufficient explanation for the comparative failure of indigenous projects. This observation, in itself, suggests the need for further research into British procurement policy across the range of aeronautical branches. As Twigge points out, 'in any historical analysis of technological development a wide spectrum of factors can be identified as influencing and shaping the process'.[12] Only when historians piece together the similarities and differences in the implementation and impact of policy across differing branches of aircraft development on a case-by-case basis will a full picture of early post-war procurement emerge. This in-depth study of the helicopter case implies that there is a requirement for such research, not least to avoid the continuation of a debate dominated largely by myths and generalisations.

THE LICENSED-PRODUCTION DIMENSION

The story of early post-war UK helicopter procurement is as much about technology transfer as it is about public policy. This dimension of the case study is relevant to debates about licensed production as a distinct procurement strategy and contemporary policy issues confronting national governments.

In the vast literature on technology transfer, licensed production is presented as a weapon of procurement strategy that can offer potential benefits over independent national R&D and production on the one hand, and direct import of defence technology items 'off-the-shelf' on the other. Compared to an independent national venture, industrial licences can provide a short-cut to the manufacture of proven production technology that would otherwise require potentially lengthy and expensive R&D. Correspondingly, unlike direct importation of complete systems, a potential benefit of licensed production is that recipient industries are involved in the process and have the prospect of the genuine technology transfer that licences can provide.

The practical experience of recipient licensed production across a range of countries and equipment types has revealed mixed results. Some states have succeeded in 'leap-frogging' the cost and time penalties of independent national development as well as assimilating technology provided under licence.[13] Correspondingly, others have found the licensed-production route extremely costly and instead of exploiting technology transfer they have become embroiled in long-term dependencies on supplier firms or industries.[14] Taken collectively, previous studies point to a relationship between the technological capability of a recipient firm and the degree to which it has been able to exploit the benefits of licensed production. States with existing industrial infrastructure have been most successful at producing licensed defence systems successful in terms of unit production costs and lead-time.[15] Similarly, recipient industries capable of initiating or expanding domestic arms production have been most successful at 'indigenising' know-how obtained under licence, in some cases improving and generating derivatives of licensed designs to the extent that it has been difficult to decide whether it 'belongs to arms transfers or indigenous production'.[16]

The observation that firms and industries with pre-existing know-how and expertise are best placed to exploit licensed production strategies is reinforced by post-war trends and developments in the UK helicopter sector. Though the relative importance of each programme performance variable varied on a contract-by-contract basis, Westland won key UK Service and civil helicopter orders because it out-competed 'all-British' government-sponsored alternatives on unit cost, lead-time and performance criteria. Westland was able to achieve this competitive edge because the firm's in-house technical expertise provided a mechanism to exploit the technological edge that the Sikorsky licences offered. Indicative of this was Westland's ability to reduce the time lag between the first delivery of a parent Sikorsky helicopter to the US armed services and UK service release to 27 months for the S-51, 40 months for the S-55 and 52 months for the S-58. Similarly, this in-house expertise enabled UK manufacture of successive licensed designs that were only marginally more expensive than the US Sikorsky parent versions.

Moreover, Westland's production success and the relative failure of MoS-sponsored R&D programmes did not mark a fundamental loss of an indigenous British helicopter technology capability. Instead, by 1960, the UK had acquired an independent national design and production expertise for two reasons. First, Westland received and exploited genuine technology transfer from Sikorsky; it acquired not only a means of winning production orders, but also an in-house R&D capability. Second, the process of industrial rationalisation brought about by Westland's absorption of its British counterparts concentrated UK helicopter design expertise under one roof, an expertise that had been dissipated over a range of underfunded MoS R&D projects.

The 'Westland model' of indigenisation, repeated with successive Sikorsky licences, was premised on a four-stage process. The first phase was replication of US Sikorsky airframes incorporated with imported American engines. The second phase was installation of British-built engines into the parent design. The third phase involved Westland in-house design modification and improvements to the airframe and subsystem blueprints obtained originally under licence. The final phase was the application of the expertise accrued through the 'anglicisation' process in Westland in-house designs. Rather than becoming technologically dependent, Westland was pragmatically producing US-designed helicopters for commercial purposes, while simultaneously absorbing Sikorsky know-how and expertise.

Between 1945 and 1960, Westland indigenisation increased over time. In 'anglicising' the S-51 during the late 1940s, Westland re-engined and reproduced, in the UK, components of essentially American specifications. Subsequently, however, it began to incorporate accumulating in-house design know-how. In the case of the S-58 Wessex, of which there were seven variants, the firm's value-added input was qualitatively different and involved the synergism of Westland in-house rotor and airframe developments with the proven Sikorsky design. Indeed, when the Wessex was given the UK government-sponsored British Napier Gazelle gas turbine, Westland had produced a helicopter of superior performance to the American S-58 parent version.17 Similarly, by the early 1950s, Westland had applied expertise obtained from its Sikorsky licences in a range of design studies and prototype developments. By 1960, Westland had established its credentials as a capable helicopter design company; credentials that were carried forward inter alia in a series of commercially successful collaborative projects with the French in the 1960s.18

Before 1960, the principal problems afflicting 'all-British' helicopter projects were the dissipation of MoS funding and government sponsorship of programmes for which there was incorrect or inadequate assessment of potential markets. The rationalisation of the industry during the late 1950s, however, concentrated design expertise under one roof. Westland's acquisition of its rivals added to the company's design and production capability.[19] Reorganisation also focused development efforts and financial resources on fewer types for which production was likely, and the outcomes were the Scout and Wasp helicopters of the early 1960s.

Consequently, Westland's long-term relationship with Sikorsky provided the UK with state-of-the-art helicopter technology and the foundations of an indigenous industry. The strength of this relationship can be measured by its subsequent endurance and consolidation after 1960. Throughout the 1960s and 1970s, Westland built on earlier licences when it manufactured and 'anglicised' the Sikorsky SH-3 Sea King.[20] During the so-called 'Westland Affair' of 1984, a factor often lost in the highly politicised debate over the future of the company was the Westland Board's clear preference for consolidating its long-term partnership with Sikorsky rather than rival European proposals for restructuring.[21] Subsequently, GKN Westland Helicopters has built on its relationship with the American firm over several decades and continues to yield world-class rotorcraft technology.[22]

There are dangers in drawing strict parallels from history to inform today's policy making.[23] However, Britain's helicopter experience and previous licensed-production studies offer salient observations for contemporary policy debates. Despite Westland's post-1945 success in indigenising helicopter technology, government-mandated licensed production remained a peripheral procurement strategy in Britain and western Europe throughout the Cold War. Between 1950 and 1989, UK firms acquired just 19 licences for defence systems, primarily in the helicopter field.[24] For the twelve European Union (EU) states over the same period, the aggregate figure was 161 licences for defence systems.[25] Instead, the procurement policies of the West European EU and/or NATO defence ministries emphasised indigenous R&D and production, and selective international collaborative ventures. Domestic sourcing of indigenous designs accounted for between approximately 70 per cent and 90 per cent of the defence equipment budgets of West Germany, France and the UK.[26] In sectors characterised by technical complexity and a relatively high proportion of development costs in total production costs, collaboration was adopted. During the 1980s, for example, in France, West Germany, Italy, Spain and the UK, collaborative projects accounted for 55 per cent of the total number of aircraft projects, 36 per cent of aero-engine projects and 48 per cent of missile developments.[27] Measured against these trends, therefore, licensed production remained a marginal procurement strategy.

The result throughout the Cold War was that the West European states' desire for independence resulted in largely separate national arms industries capable of developing a range of advanced weapons systems indigenously. The inefficiencies associated with 'self-sufficiency' procurement policies were well understood:[28] fragmentation and duplication of R&D and production,[29] short production runs in relation to US output, under-utilisation of industrial capacity and protected domestic monopolies leading to low productivity.[30] However, relatively high levels of Cold War defence equipment expenditure and the West European states' desire to source nationally where possible for domestic political reasons[31] largely outweighed the potential economic gains from procurement alternatives involving technology transfer.

Since the end of the Cold War, political and economic pressures for West European procurement rationalisation are more acute. On the demand side, reduced threat perceptions are reflected in declining equipment budgets: since 1987, procurement expenditure by the European NATO allies has fallen by over 15 per cent in real terms, and 'a further decline in the demand for major weapons systems appears inevitable'.[32] These cuts are occurring as equipment unit costs are rising in real terms: new generations of combat aircraft, for example, are between two and four times more expensive than the systems being replaced.[33] Moreover, inflationary trends in military equipment are compounded by reduced R&D outlays and unit production orders. Meanwhile, on the supply side, declining equipment orders have also been instrumental in extensive West European defence-manufacturing restructuring.[34] The significance of these trends is the challenge they present to the traditional influence and control that governments have enjoyed over domestic defence firms.

The post-Cold War scenario has led policy commentators and national governments throughout Western Europe to assess new procurement strategies to ameliorate inflationary trends in defence equipment and the increasing internationalisation of military technology. At one extreme, some commentators argue that the solution lies in efficiency improvements in procurement processes and defence manufacturing policies at the individual national level.[35] Others point to gains through innovation in the management, organisational arrangements and scope of international collaborative ventures. At the other extreme, some analysts argue that a 'pan-European' arms market is inevitable,[36] either in the form of a Single European Market (SEM) for defence contracts or, controlled by a centralised European Armament Agency (EAA) supporting a common future European defence and security policy.[37] Throughout, however, no assessment has been made of the potential for licensed production policies to alleviate the new constraints. Instead, licensed production remains a 'hidden dimension' in the current procurement debate.

Britain's early post-war experience with helicopter procurement does not imply that licensed production is a panacea for all the constraints currently affecting West European defence ministries. It suggests, though, that government-mandated licensed production may offer a more cost-effective balance between states' national interests in terms of domestic employment levels, the retention or acquisition of indigenous high-technology expertise and security of supply on the one hand, and inflationary trends in defence equipment on the other. It also suggests, in line with previous studies, that pre-existing levels of defence industrial capability in Britain and other West European states provides the necessary preconditions to exploit the maximum benefits from industrial licences. What Britain's early post-war experience with helicopter technology suggests, therefore, is that licensed production as a distinct procurement strategy should no longer remain the 'hidden dimension' of the contemporary UK and West European procurement debate.

NOTES

1. R. Fedden, *Britain's Air Survival: An Appraisement and Strategy for Success* (London: Cassell, 1957), p. 111.
2. D. Wood, *Project Cancelled: The Disaster of Britain's Abandoned Aircraft Projects* (London: Tri-Service Press, 1990), p. 240.
3. Ibid., p. 14.
4. Ibid., p. 6.
5. D. Edgerton, *England and the Aeroplane: An Essay on a Militant and Technological Nation* (London: Macmillan, 1991), p. 91.
6. F. Gregory and J. Simpson, 'The Acquisition of Military Aircraft in Great Britain and West Germany', in F.B. Horton, A.C. Rogerson and E.L. Warner (eds), *Comparative Defense Policy* (London: Johns Hopkins University Press, 1974), p. 459.
7. Ibid.
8. E. Devons, 'The Aircraft Industry', in D. Burns (ed.), *The Structure of British Industry II* (Cambridge: Cambridge University Press, 1964), pp. 45–92.
9. M. Kirby, 'British Culture and the Development of High Technology Sectors', Mimeo, Department of Economics (The Management School), Lancaster

University, 1995, pp. 1–36.

10. T. Geiger, '"The Next War is Bound to Come": Defence Production Policy, Supply Departments and Defence Contractors in Britain, 1945–57', in H. Mercer, N. Rollings and J.D. Tomlinson (eds), *The Labour Governments and Private Industry: The Experience of 1945–1951* (Edinburgh: Edinburgh University Press, 1992), p. 112.
11. Ibid.
12. S.R. Twigge, *The Early Development of Guided Weapons in the United Kingdom, 1940–1960* (Reading: Harwood, 1993), p. 235.
13. G.R. Hall and R.E. Johnson, 'Aircraft Co-Production and Procurement Strategy', *RAND Report R-450-PR*, May 1967; M.W. Chinworth and R. Matthews, 'Defence Industrialisation Through Offsets: The Case of Japan', in S. Martin (ed.), *The Economics of Offsets: Defence Procurements and Countertrade* (Reading: Harwood, 1966), p. 206; M. Moodie, 'Defence Industries in the Third World: Problems and Promises', in S.G. Neuman and R.E. Harkavy (eds), *Arms Transfers in the Modern World* (New York, Praeger, 1979), p. 17; and A. Redlich and M. Miscavage, 'The Business of Offsets: A Practitioner's Case Study: Israel', in S. Martin, *The Economics of Offsets*, pp. 321–36.
14. See for example: I. Bellany and J. Richardson,'Australian Defence Procurement' in G.H. Gelber (ed.), *Problems of Australian Defence* (Melbourne: Oxford University Press, 1970), pp. 255–56; C. Groth, 'The Economics of Weapons Co-production', in M. Edmonds (ed.), *International Arms Procurement: New Directions* (Oxford: Pergamon Press, 1981), p. 71; W. Struys, 'Offsets and Weapons Procurement: The Belgium Experience' in S. Martin (ed.), *The Economics of Offsets: Defence Procurement and Countertrade* (Reading: Harwood, 1996), pp. 75–105; D. Deng and M.W. Chinworth, 'The Teeth of the Little Tigers: Offsets, Defense Production and Economic Development in South Korea and Taiwan', in *The Economics of Offsets*, pp. 245–98; S. Markowski and P. Hall, 'Defense Offsets Policy in Australia', in *The Economics of Offsets*, pp. 49–74; and, B. Udis, 'US-Swiss F-5 Transaction and the Evolution of Swiss Offsets Policy', in *The Economics of Offsets*, pp. 321–36.
15. C. Catrina, *Arms Transfers and Dependence* (London: Taylor & Francis, 1988), p. 275. Hartley substantiates this claim with statistics that indicate the cost penalties for licensed production over direct imports are at least 10–20 per cent for developed and 40–50 per cent for developing countries, in K. Hartley, *NATO Arms Co-operation: A Study in Economics and Politics* (London: George Allen & Unwin, 1983), p. 127.
16. Catrina, *Arms Transfers*, p. 191.
17. For a discussion addressing Westland's S-58 improvements after 1960, see M.R.H. Uttley, 'British Helicopter Production, 1945–1960: A Case Study of Technology Transfer and Market Dominance', *Science and Public Policy*, Vol. 18, No. 4, August 1991, pp. 240–41.
18. See Jane's, *All the World's Aircraft, 1974–75* (London: Jane's, 1975), p. 236.
19. D. Mondey, *Westland* (London: Jane's, 1987), p. 39.
20. For a general discussion of the SH-3 Sea King, see P. Beaver, *Modern Military Helicopters* (Wellingborough: Patrick Stephens, 1987), pp. 154–59.
21. See S. Croft, 'The Westland Helicopter Crisis: Implications for the British Defence Industry', *Defense Analysis*, Vol. 3, No. 4, 1987, pp. 291–303; and, L. Freedman, 'The Case of Westland and the Bias to Europe', *International Affairs*, Vol. 63, No. 1, Winter 1986/87, pp. 1–19.
22. See M.R.H. Uttley, 'Rotary Wing Aircraft', in R. Bud and P. Gummett (eds), *Cold War, Hot Science* (Reading: Harwood, 1999), pp. 75–80.

23. For a general discussion, see K. Hartley, 'Public Procurement and Competitiveness: A Community Market for Military Hardware and Technology', *Journal of Common Market Studies*, Vol. XXV, 1987, p. 239.
24. Figures cited in S. Martin, 'Countertrade and Offsets: An Overview of the Theory and Evidence', in *The Economics of Offsets*, p. 36.
25. Ibid.
26. Statistics obtained from M. Bittleston, 'Co-operation or Competition: Defence Procurement Options for the 1990s', *Adelphi Paper*, No. 250 (London: Brassey's, 1990).
27. Statistics contained in K. Hartley and S. Martin, 'The Political Economy of International Collaboration', in R. Coopey, M.R.H. Uttley and G. Spinardi (eds), *Defence Science and Technology: Adjusting to Change* (Reading: Harwood, 1993), p. 182.
28. For a discussion of these factors, see M.R.H. Uttley, 'The Integration of West European Defense Procurement: Issues and Prospects', *Defense Analysis*, Vol. 11, No. 3, 1995, pp. 280–81.
29. See T.A. Callaghan, 'The Structural Dimension of NATO', *NATO Review*, Vol. 32, 3 June 1984, pp. 21-6.
30. See M. Chalmers, *Paying for Defence: Military Spending and British Decline* (London: Pluto, 1985).
31. For a more extensive discussion, see the collection of articles in M. Edmonds (ed.), *International Arms Procurement: New Directions* (New York: Pergamon Press, 1981).
32. W. Walker and S. Willett,'Restructuring the European Defence Industrial Base', *Defence Economics*, Vol. 4, 1993, p. 142.
33. P. Pugh, 'The Procurement Nexus', *Defence Economics*, Vol. 4, 1993, p. 180.
34. For a discussion, see W. Walker and P. Gummett, 'Britain and the European Arms Market', *International Affairs*, Vol. 65, 1989, pp. 419–42.
35. See, for example, J. Aitken, 'Defence Procurement: Past, Present and Future', *RUSI Journal*, February 1994, pp. 39–42; and J. Bourn, *Securing Value for Money in Defence Procurement*, Whitehall Paper No. 25 (London: RUSI, 1994).
36. See, for example, the collection of papers in C. Drown and K. Campbell (eds), *A Single European Arms Industry* (London: Brassey's, 1990).
37. For an overview of this debate, see P. De Vestel, 'Defence Markets and Industries in Europe: Time for Political Decisions?', *Chaillot Paper 21* (Paris: Western European Union, November 1995); and, RUSI Working Group, *1992: Protectionism or Collaboration in Defence Procurement*, Whitehall Paper No. 6 (London: RUSI, 1990).

Appendices

APPENDIX 1: BRITISH ROTARY-WING AIRCRAFT PROJECTS, 1945–60

Firm	*Project*	*Initiation Date*	*Design Approach*	*Actual/ Estimated AUW (kg)*	*Project Details*
Bristol	Type 171	1944	single rotor	2,449	MoS-sponsored
	Type 173/B191/B192	1948	tandem rotor	4,808–8,618	MoS-sponsored
Fairey	Gyrodyne	1947	compound	2,177	MoS-sponsored
	Jet Gyrodyne	1949	Gyrodyne with tip jets	2,722	MoS-sponsored
	Rotodyne	1949	compound	14,969	MoS-sponsored
	Ultra-Light	1954	tip jets	817	MoS-sponsored
Saro	Air Horse	1946	three rotor	6,804–7,938	MoS-sponsored
	Skeeter	1947	single rotor	1,043	MoS-sponsored
	P.531	1956	single rotor	2,495	MoS-sponsored
Percival	P.74	1950	single rotor tip-jet drive	3,515	MoS-sponsored
Westland	S-51	1947 on receipt of Sikorsky licence	single rotor	2,663	Private-venture licensed variant of Sikorsky design
	S-55	1951 on receipt of Sikorsky licence	single rotor	3,402	Private-venture licensed variant of Sikorsky design
	Widgeon	1954	single rotor	2,676	Private-venture in-house design
	Westminster	1954	single rotor	14,969	Private-venture in-house design
	S-58 Wessex	1956 on receipt of Sikorsky licence	single rotor	5,715–6,124	Private-venture licensed variant of Sikorsky design

APPENDIX 2: DETERMINANTS OF MOS R&D FUNDING LEVELS IN INDUSTRY IN THE 'INDIGENOUS PROCUREMENT PROCESS'

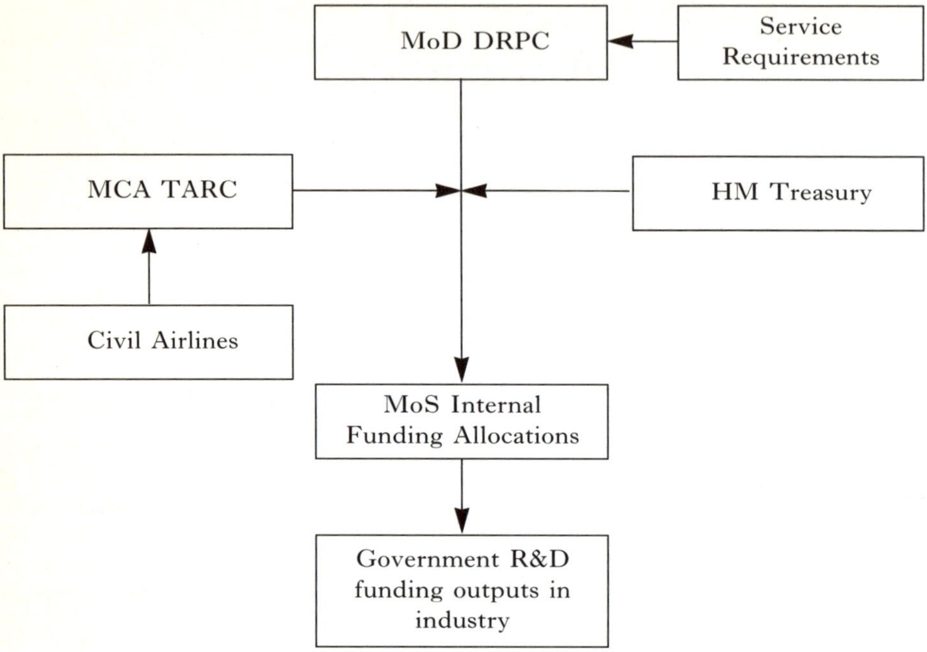

APPENDIX 3: THE ORGANISATION OF PRODUCTION REQUIREMENTS IN THE 'INDIGENOUS PROCUREMENT PROCESS'

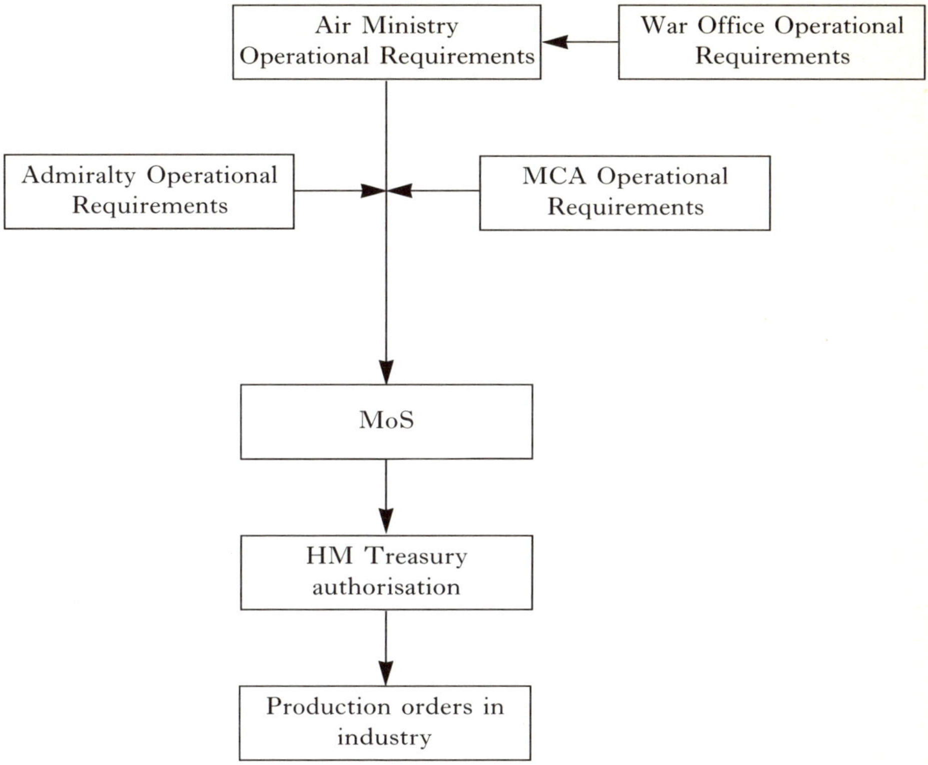

APPENDIX 4: THE 'LICENSED PRODUCTION PROCUREMENT PROCESS'

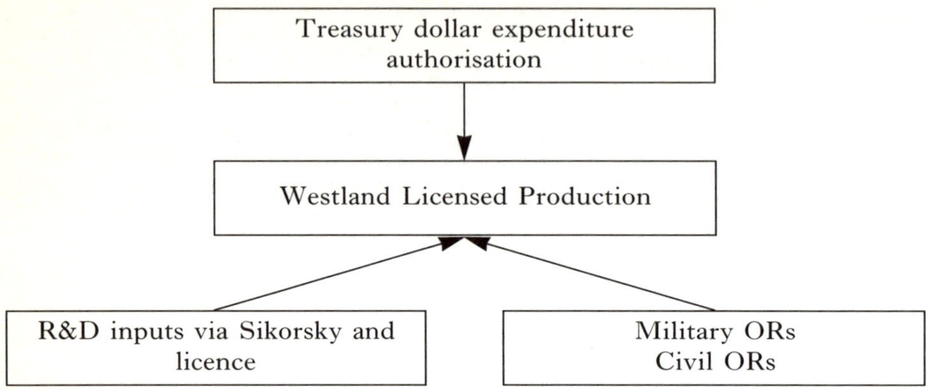

Bibliography

PUBLIC RECORDS OF THE UNITED KINGDOM

This is a summary of the main files of the Public Record Office (PRO) consulted in the course of this research. The following abbreviations are used for the location and designation of documentary sources:

ADM	Admiralty
AIR	Air Ministry
AVIA	Ministry of Aircraft Production (1940–46); Ministry of Supply (1946–60)
DEFE	Ministry of Defence
T	Treasury
WO	War Office

ADM Series

ADM 1/20428, Requirements for Helicopters in the Royal Navy (1946–47).
ADM 1/20936, Joint Paper on Sea and Air Aspects of Fleet Defence Against Submarines (1947).
ADM 1/21827, Analysis of Future Development of Naval Aviation (1950).
ADM 1/22381, Accident to Dragonfly I, VZ 961 25 June 1951: Report of Board of Enquiry (1951–52).
ADM 1/22777, Provision of Helicopter Flight for Mediterranean Fleet: Approvals for Trial to Evaluate Tactical Value (1951).
ADM 1/22804, New Aircraft: Revised Procedures for Formulation of Staff Requirements (1951–57).
ADM 264/34, Dragonfly HR1 Aircraft: Pilots' Notes (1950).
ADM 264/35, Dragonfly HR Mks 3 and 5: Pilots' Notes (1957–61).
ADM 264/36, Dragonfly Mk 5 Aircraft: Flight Test Schedule (Undated).
ADM 264/48, Whirlwind HAR Mk 1 Aircraft (1953–68).
ADM 264/60, Wessex HU Mk 5 Aircraft: Pilots' Notes (1965).
ADM 264/90, Whirlwind HAS Mk 7 Aircraft: Flight Test Schedule (1959).

AIR Series

AIR 2/5716, AOP and Rotary-Wing Aircraft: Clearance for RAF Use.
AIR 2/10797, Helicopters – Heavy Lift: Policy.
AIR 2/11428, Interservice Committee: Policy for Helicopters.
AIR 2/13518, Financial Aspects and Purchase of Skeeter Aircraft (1954–59).
AIR 2/14309, Helicopters for Use in Malaya (1954–55).
AIR 2/14410, Fairey Rotodyne: Policy, (1954–59).
AIR 2/14480, General Purpose Helicopter OR 325: Policy (1955–56).
AIR 2/14734, Helicopters for the Queen's Flight: Policy (1957–68).
AIR 2/14744, General Purpose Helicopter OR 325: Policy (1956–57).
AIR 2/14745, General Purpose Helicopter OR 325: Policy (1957–64).
AIR 2/14886, Sycamore/Whirlwind: Replacement Helicopter OR 348 (1958–60).
AIR 2/14887, British Helicopter Development (1958–60).
AIR 2/14888, Helicopter: Policy (1958–61).
AIR 2/14890, General Purpose Helicopter Air Staff Requirement No. 325: Bristol 192 Belvedere (1958–59).
AIR 2/15120, Helicopter Requirements (1952–64).
AIR 2/15149, Medium Transport Helicopters: Policy (1952–55).
AIR 2/15308, Sycamore Mks 11, 13 and 14 General Purpose Helicopter: Operational Requirements (1959–60).
AIR 2/15353, Bristol 192 Belvedere: General Purpose Helicopter (1959).
AIR 2/15354, Bristol 192 Belvedere: General Purpose Helicopter (1959–60).
AIR 2/15376, Fairey Rotodyne: Standards of Preparation (1959–66).
AIR 2/15377, Fairey Rotodyne: Policy (1959–61).
AIR 2/15693, Belvedere Helicopter: Air Staff Requirements (1960).
AIR 2/15701, Fairey Rotodyne: Standards of Preparation (1960).
AIR 2/15702, Fairey Rotodyne: Standards of Preparation (1960–61).
AIR 2/15709, Wessex Helicopter: Standards of Preparation (1960–61).
AIR 2/15891, Saunders-Roe Skeeter Helicopter (1961–63).
AIR 2/16039, General Purpose Helicopter: Air Staff Requirements (1961–62).
AIR 2/16082, Helicopters: Policy (1961–62).
AIR 2/16085, Bristol Belvedere: Operational Requirements (1961).
AIR 2/16252, ASR/OR 325: Bristol Belvedere Helicopter (1962–63).
AIR 2/16438, Wessex Helicopter: Standards of Preparation (1962).
AIR 2/16585, Air Staff Target 358, Utility Helicopter (later Chinook) (1963–65).
AIR 20/690, Development of the Autogiro and Helicopter for Operational Purposes (1933–36).
AIR 20/10294, Helicopters: ACAS Papers (1957–58).
AIR 20/10305, Transport-VIP Aircraft: Communications Flying (1958–64).
AIR 20/10927, Wessex Helicopter: Standard of Preparation (1960–62).
AIR 45/21, Review of Arnold/Evill Agreement.

AVIA Series

AVIA 15/954, Rotating Wing Aircraft Development.
AVIA 15/2245, Development of Helicopters.
AVIA 44/536, Work of the AFEE (1940–45).
AVIA 44/597, Fairey Aviation: Design Activity (1939–45).
AVIA 46/122, Westland Whirlwind (1935–46).
AVIA 46/145, Helicopters (1943).
AVIA 46/483, Supply of Ultra-Light Helicopter Requirement 144D.
AVIA 53/21, Bristol Helicopter Company: Supply of Sycamore (1948–52).
AVIA 53/27, Cierva: E24 Helicopter.
AVIA 53/32, Supply of Dragonfly.
AVIA 53/484, Invitation for Experimental Requirement 143T.
AVIA 53/485, Fairey Design.
AVIA 53/486, AV Roe Design.
AVIA 53/525–53/526, 1956–60: S-58 and Spec. Helicopter Anti-Submarine 170D.
AVIA 53/527, S-58 Supply.
AVIA 53/551, Contract for Design of Jet for Ultra-Light.
AVIA 54/163–54/174, Bristol Helicopter Spec. 34/46.
AVIA 54/340-54/345, Westland Sikorsky S-51: Naval Spec. S14/48.
AVIA 54/380, Cierva 14 (Adaptation).
AVIA 54/395, Army Version of B4/46 Helicopter Spec. No. A9/49.
AVIA 54/397, Small Helicopter for Air Observation Spec. No. A13/49.
AVIA 54/421, Helicopters for CASEVAC in Malaya: Design Action.
AVIA 54/498, Naval Target for Anti-Submarine Target.
AVIA 54/513, Hoppi-copter Helicopter.
AVIA 54/541–54/544, A13/49 Skeeter.
AVIA 54/565–54/567, S-51 and Variants.
AVIA 54/585, Sikorsky S-55 Helicopter.
AVIA 54/590–54/591, VTO Trials of Fairey E10/47.
AVIA 54/609, Firth Helicopter.
AVIA 54/619, 1946–54: General Purpose Helicopter Spec. OR.1280.
AVIA 54/626–54/627, B171 Helicopter.
AVIA 54/631, Development of the W.11 Helicopter (1947–56).
AVIA 54/662, Sycamore Helicopter.
AVIA 54/680–54/683, B171 Helicopter.
AVIA 54/687, B171 HC. Mk 11.
AVIA 54/727, 1951/52: Helicopter Requirements.
AVIA 54/731, Sycamore (1951–53).
AVIA 54/741, Conversion of B171 (1951–52).
AVIA 54/742, Large Helicopter for BEA (1951–53).
AVIA 54/768, Small Jet Helicopter Proposal (1947–49).
AVIA 54/786, Westland Sikorsky S-51 (1952).
AVIA 54/787, Fitment of Stub Wings to B171 (1952–56).
AVIA 54/790, Review of R&D (1951–52).

AVIA 54/792, Sycamore Mk1 (1952–53).
AVIA 54/795, B182 Design Action (1952).
AVIA 54/803, Westland Proposals for High-Speed Helicopters (1952).
AVIA 54/828–54/831, B171 for the Australian Navy (1952–54).
AVIA 54/832, B173 (1952–55).
AVIA 54/860, Armament for S-55 (1952–55).
AVIA 54/865, ASW Helicopter (NSR NA.43): Considerations (1952–54).
AVIA 54/873, B171 Mk10 (1952-1953).
AVIA 54/880, Design and Development of B191 to Spec. HR146 (1953–62).
AVIA 54/889, S-55 Leonides (1953).
AVIA 54/903, Sycamore Service Trials in Malaya (1952–55).
AVIA 54/916, Proposed use of B173 against NA 43 (1952–56).
AVIA 54/1065, W.11; BEA Requirements (1948–49).
AVIA 54/1123, W.11; BEA Requirements (1950–51).
AVIA 54/1299, Leonides for Bristol Helicopter E.34/64: Design (1946–50).
AVIA 54/1303, Mamba in GR.17/45 (Fairey) (1946–52).
AVIA 54/1321, Fairey Jet-Engined Helicopters: Policy (1947–48).
AVIA 54/1380, VTO; Fairey: Policy (1946–48).
AVIA 54/1458, Assistance to Industry by MoS R&D Organisations (1948–49).
AVIA 54/1573, Future Defence Research Policy (1947–48).
AVIA 54/1584, Defence R&D Priorities (1950–51).
AVIA 54/1686, Development of General Purpose Helicopter (1953–57).
AVIA 54/1972, S-51 Spec. S.14/48: General Design (1944–50).
AVIA 55/90, Use of Helicopters: Reports and Papers (1945–48).
AVIA 55/163, Dragonfly: Production Requirements (1948–53).
AVIA 55/176, Helicopters for Casualty Evacuation: Production of the Dragonfly Helicopter (1949–53).
AVIA 65/4, Bristol B191: Finance and Policy (1952–55).
AVIA 65/6, Helicopter Policy on R&D (1953–55).
AVIA 65/7, Marine Reconnaissance Helicopter: Finance and Policy (1954–56).
AVIA 65/8, Bristol B173 Development Programme.
AVIA 65/24, Westland Proposals for S-56: Finance and Policy (1954–56).
AVIA 65/39, BEA Helicopter Policy (1951–58).
AVIA 65/85, Reduction of Helicopter Noise (including Rotodyne), (1954–61).
AVIA 65/107, MoS Rotating-Wing Committee (1951–58).
AVIA 65/108, Westland HR127 (S-55): Specifications and Design.
AVIA 65/211–65/212, Engine Requirements for the Rotodyne.
AVIA 65/262, Proposals for Fairey Rotodyne (1949–51).
AVIA 65/263, Proposals for Fairey Rotodyne (1951–56).
AVIA 65/264, Percival Gas Turbine Helicopter (1950–56).
AVIA 65/265, Percival Gas Turbine Helicopter (1951–58).
AVIA 65/266, Inter-Departmental Helicopter Committee: Reports (1948–56).

AVIA 65/268, Army Helicopter Working Party: Reports (1953–54).
AVIA 65/269, Helicopter Panel (1951–57).
AVIA 65/285, Specifications: HR127P (S-58) (1952–57).
AVIA 65/602, Future Size of the Aircraft Industry.
AVIA 65/614, Rotodyne: Policy Proposals (1956–59).
AVIA 65/627, Specification H150 (1954–65).
AVIA 65/638, Specification H163P2 SARO Skeeter (1956–62).
AVIA 65/641, Specification HAS 170D: RN ASW Helicopter (1956–64).
AVIA 65/723, Helicopter R&D Policy (1955–61).
AVIA 65/784, Development of the Napier Gazelle for B191, B192 and Westland (1954–62).
AVIA 65/1302, Specification: Wessex (1956–60).
AVIA 65/1305, Specification: Whirlwind (1957–63).
AVIA 65/1309, Ultra-Light: Naval Staff Requirement and Specification (1957–58).
AVIA 65/1311, B173: Design and Performance (1947–55).
AVIA 65/1410, Engines for Helicopters: Finance and Policy (1958–67).
AVIA 65/1418, Alouette as Stop-Gap for P531 (1958–67).
AVIA 65/1446, Westland Aircraft Group.
AVIA 65/1630, Defence Research Policy Committee (1963–66).
AVIA 65/1642, Helicopter R&D Policy (1961–65).

DEFE Series

[DEFE 9: Tizard Papers]
DEFE 9/6, Research and Development Effort and Organisation (1945–49).
DEFE 9/7, Research and Development Effort and Organisation (1947).
DEFE 9/8, Defence Research Progress Report (1948–50).
DEFE 9/12, Defence Research Policy Committee: Report DRP(47) 98 on Future Defence Research Policy and other Papers (1947–48).
DEFE 9/13, Submissions and Proposals for 1950 Review of Future Defence Research and Development Policy (1948–50).
DEFE 9/34, Defence Policy: Strategy (1949–51).
DEFE 9/35, Tizard Committee: Development of Weapons (Undated).

[DEFE 10: Memoranda and Minutes of Meetings]
DEFE 10/18 – DEFE 10/20, Memoranda (1947).
DEFE 10/21 – DEFE 10/23, Memoranda (1948).
DEFE 10/24 – DEFE 10/25, Memoranda (1949).
DEFE 10/26 – DEFE 10/28, Memoranda (1950).
DEFE 10/29 – DEFE 10/30, Memoranda (1951).
DEFE 10/31, Memoranda (1952).
DEFE 10/32, Memoranda (1953).
DEFE 10/33, Memoranda (1954).
DEFE 10/34, Memoranda (1955).

DEFE 10/35, Memoranda (1956).
DEFE 10/36, Minutes of Evidence (1947–48).
DEFE 10/37, Minutes of Evidence (1949–50).
DEFE 10/38, Minutes of Evidence (1951–52).
DEFE 10/39, Minutes of Evidence (1953–54).
DEFE 10/40, Minutes of Evidence (1955–56).

[DEFE 11: Chiefs of Staff Meetings]
DEFE 11/15, Defence Research and Development (1947–53).
DEFE 11/79, Army/Air Cooperation by Ministry of Defence (1952–54).
DEFE 11/80, Army/Air Cooperation by Ministry of Defence (1954–55).

T Series

T 225/129, Information for Estimates Subcommittee on Manpower and Expenditure: Control of Research and Development (1949–51).
T 225/245, Ministry of Civil Aviation: Expenditure Estimates (1944–53).
T 225/305 – T 225/314, Defence Programme: Policy.
T 225/350, Policy Questions Relating to Treasury Control over Defence Department Expenditure (1953–54).
T 225/361, Inter-Departmental Committee on Civil Aviation Policy (1955).
T 225/369, Planning of Aircraft Industry to Maintain UK War Potential (1955).
T 225/374, Air Ministry Requirements on Postwar Production of Aircraft and Equipment (1945–47).
T 225/375, Air Ministry Requirements on Postwar Production of Aircraft and Equipment (1948–50).
T 225/376, Air Ministry Requirements on Postwar Production of Aircraft and Equipment (1950–51).
T 225/377, Air Ministry Requirements on Postwar Production of Aircraft and Equipment (1951–55).
T 225/378, Production and Development of Military Aircraft including Papers leading to White Paper on the Supply of Military Aircraft, Cmd 9388 (1955).
T 225/384, Tendering by Foreign Firms for Government Contracts in the UK (1954).
T 225/430, Design, Development and Purchase of New Civil Aircraft for the British Airways Corporation, including Memoranda, Minutes and Reports of Civil Aircraft Requirements Committee (1947–48).
T 225/431, Design, Development and Purchase of New Civil Aircraft for the British Airways Corporation, including Memoranda, Minutes and Reports of Civil Aircraft Requirements Committee (1949–52).
T 225/496, Air Ministry: Payment of Contractors for Cancellation of Contracts (1956).
T 225/511, Defence Programme: Production Priorities (1951–55).
T 225/606 (1), Treasury Participation in Defence Research Policy Committee (1951–58).

T 225/606 (2), Treasury Control over Military Research and Development (1951–58).
T 225/644, Expenditure on Research and Development of Civil Aircraft (1947–58).
T 255/653, Aircraft Industry: Postwar Financing (including capital assistance); Treatment of Surplus Aircraft and Engines; Location Policy (1943–49).
T 225/657, Government Reply to Second Report of Select Committee on Estimates on Supply of Military Aircraft (1957–58).
T 225/662, Expenditure on Defence Research and Development Programme (1956-1957).
T 225/663, Expenditure on Defence Research and Development Programme (1957).
T 225/664, Expenditure on Defence Research and Development Programme (1957–58).
T 225/665, Cancellation and Revision of Contracts following Review of Defence Programme; Payments to Contractors (1952–58).
T 225/696, Tactical Air Support for the Army: Provision of Aircraft and Equipment (1954–59).
T 225/697, Formation of Helicopter Force for Army Troop Transport (1959–60).
T 225/797, Aircraft Research and Development Programme Estimates: Correspondence on Programmes (1950–54).
T 225/798, Aircraft Research and Development Programme Estimates: Correspondence on Programmes (1954–57).
T 225/799, Aircraft Research and Development Programme Estimates: Correspondence on Programmes (1957–59).
T 225/800, Aircraft Research and Development Programme Estimates: Treasury Control of Expenditure Policy (1953–59).
T 225/819, Ministry of Supply: Development of Gas Turbines for Civil Purposes (1951–59).
T 225/840, Defence Research and Development Programme: 1959 Review (1959).
T 225/841, Cancellation of Contracts and Requisitions under the Defence Programme (1955–59).
T 225/1010–T225/1011, Royal Air Force Aeroplanes: Production Programme for Bombers and Transporters (1951–53).
T 225/1074, Air Ministry Production Programmes (1957–58).
T 225/1101, Fleet Air Arm: Provision of Aircraft (1946–49).
T 225/1102, Fleet Air Arm: Provision of Aircraft (1949–51).
T 225/1103, Fleet Air Arm: Provision of Aircraft (1951–54).
T 225/1104, Fleet Air Arm: Provision of Aircraft (1954–60).
T 225/1139, Napier Eland Engines (1953–59).
T 225/1140, Napier Eland Engines (1959).
T 225/1218, Review of the Defence Departments' Production Expenditure (1958–60).
T 225/1261, Admiralty Fleet Air Arm: Provision of Aircraft and Associated

Equipment (1958–60).
T 225/1263, Provision of Aircraft (1955–60).
T 225/1264, Provision of Aircraft (1958–60).
T 225/1296, Future of UK Aircraft Industry: Aircraft Industry Working Party (1957).
T 225/1297, Future of UK Aircraft Industry: Aircraft Industry Working Party (1958).
T 225/1307, Machinery for Control of Departmental Expenditure: Research and Development (1954–56).
T 225/1319, Admiralty: Fleet Air Arm; Provision of Aircraft (1954–56).
T 225/1376, Air Ministry: Production Programme; Transports (1959).
T 225/1504, Defence Programme: Size of UK Research and Development Effort; Special Study (1959–60).
T 225/1606, Ordering of P.531 Helicopter for Army (1959–60).
T 225/1607, Rotodyne Helicopter (1955–58).
T 225/1608, Rotodyne Helicopter (1958).
T 225/1609, Rotodyne Helicopter (1958–60).
T 225/1610, Development of Westland 'Wessex' Helicopter and Equipment (1956–60).
T 225/1611, Helicopters: RAF Production Requirements (1957–60).
T 225/1612, Helicopters: RN Production Requirements (1957–60).
T 225/1627, Recovery of Research and Development Costs: Policy (1950–57).

WO Series

WO 32/11857, Land/Air Warfare; Policy Subcommittee (1946–50).
WO 32/12214, Recognition Air to Ground (1946–55).
WO 32/13525, Evacuation of Casualties by Helicopter: Policy (1947–55).
WO 32/15177, Cargo Helicopters (1953).

UNITED STATES NATIONAL ARCHIVES

This is a summary of the main files of the United States National Archives (USNA), Washington DC, consulted during the research:

i. United States Air Corps and Army Air Forces Library Collection

File No. 452.1, Helicopters (1940–44).

ii. United States Joint Chiefs of Staff Collection

File No. 452.1, Helicopters (1940–44).

iii. United States State Department Files (1947–55)

File No. 841.3333, Manufacturing.
File No. 841.11, Manufacturing.
File No. 841.248, Aircraft.
File No. 741.5622, Military Aircraft.

iv. United States War Production Board Collection

File No. 314.228, Helicopter Production.
File No. 314.242, Helicopter Production.
File No. 314.248, Helicopter Production.
File No. 313.16, Helicopter Production..

BRITISH GOVERNMENT PUBLICATIONS

Command Papers

Central Organisations for Defence, *Cmd 6923* (London: HMSO, October 1946).
Statement Relating to Defence, 1947, *Cmd 7042* (London: HMSO, 1947).
Statement Relating to Defence, 1948, *Cmd 7327* (London: HMSO, 1948).
Statement on Defence, 1952, *Cmd 8475* (London: HMSO, 1952).
Statement on Defence, 1953, *Cmd 8768* (London: HMSO, 1953).
Statement on Defence, 1954, *Cmd 9075* (London: HMSO, 1954).
Statement on Defence, 1955, *Cmd 9391* (London: HMSO, 1955).
Statement on Defence, 1956, *Cmd 9691* (London: HMSO, 1956).
The Supply of Military Aircraft, *Cmd 9388* (London: HMSO), 1955.
Defence – Outline of Future Policy, *Cmnd 124* (London: HMSO, 1957).
Memorandum by the Secretary of State for Air to Accompany Air Estimates, 1957–58, *Cmnd 149* (London: HMSO, 1957).
Explanatory Statement on the Navy Estimates 1957–58 by the First Lord of the Admiralty, *Cmnd 151* (London: HMSO, 1958).
Air Ministry Memorandum by the Secretary of State for Air to Accompany Air Estimates, 1958–59, *Cmnd 373* (London: HMSO, 1958).
Defence Statistics 1959–60, *Cmnd 661* (London: HMSO, 1959).
Progress of the Five-Year Plan, *Cmnd 662* (London: HMSO, 1959).
Memorandum by the Secretary of State for Air to Accompany Air Estimates 1959–60, *Cmnd 673* (London: HMSO, 1959).
Report on Defence 1960, *Cmnd 952* (London: HMSO, 1960).
Report on Defence 1961, *Cmnd 1288* (London: HMSO, 1961).
Report of the Committee of Inquiry into the Aircraft Industry, *Cmnd. 2853* (London: HMSO, 1965).

House of Commons Papers

Second Report with Evidence taken before Subcommittee E of the Select Committee on Estimates of Session 1956–57, The Supply of Military Aircraft, *HCP 34* (London: HMSO, 1956).

Third Report from the Select Committee on Estimates, Expenditure on Research and Development, Session 1946–47, *HCP 132–I* (London: HMSO, 1947).

BOOKS

Alexander, A.J. and Nelson, J.R., *Measuring Technological Change: Aircraft Turbine Engines* (Santa Monica, CA: RAND Corporation, 1972).

Allen, G.C., *British Industries and their Organisation* (London: Longman, 1970).

Allen, M., *Military Helicopter Doctrines of the Major Powers, 1945–1992: Making Decisions about Air-Land Warfare* (London: Greenwood Press, 1993).

Barnes, C.H., *Bristol Aircraft since 1910* (London: Putnam, 1988).

Barnett, C., *The Audit of War: The Illusion and Reality of Britain as a Great Nation* (London: Macmillan, 1987).

Beaver, P., *Modern Military Helicopters* (Wellingborough: Patrick Stephens, 1987).

—— *Encyclopaedia of the Fleet Air Arm since 1945* (Wellingborough: Patrick Stephens, 1987).

—— *Today's Army Air Corps* (Wellingborough: Patrick Stephens, 1987).

Beer, S., *Treasury Control* (Oxford: Oxford University Press, 1956).

Bellany, I., *Reviewing Britain's Defence* (Aldershot: Dartmouth, 1994).

Bourn, J., *Securing Value for Money in Defence Procurement,* Whitehall Paper No. 25 (London: RUSI, 1994).

Brie, R.A.C. (ed.), *A History of British Rotorcraft, 1866–1965* (Yeovil: Westland Helicopters, 1968).

Burns, D., *The Structure of British Industry, Volume II* (Cambridge: Cambridge University Press, 1964).

Catrina, C., *Arms Transfers and Dependence* (London: Taylor & Francis, 1988).

Chalmers, M., *Paying for Defence: Military Spending and British Decline* (London: Pluto, 1985).

Chartres, J., *Westland Sea King* (London: Ian Allen, 1984).

Clark, R.W., *Tizard* (London: Methuen, 1965).

Coates, D. and Hillard, J. (eds), *UK Economic Decline: Key Texts* (London: Harvester Wheatsheaf, 1995).

Cockcroft, J. (ed.), *The Organisation of Research Establishments* (Cambridge: Cambridge University Press, 1965).

Dillon, G.M., *Dependence and Deterrence* (Aldershot: Gower Press, 1983).

Dowling, J., *RAF Helicopters: The First Twenty Years* (London: HMSO, 1992).

Drown, C. and Campbell, K. (eds), *A Single European Arms Industry* (London: Brassey's, 1990).

Dunstan, S., *Vietnam Choppers: Helicopters in Battle, 1950–1975* (London: Osprey, 1988).

Edgerton, D., *England and the Aeroplane: An Essay on a Militant and Technological Nation* (London: Macmillan, 1991).

Edmonds, M. (ed.), *International Arms Procurement: New Directions* (London: Pergamon Press, 1981).

Edmonds, M. (ed.), *Central Organisations of Defence* (London: Francis Pinter, 1985).

European Commission, *The European Aerospace Industry: Trading Position and Figures 1994* (Brussels: European Commission, 1994).

Everett-Heath, E.J, *British Military Helicopters* (London: Arms & Armour Press, 1986).

Everett-Heath, E.J, Moss, G.M., Mowat, A.W. & Reid, K.E., *Military Helicopters* (London: Brassey's, 1990).

Farrar-Hockley, A., *The Army in the Air: The History of the Army Air Corps* (Stroud: Alan Sutton, 1994).

Fedden, R. *Britain's Air Survival: An Appraisement and Strategy for Success* (London: Cassell, 1957).

Gablehouse, C., *Helicopters and Autogiros* (Philadelphia, PA: J.B. Lippincroft Co., 1967).

Gardner, R. and Longstaff, R., *British Service Helicopters* (London: Robert Hale, 1985).

Gibbs-Smith, C.H., *The Aeroplane: An Historical Survey of its Origins and Development* (London: HMSO, 1960).

—— *Aviation: An Historical Survey from its Origins to the End of World War II* (London: HMSO, 1985).

Gordon, C., *The Atlantic Alliance: A Bibliography* (London: Frances Pinter, 1988).

Gregory, F., Imber, M. and Simpson, J. (eds), *Perspectives upon British Defence Policy, 1945–1970* (Southampton: Southampton University Press), 1978.

Hartcup, G., *The Silent Revolution: Development of Conventional Weapons 1945–85* (London: Brassey's, 1993).

Hartley, K., *A Market for Aircraft: A Critique and a Proposal for Radical Reconstruction of British Government Procurement Policy*, Hobart Paper 57 (London: IEA, 1974).

—— *NATO Arms Co-Operation: A Study in Economics and Politics* (London: George Allen & Unwin, 1983).

Hayward, K., *Government and British Civil Aerospace: A Case Study in Post-War Technology Policy* (Manchester: Manchester University Press, 1983).

—— *The British Aircraft Industry* (Manchester: Manchester University Press, 1989).

Hitch, C.J. and McKean, R.N., *The Economics of Defense in the Nuclear Age* (Cambridge, MA: Harvard University Press, 1960).

Hobkirk, M.D., *The Politics of Defence Budgeting: A Study of Organisation and Defence Resource Allocation in the United Kingdom and the United States* (London: Macmillan, 1984).

Horton, F.B., Rogerson, A.C. and Warner, E.L. (eds), *Comparative Defense Policy* (Baltimore, MD: Johns Hopkins University Press, 1974).

Howard, M., *The Central Organisation for Defence* (London: RUSI, 1970).

Jane's, *All The World's Aircraft, 1964–1965* (London: Jane's, 1965).

—— *All the World's Aircraft, 1974–1975* (London: Jane's, 1975).

Jewkes, J., *Government and High Technology,* Occasional Paper 37 (London: IEA, 1972).

Johnson, B., *Fly Navy: The History of Maritime Aviation* (London: David & Charles, 1981).

Johnson, F.A., *Defence by Ministry: The British Ministry of Defence, 1944–1974* (London: Duckworth, 1980).

Kaldour, M., *The Baroque Arsenal* (London: Andre Deutsch), 1982.

Keesing's Contemporary Archives, 1959–1960 (London: Keesing's, 1960).

Kitson, F., *Bunch of Fives* (London: Faber & Faber, 1987).

Kitson, F., *Directing Operations* (London: Faber & Faber, 1989).

London, P., *Saunders and Saro Aircraft since 1917* (London: Putnam, 1988).

Longstaff, R., *The Fleet Air Arm: A Pictorial History* (London: Robert Hale, 1981).

McDonald, I.S., *Anglo-American Relations since the Second World War* (London: David & Charles, 1974).

Martin, S. (ed.), *The Economics of Offsets: Defence Procurement and Countertrade* (Reading: Harwood, 1996).

Mead, P., *Eye in the Air: A History of Air Observation and Reconnaissance for the Army, 1785–1945* (London: HMSO, 1983).

Mensforth, E., *Family Engineers* (London: Ward Lock, 1981).

Military Balance 1998–1999 (London: Brassey's, 1998).

Miller, R. and Sawers, D., *The Technical Development of Modern Aviation* (London: Routledge & Kegan Paul, 1968).

Milne, J.M., *Flashing Blades over the Sea* (Liskeard: Maritime Books, 1981).

Modley, R. and Caulay, T.J., *Aviation Facts and Figures 1955* (Washington, DC: Lincoln Press, 1955).

Molas-Gallart, J., *Military Production and Innovation in Spain* (Reading: Harwood, 1992).

Mondey, D., *Westland* (London: Jane's, 1987).

Munson, K., *Helicopters and Other Rotorcraft since 1907* (London: Blandford Press, 1968).

Naval Staff History of the Second World War, *The Development of British Naval Aviation, 1919–45*, Vol. 1 (London: Historical Section, Admiralty, 1954).

Nelson, R.R., *The Economics of Parallel R&D Efforts: A Sequential-Decision Analysis* (Santa Monica, CA: RAND Corporation, 1959).

Overy, R., *The Road to War* (London: Macmillan, 1989).
Peck, M.J. and Scherer, F.M., *The Weapons Acquisition Process: An Economic Analysis* (Boston, MA: Harvard University Press, 1962).
Penrose, H., *British Aviation: Ominous Skies, 1935–1939* (London: HMSO, 1980).
Polmar, N. and Kennedy, F.D., *Military Helicopters of the World: Military Rotary-Wing Aircraft since 1917* (London: Arms & Armour Press, 1981).
Postan, M.M., Hay, D. and Scott, J.D., *Design and Development of Weapons: History of the Second World War* (London: HMSO, 1964).
Pritt, D.N., *The Labour Government, 1945–51* (London: Lawrence & Wisehart, 1963).
Prouty, R.W., *Military Helicopter Design Technology* (London: Jane's, 1989).
Rawlins, E.W. and Sambito, W.J., *Marines and Helicopters, 1946–1962* (Washington, DC: US Marine Corps, History and Museums Division, 1976).
Reader, W.J., *The Weir Group: A Centenary History* (London: Weidenfeld & Nicolson, 1971).
Reed, A., *Britain's Aircraft Industry: What Went Right? What Went Wrong?* (London: Dent & Sons, 1973).
Rees, E., *World Military Helicopters* (London: Jane's, 1986).
Rich, M., Stanley, W., Birkler, W. and Hesse, M., *Multinational Co-Production of Military Aerospace Systems* (Santa Monica, CA: RAND Corporation, 1981).
RUSI Working Group, *1992: Protectionism or Collaboration in Defence Procurement*, Whitehall Paper No. 6 (London: RUSI, 1990).
Simpson, J., 'Understanding Weapons Acquisition Processes: A Case Study of Naval Anti-Submarine Aircraft Procurement in Britain, 1945–1955', unpublished Ph.D. thesis, University of Southampton, 1976.
Snyder, W.P., *The Politics of British Defense Policy, 1945–1962* (Ohio: Ohio University Press, 1964).
Sturtivant, R., *The Squadrons of the Fleet Air Arm* (Tonbridge: Air Britain, 1984).
—— *British Research and Development Aircraft: Seventy Years at the Leading Edge* (Yeovil: Haynes, 1990).
—— *British Naval Aviation: The Fleet Air Arm, 1917–1990* (London: Arms & Armour Press, 1990).
Swanborough, G. and Bowers, P.M., *United States Navy Aircraft since 1911* (London: Putnam, 1968).
Taylor, H.A., *Fairey Aircraft since 1915* (London: Putnam, 1974).
Taylor, J.W.R. and Allward, M.F., *Westland 50* (London: Ian Allan, 1965).
Taylor, M.J., *History of Helicopters* (London: Hamlyn, 1984).
Thetford, O., *Aircraft of the Royal Air Force since 1918* (London: Putnam, 1962).
—— *British Naval Aircraft since 1912* (London: Putnam, 1991).
Till, G., *Air Power and the Royal Navy 1914–1945: A Historical Survey* (London: Jane's, 1979).

Todd, D. and Humble, R., *World Aerospace: An International Survey* (London: Croom Helm, 1987).

Toumi, H. and Vayrynen, R., *Transnational Corporations, Armaments and Development* (Aldershot: Gower, 1982).

Towle, P.A., *Pilots and Rebels: The Use of Aircraft in Unconventional Warfare, 1918–1988* (London: Brassey's, 1989).

Twigge, S.R., *The Early Development of Guided Weapons in the United Kingdom, 1940–1960* (Reading: Harwood, 1993).

Weeks, J., *The Airborne Soldier* (Poole: Blandford Press, 1982).

Weinberg, G.L., *A World at Arms: A Global History of World War II* (Cambridge: Cambridge University Press, 1994).

Wettern, D., *The Decline of British Sea Power* (London: Jane's, 1982).

Williams, G., Gregory, F. and Simpson, J., *Crisis in Procurement: A Case Study of the TSR-2* (London: RUSI, 1969).

Williams, S.C., *Report on the Helicopter: The Helicopter and Its Role As a Transport Vehicle* (New York: Brundage Story & Rose, 1955).

Wood, D., *Project Cancelled: The Disaster of Britain's Abandoned Aircraft Projects* (London: Tri-Service Press, 1990).

Worcester, R., *Roots of British Air Policy* (London: Hodder & Stoughton, 1966).

Wragg, D.W, *Wings over the Sea: A History of Naval Aviation* (London: David & Charles, 1979).

—— *Helicopters at War: A Pictorial History* (London: Robert Hale, 1983).

Yin, R., *Case Study Research: Design and Method* (London: Sage, 1989).

Young, W.R., *The Helicopter* (Alexandra, VA: Time Life, 1982).

ARTICLES, BOOK CHAPTERS AND UNPUBLISHED PAPERS

Aitken, J., 'Defence Procurement: Past, Present and Future', *RUSI Journal*, February 1994, pp. 39–42.

Bellany, I. and Richardson, J., 'Australian Defence Procurement' in Gelber, H.G. (ed.), *Problems of Australian Defence* (Melbourne: Oxford University Press, 1970), pp. 255–6.

Bennett, J.A.J., 'Rotorcraft Achievements', in R.A.C. Brie, (ed.), *A History of British Rotorcraft 1866–1965* (Yeovil: Westland Helicopters, 1968), pp. 81–2.

Bittleston, M., 'Co-operation or Competition: Defence Procurement Options for the 1990s', *Adelphi Paper*, No. 250 (London: Brassey's, 1990).

Bourn, J., *Securing Value for Money in Defence Procurement*, Whitehall Paper No. 25 (London: RUSI, 1994).

Brie, R.A.C., 'The Cierva Autogiro Company 1930–1940', in R.A.C. Brie, (ed.), *A History of British Rotorcraft 1866–1965* (Yeovil: Westland Helicopters, 1968), pp. 41–4.

—— 'Bristow Helicopters', in R.A.C. Brie, (ed.), *A History of British*

Rotorcraft 1866–1965 (Yeovil: Westland Helicopters, 1968), p. 50.

—— 'B.E.A. Helicopter Experimental Unit 1947–1954', in R.A.C. Brie (ed.), *A History of British Rotorcraft, 1866–1965* (Yeovil: Westland Helicopters, 1968), p. 47.

Brie, R.A.C. and Caunter, C.F., 'References to Rotary Wing Aircraft in the Annual Reports and Journals of the Royal Aeronautical Society, 1866–1965', in R.A.C. Brie (ed.), *A History of British Rotorcraft 1866–1965* (Yeovil: Westland Helicopters, 1968), pp. 1–22.

Bryson, L.B., Heenan, F.E. and Johnson, C.A., 'Helicopters in the Royal Navy', *Royal Aeronautical Society Journal*, Vol. 76, August 1972, pp. 469–500.

Callaghan, T.A., 'The Structural Dimension of NATO', *NATO Review*, Vol. 32, 3 June 1984, pp. 21–6.

Cheeseman, I.C., 'Rotary Wing Aircraft', in F. Gregory, M. Imber and J. Simpson (eds), *Perspectives upon British Defence Policy 1945–1970* (Southampton: Southampton University Press, 1978), pp. 191–202.

Cheeseman, I.C., Edmonds, M. and Simpson, J., 'The Procurement of Military Aircraft, 1945–1970', in F. Gregory, M. Imber and J. Simpson, (eds), *Perspectives upon British Defence Policy 1945–1970* (Southampton: Southampton University Press, 1978), pp. 145–212.

Chinworth, M.W. and Matthews, R., 'Defense Industrialisation Through Offsets: The Case of Japan', in S. Martin (ed.), *The Economics of Offsets: Defence Procurement and Countertrade* (Reading: Harwood, 1996), pp. 177–218.

Ciastula, T.L., 'The Development of the P.531', *Journal of the Royal Aeronautical Society*, Vol. 68, June 1964, pp. 399–417.

—— 'Saunders-Roe Helicopter Activities, 1951–1959', in R.A.C. Brie (ed.), *A History of British Rotorcraft 1866–1965* (Yeovil: Westland Helicopters, 1968), pp. 129–33.

Coates, D., 'UK Underperformance: Claim and Reality', in D. Coates and J. Hillard (eds), *UK Economic Decline: Key Texts* (London: Harvester Wheatsheaf, 1995), pp. 3–24.

Crawford, C.C., 'The Light Observation Helicopter Programme of the United States Army', *Journal of the Royal Aeronautical Society*, Vol. 68, December 1964.

Croft, S., 'The Westland Helicopter Crisis: Implications for the British Defence Industry', *Defense Analysis*, Vol. 3, No. 4, 1987, pp. 291–303.

Crookenden, N., 'Aviation in the British Army Today', *RUSI Journal*, August 1956, p. 205.

—— 'The British Army Unit Light Helicopter Project', *Journal of the Royal Aeronautical Society*, Vol. 69, 1965, pp. 489–92.

De Vestel, P., 'Defence Markets and Industries in Europe: Time for Political Decisions?', *Chaillot Paper 21* (Paris: WEU, November 1995).

Deng, D. and Chinworth, M.W., 'The Teeth of the Little Tigers: Offsets, Defense Production and Economic Development in South Korea and Taiwan', in S. Martin (ed.), *The Economics of Offsets: Defence Procurement and Countertrade* (Reading: Harwood, 1996), pp. 245–98.

Devons, E., 'The Aircraft Industry', in D. Burns (ed.), *The Structure of British Industry II* (Cambridge: Cambridge University Press, 1964), pp. 45–92.

Edmonds, M., 'Central Organisations of Defence in Britain, 1945–85: The Federal-Unification Debate', in idem. *The Defence Equation: British Military Systems, Policy, Planning and Performance* (London: Brassey's, 1986).

Edmonds, M., 'Strike Aircraft', in Gregory, F., Imber, M. and Simpson, J. (eds), *Perspectives upon British Defence Policy 1945–1970* (Southampton: Southampton University Press, 1978), pp. 169–91.

—— 'International Military Equipment Procurement Partnerships: The Basic Issues', in M. Edmonds (ed.), *International Arms Procurement: New Directions* (Oxford: Pergamon Press, 1981), pp. 1–23.

—— 'Central Organizations of Defence in Great Britain, 1945–1985', in M. Edmonds (ed.), *Central Organizations of Defense* (London: Frances Pinter, 1985), pp. 85–107.

Edmonds, M., Uttley, M.R.H. and Hayhurst, G., 'UK and US Dependence on Foreign Technology in Defence Research and Development', *Science and Public Policy*, Vol. 17, No. 3, June 1990, pp. 157–69.

Fitzwilliams, O., 'Westland Helicopter Activities, 1946–1960', in R.A.C. Brie (ed.), *A History of British Rotorcraft 1866–1965* (Yeovil: Westland Helicopters, 1968), pp. 115-23.

Freedman, L., 'The Case of Westland and the Bias to Europe', *International Affairs*, Vol. 63, No. 1, Winter 1986–87, pp. 1–19.

Geiger, T., '"The Next War is Bound to Come": Defence Production Policy, Supply Departments and Defence Contractors in Britain, 1945–57', in H. Mercer, N. Rollings and J.D. Tomlinson (eds), *The Labour Governments and Private Industry: The Experience of 1945 to 1951* (Edinburgh: Edinburgh University Press, 1992), pp. 95–118.

Gregory, F. and Simpson, J., 'The Acquisition of Military Aircraft in Great Britain and West Germany', in F.B. Horton, A.C. Rogerson and E.L. Warner (eds), *Comparative Defense Policy* (London: Johns Hopkins University Press, 1974), pp. 453–64.

Groth, C., 'The Economics of Weapons Co-Production', in M. Edmonds (ed.), *International Arms Procurement: New Directions* (Oxford: Pergamon Press, 1981), pp. 71–83.

Gummett, P., 'Civil and Military Aircraft in the UK', in J. Krige (ed.), *Choosing Big Technologies* (Reading: Harwood, 1993), pp. 203–22.

Hafner, R., 'British Rotorcraft', *Journal of the Royal Aeronautical Society*, Vol. 70, Part 1, January 1966, pp. 235–42.

—— 'Four Decades of Rotating Wing Activity, 1928–1965', in R.A.C. Brie (ed.), *A History of British Rotorcraft 1866–1965* (Yeovil: Westland Helicopters, 1968), pp. 37–41.

Hall, G.R. and Johnson, R.E., 'Aircraft Co-Production and Procurement Strategy', *RAND Report R-450-PR*, May 1967.

Hartley, K., 'The Mergers of the UK Aircraft Industry, 1957–60', *Journal*

of the Royal Aeronautical Society, Vol. 69, December 1965, pp. 846–53.
—— 'The Political Economy of NATO Defense Procurement Policies', in M. Edmonds (ed.), *International Arms Procurement: New Directions* (Oxford: Pergamon Press, 1981), pp. 98–114.
—— 'Efficiency, Industry and Alternative Weapons Procurement Policies', in C. Schmidt (ed.), *The Economics of Military Expenditures: Military Expenditures, Economic Growth and Fluctuations* (London: Macmillan, 1987), pp. 283–300.
—— 'Public Procurement and Competitiveness: A Community Market for Military Hardware and Technology', *Journal of Common Market Studies*, Vol. XXV, 1987.
Hartley, K. and Martin, S., 'The Political Economy of International Collaboration', in R. Coopey, M.R.H. Uttley and G. Spinardi (eds), *Defence Science and Technology: Adjusting to Change* (Reading: Harwood, 1993), pp. 171–206.
Hayes, I., 'Choppers over Malaya', *Aeroplane Monthly*, August 1989, pp. 472–6.
Head, R., 'The Weapons Acquisition Process: Alternative National Strategies', in F.B. Horton, A.C. Rogerson and E.L. Warner (eds), *Comparative Defense Policy* (London: Johns Hopkins University Press, 1974), pp. 412–26.
Hewin, L.M., 'The General Requirement of the Three Armed Services for Helicopters and other VTOL Aircraft', *Journal of the Royal Aeronautical Society*, Vol. 69, July 1965, pp. 482–8.
Hislop, G.S., 'Helicopter Activities of Fairey, Westland and British European Airways, 1947–1965', in R.A.C. Brie (ed.), *A History of British Rotorcraft 1866–1965* (Yeovil: Westland Helicopters, 1968), pp. 125–9.
Hobson, C.M., 'Gate Guardians No. 9: Westland Whirlwind HAR10 XP361 RAF Valley', *Air Clues*, Vol. 39, No. 9, September 1985, pp. 347–8.
'Hunting Percival P.74', *Flight*, 23 December 1955, pp. 938–41.
Katz, J.E., 'Understanding Arms Production in Developing Countries', in J.E. Katz (ed.), *Arms Production in Developing Countries: An Analysis of Decision Making* (Lexington: Lexington Books, 1984), pp. 3–13.
Kirby, M., 'British Culture and the Development of High Technology Sectors', Mimeo, Department of Economics (The Management School), Lancaster University, 1995, pp. 1–36.
Lighthill, M.J., 'The Royal Aircraft Establishment', in J. Cockcroft (ed.), *The Organization of Research Establishments* (Cambridge: Cambridge University Press, 1965), pp. 28-54.
Liptrot, R.N., 'Rotary Wing Survey, 1842–1954', in R.A.C. Brie (ed.), *A History of British Rotorcraft 1866–1965* (Yeovil: Westland Helicopters, 1968), pp. 23–34.
McClements, A., 'The Westland Belvedere Mk1', *Journal of the Royal Aeronautical Society*, Vol. 66, August 1962, p. 521.
—— 'A Review of British Helicopter Activities, 1943–1946', in R.A.C. Brie (ed.), *A History of British Rotorcraft 1866–1965* (Yeovil: Westland

Helicopters, 1968), pp. 103–14.
McTaggart, A.W., 'Helicopter Air Power', *Air Clues*, Vol. 43, No. 3, March 1989, pp. 83–8.
Markowski, S. and Hall, P., 'The Defence Offsets Policy in Australia', in S. Martin (ed.), *The Economics of Offsets: Defence Procurement and Countertrade* (Reading: Harwood, 1996), pp. 49–74.
Martin, S., 'Countertrade and Offsets: An Overview of the Theory and Evidence', in S. Martin (ed.), *The Economics of Offsets: Defence Procurement and Countertrade* (Reading: Harwood, 1996), pp. 15–48.
Mead, P.W., 'Army Aviation', *RAF Quarterly*, Summer 1962, pp. 189–93.
Moodie, M., 'Defense Industries in the Third World: Problems and Promises', in S.G. Neuman and R.E. Harkavy (eds), *Arms Transfers in the Modern World* (New York: Praeger, 1979), pp. 294–312.
Morain, P.H.L., 'The Development of French Helicopters', *Journal of the Royal Aeronautical Society*, Vol. 68, October 1964, pp. 675–82.
Morley, A.W., 'Some Aspects of Turboshaft Engine Installation in Multi-engined Helicopters', *Journal of the Royal Aeronautical Society*, Vol. 68, June 1964, pp. 429–45.
Motley, C.F., 'Naval Air Power in Korea', *Aviation News*, August 1989, pp. 248-57.
Nailor, P., 'British Defence Policy in the 1960s', in F. Gregory, M. Imber and J. Simpson (eds), *Perspectives upon British Defence Policy 1945–1970* (Southampton: Southampton University Press, 1978), pp. 62–7.
Neuman, S.G., 'Arms Transfers, Indigenous Defence Production and Dependency: The Case of Iran', in A. Hossein (ed.), *The Security of the Persian Gulf* (London: Croom Helm, 1981), pp. 131–50.
—— 'International Stratification and Third World Military Industries', *International Organization*, Vol. 38, No. 1, 1984, pp. 167–97.
Norman-Walker, R.A., 'The Formation of the AAC – 1955–1957', *Army Air Corps Journal*, 1982, pp. 9–16.
Pribram, E., 'British Helicopter Engines, 1945–1965', in R.A.C. Brie (ed.), *A History of British Rotorcraft 1866–1965* (Yeovil: Westland, 1968), pp. 99–102.
Pugh, P., 'The Procurement Nexus', *Defence Economics*, Vol. 4, 1993, pp. 179–94.
Redlich, A. and Miscavage, M., 'The Business of Offsets: A Practitioner's Perspective Case Study: Israel', in S. Martin (ed.), *The Economics of Offsets: Defence Procurement and Countertrade* (Reading: Harwood, 1996), pp. 381–406.
Reid, B.H., 'Civil War Between Services', *Military History*, January 1984, pp. 1–7.
'Rotary-Wing Power', *Flight*, 12 March 1954, pp. 318–22.
'Rotodyne Report: Development Aspects and Commercial Applications of Fairey's VTOL Transport', *Flight*, 20 December 1957, pp. 953–60.
Royal Air Force, 'Rotary Wings in the RAF', *The Aeroplane and Astronautics*, 18 March 1960, pp. 336–9.

Saviotti, P.P. and Trickett, A., 'The Evolution of Helicopter Technology, 1940–1986', Mimeo, University of Manchester, 1987, pp. 1–27.

Scott, J.F., 'Joint Experimental Helicopter Unit', *Air Power*, Spring 1959.

Self, H., 'The Status of Civil Aviation in 1946', *Journal of the Royal Aeronautical Society*, September 1946, pp. 719–61.

Shapiro, J., 'Cierva Autogiro Company, 1943–1951', in R.A.C. Brie (ed.), *A History of British Rotorcraft 1866–1965* (Yeovil: Westland Helicopters, 1968), pp. 85–91.

—— 'Servotec Ltd., 1952–1964', in R.A.C. Brie (ed.), *A History of British Rotorcraft 1866–1965* (Yeovil: Westland Helicopters, 1968), pp. 93–4.

Simpson, J., 'The Procurement of Military Combat Aircraft, 1945–1970: Introduction', in F. Gregory, M. Imber and J. Simpson (eds), *Perspectives upon British Defence Policy 1945–1970* (Southampton: Southampton University Press, 1978), pp. 145–9.

Smith, R., 'Defence Procurement: A European Identity?', *RUSI Journal*, February 1992, pp. 42–8.

Stevens, T.M.P., 'Helicopters', *RUSI Journal*, February 1959.

Struys, W., 'Offsets and Weapons Procurement: The Belgium Experience', in S. Martin (ed.), *The Economics of Offsets: Defence Procurement and Countertrade* (Reading: Harwood, 1996), pp. 75–105.

Tobin, P.A., 'Westland Prize Essay', *RUSI Journal*, August 1956, pp. 540–56.

Towle, P.A., 'The RAF and the Malayan Insurgency', *Air Clues*, Vol. 43, Number 8, August 1989, pp. 284–90.

Udis, B., 'US–Swiss F-5 Transaction and the Evolution of Swiss Offsets Policy' in S. Martin (ed.), *The Economics of Offsets: Defence Procurement and Countertrade* (Reading: Harwood, 1996), pp. 321–36.

Uttley, M.R.H., 'British Helicopter Production, 1945–1960: A Case Study of Technology Transfer and Market Dominance', *Science and Public Policy*, Vol. 18, No. 4, August 1991, pp. 235–43.

—— 'British Helicopter Developments, 1945–1960: Government Technology Policy in a Changing Defence Environment', in R. Coopey, M.R.H. Uttley and G. Spinardi (eds), *Defence Science and Technology: Adjusting to Change* (Reading: Harwood, 1993), pp. 125–41.

—— 'The Integration of West European Defense Procurement: Issues and Prospects', *Defense Analysis*, Vol. 11, No. 3, 1995, pp. 275–91.

—— 'Rotary Wing Aircraft', in R. Bud and P. Gummett (eds), *Cold War, Hot Science: Applied Research in the UK's Defence Research Laboratories, 1945–90* (Reading: Harwood, 1999), pp. 59–84.

Varas, A., Portales, C. and Aguero, F., 'The National and International Dynamics of South American Armamentism', *Current Research into Peace and Violence*, Vol. 3, No. 1, 1980, pp. 1–23.

Waddy, J. and Moss, S., 'The Saga of the Soldier and His Helicopter', *The Army Quarterly and Defence Journal*, Vol. 116, No. 4, October 1986, pp. 391–6.

Walker, G.E., 'Activities of Weir, Hafner and Bristol, 1933–1960', in R.A.C.

Brie (ed.), *A History of British Rotorcraft 1866–1965* (Yeovil: Westland Helicopters, 1968), pp. 65–78.

Walker, W. and Gummett, P., 'Britain and the European Arms Market', *International Affairs*, Vol. 65, 1989, pp. 419–42.

Walker, W. and Willett, S., 'Restructuring the European Defence Industrial Base', *Defence Economics*, Vol. 4, 1993, pp. 141–60.

Watson, K., 'Activities of Weir, Cierva and Saunders-Roe, 1933-1962', in R.A.C. Brie (ed.), *A History of British Rotorcraft 1866–1965* (Yeovil: Westland Helicopters, 1968), pp. 51–63.

Wilby, P., 'Helicopter Research at the RAE', *Air Clues*, Vol. 44, No. 2, February 1990, pp. 67–72.

Willson, F.M.G., 'Defence Organisation – 1958 Style', *Public Administration*, Winter 1958, pp. 385–90.

Index

Note: Italic page numbers refer to Tables.